{ The Truth of Tao

The Truth of Tao

Alex Anatole

Anatole, Alex.
The Truth of Tao / Alex Anatole.—1st ed.
p. cm.
LCCN 2003111150
ISBN 0-9742529-0-5

1. Taoism. 2. Laozi. Dao de jing—Criticism and interpretation.
I. Title.

BL1920.A53 2005   299.5'1444
                     QBI04-200174

First edition published in 2005 by the
Center of Traditional Taoist Studies, P.O. Box 134, Weston,
Massachusetts 02493, www.tao.org.

Copyright 2005 Alex Anatole. All Rights Reserved.

All rights reserved. No part of this publication may be reproduced or utilized in any form or by any means, electronic or mechanical, including photocopying, recording, or by any information storage and retrieval system, without prior written permission from the publisher.

Unless otherwise noted, all quoted material is taken from *The Wisdom of Laotse* by Lin Yutang, copyright 1948 by Random House, Inc. Used by permission of Modern Library, a division of Random House, Inc.

Photographs by various members of the Temple of Original Simplicity and Jean Renard.

All photographs are reprinted herein by permission of the respective photographers, who reserve all rights in the original photographs.

Design and layout by Adele Levitan

Printed in the United States of America.

Who can find repose in a muddy world?
—The Wisdom of Laotse, 106

With special thanks to Kim Mayyasi for his tireless efforts and assistance in transferring my words to paper, and for his encouragement during the editing process. Thanks also to Jack McDonough, Chris Kilham, Tom Champagne and everyone else who read earlier manuscrips and provided helpful comments.

Alex Anatole

Contents

About the Author   xi
Preface   xiii
    Enlightenment and You   xiii
    Translating the Tao across Time,
       Culture, and Language   xx

1. Enlightenment   1
    What Is Enlightenment?   1
    Sources of Confusion   7
    The Process of Enlightenment   10
    Sensitivity   13
    Recognize the Sources of Confusion   17
    Fight Confusion with Action   22
    Build a Life of Contentment   26
    The Final Tuning   30

2. Dealing with Western Confusion   33
    Confusion #1: Mind over Body   35
    Confusion #2: The Family Unit   40
    Confusion #3: Engines of Hypocrisy   49
    Confusion #4: Money and the Work Ethic   69
    Confusion #5: Fate and the Futility of Planning   72
    Confusion #6: It's Never Too Late   75
    Confusion #7: Unrealistic Expectations   77
    Confusion #8: The Power of Positive Thinking   80

Confusion #9: Universal Love	81
Confusion #10: Avoid Conflict at All Cost	86
Conclusion	89
3. Dealing with Eastern Confusion	**95**
Why Do We Need This Chapter?	95
Buddhism	98
Confucianism	111
4. The Principles of Tao	**131**
The Diamond of the Tao	131
Classical Taoist Principles	137
Oneness	140
Yin and Yang	141
Life and Death	145
Reversion	147
Inaction	149
The Coiled Spring Phenomenon	153
Noninterference	155
Humanity and Justice	158
The World and I	165
The Common Man and the Man of Tao	166
Knowledge and Chaos	173
The Futility of Plans	181
The Individual Path	184
Nature Is Unkind	185
The Three Treasures	197
5. Applying Taoist Principles	**209**
The Application Imperative	209
Chi	217
Developing Individual Chi	223

Physical Chi Quong	226
Mental Chi Quong (Meditation)	238
Practical Immortality	250
Martial Arts	254
The Warrior Way	260
True Martial Arts	265
Key Principles Reinforced by Martial Arts	271
Metaphysical Aspects of Martial Arts	284
Religion	289
Taoism's Shamanistic Roots	299
Celestial Evolution	303
The Taoist Temple	311
Pantheon of Gods	316
Religious Ceremonies	323
The Theological Mission Redux	325
6. The Conduct of Life	**327**
Grasp the Tao	327
The Perfect Day	335
Achieving the Perfect Day	339
Desires and Expectations	342
Dealing with Society	348
The Futility of Argument	349
Borrowing: The Ultimate Clarifier	355
Physical Conduct of Life	357
Mental Conduct of Life	361
Spiritual Conduct of Life	368
The Purpose of Life	374
Afterword	**381**

About the Author

The Master came, because it was his time to be born; he went, because it was his time to go away.

—*The Wisdom of Laotse*, 181

Alex Anatole was born in Moscow in 1948. At the age of eight, Alex met Master Lu Yang Tai, the "Enlightened One", a Taoist sage whose lineage extended to the ancient origins of Taoism. For twenty years, this great teacher instructed young Alex—his only disciple—in all aspects of the Tao and ultimately ordained him a Taoist priest, sending him to the West as a Grand Master.

In 1976, Grand Master Anatole immigrated to the United States and settled near Boston, Massachusetts, fulfilling the destiny foretold by his given Taoist name,

开辟真理道往西

"He who builds the true path of Tao in the West". He built a traditional Taoist temple, which is officially recognized as one of the few authentic temples outside China (both mainland and Taiwan), and began to teach a select group of dedicated students. Grand Master Anatole maintains close ties to temples in China, whose roots extend to Taoism's earliest beginnings. Today, he continues the tradition of imparting the Tao through a classical program of philosophy, religion, meditation, chi quong, and martial arts.

While Grand Master Anatole continues his quiet approach to teaching Taoism, he has observed with great concern the confusing and hypocritical teachings of modern teachers and philosophers—some of whom even use the name of his beloved Tao. Motivated by his desire to help preserve the classical teachings of Taoism, he has written this book to explain clearly and unambiguously the wisdom of the Tao to Americans, using language and imagery specifically tailored to the Western mind.

—Kim Mayyasi
May 20, 2004

Preface

Because if you haven't got it in you,
you could not receive Tao.

—*The Wisdom of Laotse*, 317

Enlightenment and You

This book may not be for you. It is meant for those rare individuals who ponder the answers to life's big questions and have the strength to stare reality boldly in the face. It deals with topics ranging from the fear of death to the mystical connection of man to the gods. It imparts the pragmatic principles of physical confrontation and the power to heal oneself. It is a manual for achieving a content life.

As a book written for a select few, it explains a system of remarkable simplicity and power that requires you to throw

The Truth of Tao

away beliefs cherished since childhood. It destroys the myths of universal love, social status, and money. It is not a book for cowards, as you will have to deal unflinchingly with reality. And, because the system is integrated, there is no flexibility to pick and choose only those principles that make you comfortable. It is all or nothing. There is no halfway.

Several millennia ago in China, a sage named Lao Tzu* appeared. He created one of the most mystical yet pragmatic systems ever known. In studying this book, you are attempting to embrace the Tao, or "the Path," your spiritual road through life. Your life can be the confused path you have followed since birth, the path prescribed by popular convention. Or you can follow a path in concert with the natural core of man. Indeed, there is an ongoing war for possession of your soul. The combatants are society versus nature, confusion versus clarity. This book is a battle plan to recapture your soul. It prescribes a warrior's path that may be difficult for you.

Why are you considering such a quest? Why should you challenge beliefs taught to you by your parents, teachers, and clergy? Why address the ugliness of death and man's instinct to kill? Worse still, if you make this journey and become a true man of Tao, you will eventually become a stranger in your own land. Why invest intellectual and emotional energy in such a lonely venture? What could be the purpose of such a voyage?

---

* The spelling of Chinese names and terms varies among authors. For example, this book uses Lao Tzu instead of Laotse (as in *The Wisdom of Laotse*), Chuang Tzu instead of Chuangtse, and Mao Tzu instead of Maotse.

Preface

Throughout history, all theological systems—regardless of their structure—have delineated a process of enlightenment designed to relieve the sufferings of their followers. For example, Buddha explained that there is suffering in this world because of our material and spiritual desires. He then prescribed a process for his followers to remove their desires. Therefore, Buddha, like all other spiritual guides, recognized that the journey to enlightenment first required an individual to acknowledge his suffering and then deal with it. Simply put, if there is no suffering, what's the point in enlightenment?

Like many Americans, you may not acknowledge suffering as part of your daily life. This is largely the result of the security and prosperity of America, the most powerful industrial nation in history. Unlike Europe, Asia, and Africa, which have regularly experienced the horrors of war, American soil has not hosted widespread bombings, fires, and famine for over a century. As such, the American sense of suffering has become ever more abstract. Except for a few combat veterans, most have only experienced war vicariously in glamorized renditions created by Hollywood. Even with the tragedy of September 11, 2001, recent generations tend to view life's difficulties as a dark shadow of the distant past.

If you are a fortunate American who is content with your life, happy with your job, satisfied with great relationships with loved ones, and secure in the belief that the world is a beautiful place, then the journey to enlightenment is not for you. Without the daily recognition that you are suffering, enlightenment is just a hollow quest.

Lao Tzu cautioned that exposing satisfied members of society to the harsh reality of the Tao would be a disservice.

The Truth of Tao

He taught that his principles might breed discontent among the masses, who are unwilling and incapable of understanding them. For all its simplicity, the Tao would be akin to advanced calculus for the majority. Consequently, Lao Tzu labeled the masses "the herd," because he viewed society as a herd of grazing cattle, happily chewing their cud and blind to the slaughterhouse down the road. Wise Lao Tzu knew that enlightening the cattle of society was a futile exercise that could easily backfire. He understood that most people need to remain unaware. Indeed, for the majority, ignorance is bliss.

However, there is a small segment of the populace—possibly including you—that senses something is wrong. These people observe regular contradictions between society's popularly held beliefs and the clues provided by reality. They listen to religious leaders preach the inherent goodness of man while terrorists fly hijacked planes into buildings. They notice the hypocrisy of world leaders who evaded military service in their youth but later send soldiers to fight in distant lands. They see the elderly, who invested everything in raising their children, not even receive a birthday card from their offspring. They shake their heads at lying, corrupt politicians who get reelected. They watch their debt grow with mortgages, car loans, college savings, and retirement plans, forcing both spouses to work until they are exhausted.

The list is virtually endless: priests in ornate attire telling the poor how to live, murderers being set free, shallow friendships disappearing when times get tough, a good-hearted thirty-year-old unexpectedly developing terminal cancer. The violent deaths of innocent children, the deception of politicians, marriages without love, no free time, and

Preface

finally, death—the only thing on which you can absolutely depend.

For the rare individual who observes what is happening around him, doubt creeps into his mind. He wonders if something is very wrong. Maybe rational people don't govern the world. Maybe the good guys don't always win. Maybe his neighbor's smile isn't sincere. Maybe making it to retirement isn't guaranteed. Maybe "turning the other cheek" only results in a slap to the other cheek. Maybe his view of life, supported by all society, is a fraud. Maybe, as Burton Watson wrote, life is "dominated by chaos, suffering, and absurdity."*

If witnessing the everyday symptoms of a dysfunctional society has you questioning what's going on, then this book is for you. While you may not suffer materially, your soul is in conflict. If you are sensitive enough to be affected by the "chaos, suffering, and absurdity" around you, then discontent has infected your life and this book is the prescription. If you are strong enough to take a bitter dose of reality and can reason outside the conventional parameters of society, then the Tao is your path. If you are a "seeker" of unambiguous answers to life's questions, then Lao Tzu is your teacher. This book has the tools to transform you into a truly spiritual person and help you find contentment in our bizarre world.

You, sensitive to the "chaos, suffering, and absurdity" of life, have a wonderful gift that is also a lifelong curse. You lack the shield of numbness that provides the herd of humanity with the bliss of ignorance. You are aware and thus exposed.

---

* Burton Watson, trans., *Chuang Tzu Basic Writings* (New York: Columbia University Press, 1964), 3.

The Truth of Tao

For the thinking man, enlightenment is not merely a silly search for New Age foolishness. It is an essential journey to find contentment. This book is dedicated to helping those rare individuals—people with intelligence, sensitivity, and perseverance—recapture their souls from society and lead happier lives. And it is this goal that casts Taoism in its most romantic light, as it defines a journey rivaling any of the greatest quests.

Lao Tzu's writings inform both a philosophy and a religion. Based on the precept that "nature is unkind," a model emerges that initially appears pessimistic and dour. However, Lao Tzu's strength was that he created a philosophical system that is simultaneously optimistic and pragmatic. For while he warns that a clear view of nature is essential and that man will always be a link in the food chain, he describes a means to embrace this reality and navigate a life of contentment.

Lao Tzu asks us to see nature for what it is. By avoiding the labels of good or bad, he teaches us that we can comprehend our immutable environment. The resulting mental clarity is an antidote to the confusions of conventional values. As a clearer picture of the world emerges, the budding Taoist can fight his way to calm amid a sea of turmoil.

For this reason, Lao Tzu's teachings are quite romantic. Walk into any classical Taoist temple and you're surrounded by armor-clad statues of deities wielding a variety of weapons. The message may be harsh—life is a war and nature is unkind—but these are only the basic principles on which Taoism is built. While most philosophies and religions acknowledge the pain of mortal existence, they then espouse various means for trying to change what can't be changed.

Preface

Taoism, in contrast, takes the opposite approach, giving individuals those tools necessary to coexist with the laws of nature and find contentment in an uncaring environment.

In the tradition of the great mythologies that celebrate the power of an individual to overcome enemy hordes, the optimism of Taoism stems from its similar romantic belief that it is possible for an individual to successfully navigate through a faceless society and its seductive confusions. At its core, Taoism is a testament to the possibility of fighting one's way out of society's ignorance and dwelling within a realm of clarity.

Philosophy has been called "the mother of all sciences." Therefore, it is not surprising that as Taoism provides a clear picture of reality, its principles have spawned pragmatic applications that span all the sciences. Taoist practitioners invented gunpowder, porcelain, the compass, herbal remedies, matches, rudders for boats, and a host of strategic methods used in everything from physics to the military arts and holistic medicine. In a true sense, the Taoist dedicated to principles grounded within observed reality becomes a de facto Renaissance man, constantly inquiring as to the workings of nature and applying them in practical ways.

Perhaps the most romantic notion of Taoism is derived from its mystical shamanistic origins. While the philosophy of the Tao clarifies man's view of mortal existence, the religion of the Tao purifies his corrupted soul. As civilization and its soldiers of confusion have destroyed man's natural instincts, so too have they destroyed our human essence. Label this essence whatever you want—some call it "soul." And if that soul is encased within a confused mortal creature, it mirrors that conflicted exterior housing. This torment carries metaphysical consequences as the soul readies itself for the death of its body. Thus, the sin of confusion results in an unhappy mortal existence, as well as a doomed hereafter.

Taoists view the physical world as a manifestation of heavenly principles. For this reason, praying to the gods for guidance in dealing with mortal existence is simultaneously asking for their help to clarify one's own soul. While Lao Tzu is undeniably harsh in his description of reality, he provides life secrets that enable individuals to fight through the forces of confusion and enter a realm of contentment where salvation truly touches the soul.

Translating the Tao across Time, Culture, and Language

This is not a history book filled with dates, names, and detailed analyses of the great Chinese dynasties. Nor is it a new translation of the Tao Te Ching or of Chinese philosophers like Chuang Tzu and Mao Tzu. For those interested in such topics, there are many excellent books by learned historians with translations by brilliant linguists. Instead, this book's single focus is to communicate, in plain language, the most ancient, mystical, and pragmatic philosophy of life: the Tao. As Burton Watson wrote in his *Chuang Tzu Basic Writings*, "While most of the philosophies of ancient China are addressed to the political or intellectual elite, Chuang Tzu's is addressed to the spiritual elite."*

---

* Watson, 5.

Preface

Unlike the works of Lao Tzu and Chuang Tzu, which were written exclusively for ancient Chinese rulers, this book has been tailored to the American consciousness. Since each culture has its own mentality, this book is not simply for all English-speaking people; the information presented has been adapted to the American mindset for easier comprehension.

Ordinary Americans do not know much about the history of China, its great dynasties, and its important historical events. It is also difficult to remember Chinese names, dates, places, and concepts if one doesn't speak Chinese. Understanding ideas in any foreign language is challenging, even after reading a translation. An accurate but dry translation often loses the essence of the original. Semantic and linguistic nuances in one's native tongue are clear, but such is not the case in a second language. Language represents culture and vice versa. One or both are frequently lost in a bad translation.

Often these translations are even worse than they initially appear. Translators may have brilliant linguistic capabilities but be ignorant of the material they translate. For example, a capable translator of poetry must not only be a brilliant linguist with an understanding of the grammar, semantics, and nuances of the language, but he must also be a poet. The same is true of philosophy. The person who translates philosophy from Chinese to English must not only be competent in both languages, but must also be a philosopher and scholar in each culture. With such requirements, it is clear why there are so many confusing and contradictory interpretations of the Tao Te Ching.

Therefore, in explaining the works of great Chinese sages, we must both translate the language and convey the knowledge. This book brings these two translations—the linguistic and the cultural—into focus as one so the reader can fully comprehend the power of the material. This text draws mostly on a professionally translated version of the Tao Te Ching and then provides explanations of its essential philosophy. This requires bridging the gap between modern American and ancient Chinese cultures. We spare the reader the unnecessary task of learning foreign names and phrases and translate most of the technical terms into everyday English. There are many books available today, written by various so-called gurus and teachers, that gratuitously employ foreign names and terms. Obviously these sayings and writings can be translated into plain English, but the authors attempt to create an aura of sophistication by using exotic language— a cheap way to persuade the reader that the author is erudite.

Such specious intellectual persuasion not only creates difficulties in comprehension—it also frustrates the reader. Lao Tzu says in the Tao Te Ching,

> **My teachings are very easy to understand and very easy to practice,**
> **But no one can understand them and no one can practice them.**
>
> —*The Wisdom of Laotse,* 297

For America's charlatans of modern Eastern philosophy, simplicity isn't the goal; these spiritual con men must hide behind exotic terminology to disguise their ignorance and fraudulence.

Preface

This book is called *The Truth of Tao* because, while there are hundreds of translations of the Tao Te Ching, there are no accurate interpretations that Americans can understand. *The Truth of Tao* is for the American interested in the secrets of the Tao. It takes concepts that most writings have made overly complex or blatantly wrong and turns them into simple, elegant principles of life.

Taoism is both a philosophy and a religion. The Tao Te Ching, Lao Tzu's five thousand characters of poetry, conveys a unique philosophical system. It is the "bible" for one of the world's most ancient and mystical religions. It is a testament to the power of Lao Tzu's teachings that his principles have a variety of practical applications, from holistic healing to military tactics to warnings that enable the Taoist to prosper throughout life. Equally remarkable, Lao Tzu created a religion that codified early shamanistic beliefs into an organized structure for interacting with the unknown world of Higher Energy, including spirits and gods.

This book focuses on the philosophical aspects of Lao Tzu's teachings and only briefly touches on its theology. Ideally, these two domains of the tangible and the intangible worlds would be taught in an integrated manner that reflects their symbiotic nature. However, without the personal guidance of a master, there is too much opportunity for misunderstanding and confusion.

The Truth of Tao is structured to lead the reader to ever-deeper levels of understanding. Chapter 1 defines the goal of enlightenment and identifies the root causes for man's discontent. Chapter 2 debunks common Western beliefs that create suffering throughout American society. Chapter 3 examines Eastern beliefs that do the same and eliminates the confusion caused by the intermingling of Buddhist and Confucian beliefs with popular Taoism over the past two millennia. Chapter 4 explains Lao Tzu's basic principles, and chapter 5 explains how to apply them. Finally, chapter 6 defines the conduct of life.

Throughout this text, the use of male pronouns or phrases such as "a man of Tao" are not intended to exclude women from the process. Taoism is deeply rooted in the balance of female and male, yin and yang, although explanations using traditional language tend to be male oriented.

Overall, *The Truth of Tao* performs an important task. It explains, in simple and concrete terms, how to use a profound and mystical philosophy on a daily basis to achieve a life of contentment.

CHAPTER 1

Enlightenment

Among mortals who attain happiness,
such a man is rare.

—*The Wisdom of Laotse*, 96–97

What Is Enlightenment?

Man has always been in search of an elusive goal—
"enlightenment." This yearning has manifested itself in
mythology as the great quests. Often requiring the seeker
of enlightenment to endure brutal physical hardship and
mental anguish, these quests demanded self-sacrifice.
Invariably, a quest culminated in the discovery of a precious
artifact containing the secrets to life's big questions or a short
audience with a reclusive holy man who had hidden himself

in the remote regions of a far-off land. Most ended in sadness, with the searcher's discovery that true enlightenment remained beyond his grasp and that his rigorous quest had been genuine but misguided.

One of the great quests' lessons is that the goal of any journey must be clearly defined or there is little chance for success. For example, a precise destination must be selected before navigating a boat. Similarly, a clear definition of enlightenment's goal is a necessity. Most philosophers and prophets have vaguely described the state of enlightenment as a bewildering collection of mystical, religious, and philosophical concepts. Remarkably, entire belief systems—religious and political—have been built around such ill-defined concepts. Man's ingenuity has been unlimited in conceiving *and implementing* absurd societies based on mere intellectual flights of fantasy. And individuals who have challenged such a belief system's logical contradictions (which were caused by its obscure goals) have been labeled heretics and suffered expulsion, torture, or death. When faulty belief systems are challenged with logic, leaders mandate that their followers must have "faith" and turn off their logical minds. "Blind faith" becomes the great cover-up for irrational thinking and undefined goals. Chuang Tzu noted this behavior:

> **The clever people become lost in their own devices, while the divine man can go straight to the truth.**
>
> —*The Wisdom of Laotse,* 308

For this reason, Taoism's pragmatic core requires a definition of its purpose. Once we have a clear understanding of the goal, we can explain all the principles without relying on "faith." This also means that there is no room for individual interpretations. Similar to the science of bridge building—which is based on the unambiguous principles of physics—there are no "maybe" answers in Taoism. Something is either correct or incorrect. Just as faulty formulas in engineering yield bridges that collapse, an ill-conceived definition of enlightenment produces a doomed philosophical system. Indeed, the clear definition of Taoism's goal is the bedrock on which all of its teachings stand. Precise definitions for all philosophical terms must become a divine, guiding principle to students of the Tao. As the saying goes, "One who thinks clearly, speaks clearly."

One illustration of Taoism's solid core is that for millennia its principles have been applied beyond philosophy and religion to the practical development of holistic healing, martial arts, and physical sciences. It is a testament to its clarity that it bridges the gap between the apparently intangible world of religion and philosophy and the physical world with concrete applications. This remarkable achievement has not been duplicated by any other philosophical system for three millennia; for many, this is evidence of Taoism's mystical origins. Nevertheless, with such a powerful system emerging from unambiguous definitions, let's make sure we understand our goal of "enlightenment."

Enlightenment is the highest state of spirituality. The achievement of a spiritual state allows you to live contentedly and find happiness in a world full of chaos, suffering, and absurdity. By becoming a spiritual person, you transcend the pain of the common masses and achieve a true "state of grace." You relieve your mental, physical, and spiritual suffering. This is the true goal of enlightenment— a holy quest to become a spiritual person. What could be a worthier journey than to discover the hidden secrets to living a content life during your short stay on this planet? Since achieving spirituality is the result of enlightenment, it too must be completely understood in order to give Lao Tzu's principles context. You must understand what it is to become an enlightened, spiritual person.

Many times we use words without thinking about their precise meaning. Ask, "Who is a spiritual person?" and you'll rarely hear a clear answer. Some respond that a spiritual person is one who communicates with God. But is it not a fact that we all communicate with God? We communicate with God in our temples and churches. We can also communicate with God while walking down the street or staying home. Anyone can communicate with God anytime he wishes. Thus, speaking to God does not define spirituality.

Others say that spirituality occurs when one thinks about the soul or the spirit. But what is the soul or the spirit, and how much do we know about them? They are, by definition, invisible objects. How can we bring invisible and intangible things into our material world? More important, how can we test intangible and immeasurable phenomena to validate our concepts? Attempting to take unknown forces from the world of the intangible and apply them in the tangible, physical world yields only confusion.

Enlightenment

> **If peace, order, and the pursuit of happiness are invisible things, obviously they cannot be really obtained by visible means.**
>
> —*The Wisdom of Laotse,* 157

How do you define spirituality in practical terms? Try to identify the most spiritual person you know and examine his characteristics. For example, if we say that person A is more spiritual than person B, or that person C is the most spiritual person of all, what is the litmus test used to determine these degrees of spirituality? How can you judge who is spiritual and who is not?

The Taoist definition of a spiritual person comes from its root word, *Tao*, which translates to "the path," "the way," or "the road." In Taoism, as in life, you should see the road clearly. You cannot walk down a road with blinders on your eyes. Similarly, how can you drive a car with a dirty windshield? If you cannot see the road, injury or death is imminent. A driver eliminates poor visibility by cleaning the windshield, improving his vision and permitting safe travel. The same is true of spirituality—we need to see our "path" clearly. We need to see where we are going and what is around us. Confusion obscures our vision and makes the road through life dangerous. Confusion is a dirty windshield. Getting rid of confusion, understanding our own limitations, and having the correct expectations is the path to spirituality.

Now, we can see why person A is more spiritual than person B. If person A walks on his path of life and sees his path clearly, he is not confused. He does not take one step forward and two steps backward. He moves slowly ahead with his eyes open, observing his road and all that surrounds him. Person A has an understanding of his limits, which leads to peace of mind. He understands what he can do and what he cannot do, and this creates contentment. He has an understanding of his expectations. He knows that his car can't go 200 miles per hour, turn on a dime, or drive endlessly on a tank of gas. With this knowledge, person A has the correct reactions to his environment, responses based on reality and not fantasy or desires of the mind. Therefore, a spiritual person is one who sees the world around him clearly, understands his limits, and knows how to operate within them.

With this clear definition of spirituality, one can understand why the path to spirituality is such an important quest. Enlightenment is not just a nice thing to achieve; it is an essential prerequisite for life. Becoming enlightened or content is a goal that permeates everything in your life. It has nothing to do with communicating with gods or spirits (like a medium or channeler), but instead is a state of practical awareness that helps you navigate through life.

Defining an enlightened and spiritual person as one with a clear vision of the world also helps us define the greatest sin in classical Taoism: confusion. Like dirt on the windshield of a car, confusion prevents clear vision and represents the primary obstacle to enlightenment. Many passages written by Lao Tzu and Chuang Tzu treat confused individuals in a rough manner.

For example, Chuang Tzu writes of a former duke under Emperor Yao, who explains that he has given up his title because the emperor has created so many laws that people have become confused and "lost their natural humanity." This, he continues, "is going to be the beginning of world chaos." Despite protests from the emperor and his court, the duke, disgusted at the confusion he witnesses, tells them to "go away and leave me alone" (p. 116*). Lao Tzu and other great masters throughout history have treated confusion with disdain, abandoning societies infected with incurable confusion. For the great masters, confusion is the opposite of spirituality, yielding only bad consequences for which they have little tolerance.

Sources of Confusion

> **When you are disturbed by the external senses and worried and confused, you should rest your mind and seek tranquility inside.**
>
> —*The Wisdom of Laotse,* 85

For enlightenment to work, the student of the Tao must understand the source of this disease called confusion. Where does it originate? By understanding its source, the Taoist can then amass a collection of tools (philosophical principles) to remove confusion and prevent further contamination.

To discover the source of your confusion, begin with the observation that animals are not confused. When was the

---

* All in-text quotes followed by page numbers are taken from Lin Yutang, ed., *The Wisdom of Laotse* (New York: Modern Library, 1976).

last time you heard of a confused bird or squirrel? Confusion is the state of mind that exists when we do not understand what is around us and cannot evaluate the information we receive. What is it about *Homo sapiens* alone among all earth's species that enables confusion to take hold and flourish? What in particular about human nature allows confusion to reduce us to blind men in a strange forest, where sooner or later we will fall into a hole and perish?

Lao Tzu provides the clear answer:

> **On the decline of the great Tao,**
> **The doctrines of "humanity" and "justice"**
> **arose.**
>
> —*The Wisdom of Laotse,* 119

Lao Tzu's explanation is that the artificial values of society (humanity and justice) caused mankind's loss of its original clarity as an animal (or unspoiled man). The values promulgated by society are the source of confusion in modern man. In essence, societal values replace natural individual desires and needs, resulting in a confused vision of the world. Society uses seemingly benign values, like love, patriotism, and material achievement (see chapter 2) to confuse you and control your behavior.

Chuang Tzu extends this theory:

> **Then came confusion between joy and anger, fraud between the simple and the cunning, recrimination between the virtuous and the evil-minded, . . .**
>
> —*The Wisdom of Laotse,* 126

Enlightenment

Lao Tzu's disciple explains that society's values cause so much confusion that they can lead the individual to act against his own interests. These societal values appear good on the surface but don't work in real life; they are a prescription for confusion. How can Christianity explain how, thousands of years after the creation of the Ten Commandments, we still live in a violent world where Christians kill fellow Christians with as much enthusiasm as before the coming of Christ? How can a good Christian turn his cheek against the blow of an attacker, only to receive another blow, again and again? Isn't "turn the other cheek" a central principle to the humanity of the New Testament? How can a veteran soldier serve his country honorably, lose both legs in battle, and then return to an uncaring society with underfunded VA hospitals? It is the disconnection between the values of society and brutal reality that causes confusion. With expectations built on values that are not borne out in the real world, navigation through life is severely impaired. We have lost our clear view of reality.

The uniqueness of Lao Tzu's philosophy is its identification of society as the source of confusion. All other philosophies and religions try to change human nature. They describe wonderful fantasy worlds of universal love in which an abundance of material resources allows for the elimination of suffering. According to these philosophies, the world would become a better place as each convert adopted their artificial values. Change occurs one person at a time until the world's suffering is eliminated. What a wonderful, logical, compelling approach: to fundamentally change human nature—beginning with you. Unfortunately, that one requirement is the catch! As Chuang

Tzu wrote, "... (since human civilization began), there is no man but has changed his nature... ." (p. 91).

Society, the prime suspect in creating confusion, is a social structure built on a hierarchy of classes dedicated to a set of ethical values—maintained primarily through a judicial system. Throughout history and in all corners of the globe, societies have created their own unique brand of confusion. The variations come and go, but one set of confusing values always replaces another in a cycle repeated time and again. Lao Tzu understood this thousands of years ago and developed a system to eliminate confusion for each individual dealing with the diseased society around him. Lao Tzu was the only philosopher who knew that the majority should be left in its confused state and that only a few true Taoists could enlighten themselves. Society at large was a terminal patient, but there was hope for those rare individuals willing to become spiritual and leave society to its endemic confusion.

The Process of Enlightenment

> "You rectify what can be rectified." When a man's heart cannot see this, the door of his divine intelligence is shut.
>
> —*The Wisdom of Laotse,* 318

The process of enlightenment is not an easy one. There is no magic pill. Eliminating the disease of confusion that has infected your natural being (your soul) requires rare dedication and focus. It would be ludicrous to think such a profound change to your outlook could be achieved with anything less than total commitment. In ancient China, a student wishing to learn from a true master first had to perform menial chores for years. Only then was he considered a worthy candidate. This ordeal tested the potential student's desire before a master expended valuable time and energy on him. Likewise, in mythology, any worthy quest requires dedication and self-sacrifice—and enlightenment is the greatest of the great quests.

> **He who lightly makes a promise**
> **Will find it often hard to keep his faith.**
>
> —*The Wisdom of Laotse,* 282

In the Far East, the process of enlightenment is not considered complete until the student absorbs the teachings, incorporating them into the natural core of his being. This state—called "ch'an" by the Chinese and "Zen" by the Japanese—is reached when teachings are no longer an intellectual exercise, but rather instinctual principles on which one automatically operates. For example, when you first learn to drive a car, you must think about shifting gears, braking, and turning the steering wheel. Over time, the process becomes second nature or ch'an—with no conscious thoughts required. To become a spiritual person, the principles of Tao *must* become ch'an, a part of your nature, or the effort is purely an intellectual exercise.

The implications of ch'an extend beyond the ability to act without thought to one of the most important principles in life: living in the moment. Once we recognize that reacting to the current moment is everything, we can have instantaneous action. The past is history and the future is unknown. You drive a car by reacting to road conditions and other cars immediately in front of you, not those you passed ten minutes ago or those that are ten minutes away. And so it is in life. You should react and live for the current day and not dwell in the past or fret over the future. The Bushido code of the Japanese samurai says it best with "live every day as if it were your last." This attitude results in appreciation for life and a passion to enjoy every minute. It is a cornerstone to achieving contentment.

In China, enlightenment is believed to occur in one of two ways. One branch believes the ch'an state will, after years of preparation, suddenly manifest itself in a brilliant flash of comprehension. Another branch believes the achievement of this ch'an state occurs gradually as Taoist principles are learned and absorbed over time. Despite the disparate approaches, however, both schools of thought agree on one important point: enlightenment only occurs after years of work and dedication.

In America, the notion of dedicating years of hard work to a goal is difficult to understand. Americans are used to a world of fast food, instant replay, fifteen-day diets, thirty-second political sound bites, microwave dinners, instant millionaires, world history in ten pages, and diplomas by mail. Whereas Chinese medicine emphasizes prevention practiced over many years, Americans want to be cured with a pill and a quick operation. Intense dedication is as foreign to the average American as hieroglyphics. Sadly, it seems the only area where Americans can understand the concept of total dedication is in the pursuit of money.

Enlightenment

Sensitivity

> To adjust oneself to events and surroundings casually is the way of Tao.
>
> —*The Wisdom of Laotse*, 78

To be a *dedicated* student of the Tao you must want the teachings of Lao Tzu in a deep and profound way. Many classical philosophers have attributed an individual's thirst for enlightenment to personal suffering. Without suffering as motivation, the pursuit of enlightenment is reduced to entertainment. And it is important to understand that your personal suffering is the result of two factors: (1) the environment in which you live and operate every day and (2) your sensitivity to the physical and mental effects of that environment.

Most great teachers have created their philosophies in times of chaos, when physical suffering was part of everyday life. In the ancient times of Lao Tzu and Christ, the average man lived thirty years, disease was rampant, famine occurred regularly, and war was routine. Women regularly died during childbirth, and most children died before the age of five. Death was witnessed daily. Physical discomfort and pain produced mental anguish, which in turn became the motivation behind the emergence of the world's major religions. Later in history, civilization produced "great architects" of social engineering who strove to reduce suffering. These failed social engineers unfortunately include the likes of Hitler and Stalin.

By contrast, modern America—built on the backs of generations of tough, determined immigrants—is a wealthy country of security and prosperity. In this era, physical suffering is not a regular factor of daily life; the average American doesn't directly experience violence, hunger, or warfare. For most of us, suffering is abstract. This obliviousness to surroundings, exacerbated by the comforts of prosperity, is addressed by Chuang Tzu's observation:

> **Many are the people who have a head and toes, but are deficient in hearing and in understanding.**
>
> —*The Wisdom of Laotse,* 322

Without the concrete motivation of physical hardship to drive the desire for enlightenment, only mental anguish can inspire the search for spirituality. In this regard, most Americans are happy with their lives. For them, a regular paycheck, a thirty-year mortgage, several kids, a car, and two TVs is "heaven on earth." The typical American does not need spirituality, because life's path is prescribed by social convention. Everyone follows this path, which is reinforced by teachers, clergy, and TV programs.

However, a few rare individuals are unhappy with this predefined structure. For those few individuals who can observe what is happening around them, doubt creeps into their minds and alerts them that something is wrong with the picture. Maybe rational people don't govern the world and good guys don't always win. Maybe universal love is a joke. Maybe laws protect the powerful at the expense of the masses. Perhaps the hypocrisy around them is symptomatic of a deeper disease. Maybe the conventional view of life, supported by all society, is a fraud.

If an American—despite affluence and security—can still be affected by the absurdity of life, then he has the sensitivity to perceive the things that the common masses do not. Typical Americans have a thick skin that is impervious to the hypocrisy of modern life. Without actual physical threats or discomfort, it is impossible to slap them back into reality, for this thick skin allows them to wallow in a fantasy world of bogus life principles. In essence, the thick skin is a shield and the lack of sensitivity to their surroundings provides the bliss of ignorance.

Sensitivity is a prerequisite for enlightenment. You cannot become a spiritual person without a sensitive nature, one that *needs* the teachings of Lao Tzu to find contentment. The forces of the Tao cover everything—planets, gods, even ambitious Americans. The thick-skinned American lives in a fortress as impenetrable to the forces of the Tao as a castle is to the weather. Inhabitants of such a castle are ignorant of the inclement weather, while the sensitive man lives in a shack with the rain and cold. The weather is the same for both the insensitive and the sensitive, but only the latter suffers. This sensitive man is now a candidate for enlightenment, for he seeks shelter from the battering of the weather and a path to warmth.

The insensitive castle dweller remains blissfully ignorant until his castle is attacked or he suffers a catastrophe. Only a severe illness, economic reversal, serious crime, or the ravages of war can awaken the thick-skinned man. Witness the chaos at your neighborhood supermarket when a severe snowstorm is en route. Note how crime skyrockets in New York City during a three-day power outage. Recall suburban America fighting in gas lines during the fuel shortages of the 1970s or the rioting and looting in Los Angeles after high-profile trials yielded unpopular outcomes. Just a mild disruption to the typical American's sense of security blows away the dust of civilization.

Social values go out the window when the forces of the Tao manifest themselves and insensitive people glimpse reality. Appropriately, the insensitive person will be ill prepared when the forces of the Tao make their inevitable appearance. Chuang Tzu's disdain for these insensitive members of mankind is evident when he labels them "snugs." He gloriously describes snugs as insects burrowed within the fleshy folds of pigs, living in comfortable ignorance until the pig is slaughtered and roasted:

> **The snugs are lice on the bodies of hogs. They choose their abode in the long mane and hair of the hogs and believe themselves to be living in a grand palace with a big garden. They hide themselves in the corners, armpits, breasts and legs of the pigs and think that they are living in security. They do not realize that one day the butcher may come and rolling up his sleeve begin to lay hay under it and set fire to singe the pig, and both themselves and the pig will be scorched to death.**
>
> —*The Wisdom of Laotse*, 79–80

Enlightenment

This statement colorfully summarizes Chuang Tzu's true feelings toward the insensitive person. It should be a wake-up call to all of us. Sadly, it will take a catastrophic event—even more traumatic than the events of September 11, 2001—to shake us out of our self-induced stupor.

Sensitivity is the key to enlightenment. Sensitivity produces the legitimate desire for enlightenment and must be cultivated to achieve spirituality. Sensitivity is necessary to see the world as it really is. Sensitivity causes your mental suffering but is also your salvation. Sensitivity is key to survival in both the business world and in combat. Sensitivity to your body and loved ones is essential for happiness. Sensitivity to the forces of the Tao is precisely what a Taoist cultivates over a lifetime. Superlative sensitivity distinguishes a great Taoist master.

Recognize the Sources of Confusion

> **And then when [social] Sages appeared, straining for humanity and limping with justice, doubt and confusion entered men's minds.**
>
> —*The Wisdom of Laotse,* 120

Confusion destroys sensitivity. It numbs your perception of reality. By recognizing the sources of confusion, Taoists train themselves to remove confusion as an obstacle to enlightenment. Confusion comes from those unrealistic expectations and desires that are divorced from everyday reality. The confused people surrounding us are like a contagious virus. Just one diseased person can infect thousands of people. And the newly diseased can infect thousands more, creating a never-ending escalation of confusion. As the ancient philosophers stated, "Tell me who your friends are and I will tell you who you are." If your friends, acquaintances, or surroundings are totally confused, it is easy to become confused yourself.

It is now fashionable to be confused. Movies, books, and our popular culture celebrate the confused person. All of the "in" people have analysts. We all know people who are aware of their confusion and announce it with pride—"confused and proud of it." When asked, "Why are you so proud of your confusion? Don't you feel it is wrong to be proud of these feelings?" they respond that everyone is confused, so they are just part of the world's fabric. This is similar to arguing that, since there are so many fat people in this world, I too can be fat and happy about it. Even if the whole world is sick and awash in confusion, it does not mean the man of Tao must join in this dance of insanity.

> **The truly confused can never get out of their confusion, . . .**
>
> —*The Wisdom of Laotse,* 130

While those around us are one source of confusion, there are other, more structured sources of this disease. These include the family unit and social institutions built over centuries to impose the values of society on its populace. These social institutions include churches, temples, political organizations, schools, universities, and a host of other value-infecting sources.

Enlightenment

One of the tragedies of modern life is its effect on the family unit. Not long ago, when the family unit was a structure necessary to survive, children—whether raised on a farm or in a city—supported the efforts of hard-working parents. Sons learned a trade from their fathers or participated in hunts for meat. Daughters helped in the hours-long rituals of cooking, watched younger siblings, and assisted their mothers in hand-washing clothes and dishes. All children helped in the gathering of food.

The family unit had its hard physical existence to reinforce reality-based values. Natural death was a common part of family life, as grandparents lived in the same household with children and grandchildren. When the grandparents passed away, they imparted a lesson on the circle of life to their offspring.

Modern American life has eliminated any physical need for a family unit. It has allowed parents to abdicate their responsibility to teach their children how to survive in the real world. The result is confused family relations and children raised with values that are out of sync with reality. American family values are no longer based on survival. Instead, they are derived from the musings of social institutions and the confused chatter of manipulative clergy, politicians, and teachers.

Throughout history, social institutions have been created for the benefit of the ruling class to ensure that society operates smoothly and its members behave like good robots. Often, these institutions threaten imprisonment or death to reinforce their artificial pet values. At other times, these social institutions, especially religious ones, resort to seductive values, like "universal love," to accomplish their goals. Invariably, these values defy reality, because the institutions want individuals to act against their self-interest. "Faith" covers illogical concepts and eliminates doubt. These institutions hypocritically impart confusing values to their populaces.

True to form, American schools deviate from teaching the "three Rs" (reading, writing, and arithmetic), devoting time instead to training students in political correctness. Education is increasingly an indoctrination program for popular values. And on the religious front, the hypocrisy continues. Priests—sermonizing from marble palaces while garbed in gilded robes—tell the poor how to live.

In an industrial society, institutions need to maintain daily control of the populace. The machine of society uses sophisticated channels of communication: television, film, radio, magazines, and newspapers—even the Internet. At its extreme, mass communication blatantly controls the population, often to extraordinary effect. We call this "propaganda."

Although not as blatant as the propaganda of history's many totalitarian regimes, American television—our strongest and most pervasive medium of mass communication—promotes societal values at odds with the everyday reality. While television in the United States is perceived as relaxing entertainment, its effects are insidious and hardly benign. The typical American watches more than five hours of television each day, absorbing its fantasy values as accurate reflections of reality.

While television viewers understand that television is not real, they nevertheless assimilate programs' underlying values.

Enlightenment

For example, most detective shows have nothing to do with the reality of police work. The stars drive fast cars, shoot up bad guys, meet beautiful women, and leave no crime unsolved. These fantasy heroes always demonstrate good American values; they are tanned and muscular, with perfect teeth. They live in million-dollar houses and act as if, for the most part, they are just having fun. And no matter how much trouble the hero gets into, the ending is always happy. The programs close with our stars rich, in love, and assured of a bright future.

Watching these shows is akin to taking drugs. Viewers grow intoxicated with the exciting lifestyles of beautiful people. While we understand that television is entertainment, it slowly poisons us with its implicit messages: winners must be aggressive and cocky; to find love and respect, you must have a lot of money; nobody is interested in a loser who cannot make money; heroes are young, handsome, and athletic; heroines are young, thin, and beautiful. In short, personal value is linked to good looks, wealth, and power.

What if one doesn't look like a Hollywood star? Or can't make the kind of money that they do? How can the common person live without these measures of success? How can people keep up with their role models in film and television?

This is how suffering is born. The harder one attempts to keep up with these make-believe role models, the harder it becomes to equal their unattainable images. This creates a deeper gap between the entertainment hero and one's own real-life situation. And the longer this goes on, the worse the situation becomes. Meanwhile, all of society's channels of mass communication—not only television, but also magazines, newspapers, film, and Web sites—bombard the common man with values promoting this ideal lifestyle which has no basis in reality.

Fight Confusion with Action

> **Action is man's nature in motion. When man's actions are false, it is called the loss of Tao.**
>
> —*The Wisdom of Laotse,* 120

Although society hammers away at citizens' natural desires, and society's teachers, clergy, and media blabber their hypocritical values, the Taoist cannot blame anyone other than himself for his confusion. Taoism is a philosophy of individual responsibility. Inscribed above the entrance to all classical Taoist temples is the phrase "Every man is responsible for his own actions." Classical Taoism has no place for the weak. Once confusion is identified, it's up to you to employ Taoist principles to achieve a spiritual position in life. Enlightenment is not handed to you on a platter.

This book introduces you to simple concepts for conduct that can strip away life's confusions and improve your daily contentment. However, for those who are moved to achieve spirituality, action begins with a search for a good teacher.

We've described spirituality as the ability to see reality clearly. And we now understand that confusion is akin to driving a car with a dirty windshield. It is thus the role of a student's teacher, or master, to help the student clean the windshield. Over time, the student learns how to apply Taoist principles to develop a clear vision of the world and the skills needed to operate within it. Ultimately, these principles become ch'an, and the student can clean his own windshield.

With a good master, the process works. With a bad teacher, the process is doomed before it begins. Selecting a good teacher is essential. Oddly enough, it is a two-way street. As you look for a good teacher, the teacher searches for a few good students. This quest for a good master can be an arduous but crucial one. It represents the first and most important step in achieving spirituality.

How does one distinguish a good master? Since there are thousands of self-proclaimed gurus and teachers, how does a student distinguish a legitimate master from a charlatan? It is difficult to find a true master, but once you find one, it is easy to recognize him or her as a teacher of the great art of navigating through life.

Begin by understanding that a legitimate teacher of classical Taoism will not have hundreds of students. The notion that there can be mass instruction of the Tao is absurd. Mass teaching of classical Taoism is akin to going to McDonald's for gourmet food. The master must work personally with a few students, slowly imparting a profound system that removes confusion. There must be an exchange of chi (life energy) between master and student. Obviously, a teacher cannot share limited chi with hundreds of students and expect any significant effect. When was the last time you heard of a concert pianist learning from a maestro in a class of fifty students? The transmission of Lao Tzu's principles is a deeply personal and time-consuming process that classically takes about twenty-one years. Your search for a legitimate master begins by avoiding mass-production teachers.

The next criterion for a legitimate teacher of the Tao is the ability to demonstrate mastery of it. First, his lifestyle must be consistent with Lao Tzu's principles. He must live as he preaches. He must be humble and shun fame, and yet he must have carved out a comfortable life. He can be rich or poor, but since the goal of enlightenment is contentment, the master must display a life reflecting his mental and physical mastery of his environment.

Second, the training system for a student of the Tao involves mental *and* physical instruction. Since words mean nothing without action, prospective students should witness the master (or his student) demonstrate mastery of Taoist principles with physical manifestations, including martial arts and chi quong (a form of tai chi that employs coordinated breathing). This emphasis on Taoism's physical aspects is important because a true master must be able to control the body with the mind. That is, the mind gives commands and the body obeys those commands. Without mind-body discipline, how can a student trust the master's ability to teach the more intangible subject of philosophy? A master must demonstrate that he has harmoniously combined the physical with the intellectual and spiritual. Without the integration of these three disciplines, the teacher is nothing more than a shadow of a true master.

Finally, the student should check out the teacher's ability to communicate clearly. Ask the teacher (or his student) about meditation, its purpose, and how to do it. Regardless of the depth of the master's knowledge, it is useless if he cannot impart this wisdom coherently.

Amazingly, the Tao's philosophical principles can be tested by their applications in the martial arts and healing sciences. Constant verification of these applications will, over time, forge trust between student and teacher. But it won't be blind faith: the student will constantly see concrete manifestations of the teacher's ability. Likewise, the student will demonstrate loyalty to the master with tangible proof: money, time, and respect.

The next step in identifying a master is verifying that his integrated system of training is based on consistent and clear principles. Most great teachers first define the source of suffering and then define a process to eliminate that suffering. For example, Buddha identified the source of man's suffering as material and mental desires. Therefore, Buddha's path to enlightenment required the student to give away all of his possessions, seclude himself within a monastery away from society, and deprive his body of food and sex. Lao Tzu's Taoism is based on clarifying the forces of reality to relieve suffering. Its program of instruction uses mental and physical training first to sensitize the student to the forces of the Tao and then to teach the student to deal with them.

Sensitivity increases with the development of your "third eye." This nonphysical manifestation of your ability to see and react appropriately to your surroundings is prized in Asian cultures. Notice the spot marked in the center of the foreheads of Hindu, Buddhist, and Taoist deities. Often, this spot appears as another, or "third," eye. This representation is a reminder that the gods possess well-developed third eyes that see and understand the forces driving the universe. The goal of any legitimate Taoist instruction will therefore work to develop your third eye with physical and mental training.

The training will initially center on developing the body with martial arts and chi quong. Students pursue mental development through meditation and instruction. As students develop their third eye, they are exposed to more mystical aspects of Taoism with religious and "magic" ceremonies. A good Taoist master will provide students with teachings that yield tangible results almost immediately. Any teacher claiming that results come only after many years of instruction is probably a fraud. While true enlightenment takes years of dedication, the student should experience incremental improvements in a short time.

Build a Life of Contentment

> **Perfect happiness is described as success. When the ancients spoke of success, they did not mean the symbols of rank and honor; they meant by success the state wherein one's happiness was complete.**
>
> —*The Wisdom of Laotse*, 94

Enlightenment means nothing without action. Taoism operates in the real world, leaving fantasies to Hollywood and organized religion. Central to this tenet is the conviction that enlightenment that does not result in a daily

Enlightenment

life of greater contentment is a waste of time. In this context, a simple goal helps define the purpose of spirituality: articulating and then creating a "perfect day."

Ask anyone to define the perfect day—one he would wish to experience every day for the rest of his life and which excludes work—and you're likely to receive no answer. While typical Americans can talk endlessly about the perfect vacation, they have no idea what to do with themselves if granted twenty-four hours of free time every day for the rest of their life.

This simple test demonstrates the shallowness of human nature. It also explains why people deteriorate so quickly after retirement—they are so spiritually void they don't know what to do with themselves. Suffering in America is largely due to individuals empty-headedly allowing society to define their personal goals. Society's goals become theirs. How ridiculous that our short life is driven by the confusing ideals shaped by mass media—the puritanical work ethic and ever-expanding wealth. Chuang Tzu witnessed this identical shallowness in ancient China:

When men's attachments are deep, their divine endowments are shallow.

—The Wisdom of Laotse, 107

The American dedication to work is the best example of society's goals taking over those of individuals. Derived from this country's Protestant founders, who preached that idle hands make for the devil's work, the professed love of the job manifests itself in the "work ethic." The term *work* has had its meaning twisted from being a necessary task to make money and pay bills to an effort to be enjoyed. Frequent pronouncements of "I love my job!" mimic a society that labels the hard worker as a "good person." The line between work and its antithesis, leisure time, has become blurred. Leisure time is that precious period when you are supposed to enjoy life—it isn't work, it's pleasure. Somehow, work has become pseudofun. It's all the worker knows and, while professional pride is all right, his entire self-worth is tied to his profession. The new definition of work has turned it into a game with money and power as points on a hypothetical scorecard of life. For the modern American, the emotional satisfaction of this game is tied to acquiring more money and prestige—all to the admiring applause of society. Sadly, society's cheerleaders push the blind competitor to act against his own self-interests. Like a professional football player who retires after five years to a life with a broken body, the burned-out American spends his last days with anger, knowing he was fooled into wasting his short life to build a bank account.

As a Taoist learns to deal with the world, he also develops an understanding of his own internal desires. He develops techniques to shrug off society's bogus values and becomes synchronized with his natural wants. Under the tutelage of a good master, he absorbs philosophical principles necessary for a content life. The final step in enlightenment is to live the perfect day—or as close as he can get given his material wealth.

One discovery in defining your perfect day is that many things you enjoy don't cost much money. If you enjoy

Enlightenment

reading, libraries are free. If you enjoy walking, it costs nothing to walk in a park. If you love fishing, bait is inexpensive. If you love to paint, paint is affordable. Long dinners with friends cost only the price of a good bottle of wine. Smell the air, visit art galleries, or garden—it all costs little.

The challenge is to "buy" free time. The real price of the perfect day is the cost of your time. Time is money, and money is time. This means the conventional path of modern life—committed to acquiring a bigger house, pricier car, and more children—results in a commitment of time and money that steals free time. Sought-after promotions mean more money but also more responsibility, more stress, and less freedom.

As you get older, the conventional American path moves you further from the perfect day. Get a bigger house by signing a thirty-year mortgage. Buy a Porsche with a five-year lease. Have a couple more children and begin saving for their college tuitions. It is no accident that financial planning doesn't include "free time" on the balance sheet—in America, it has no value. One of the great American lies is that the perfect day arrives after retirement. Modern retirement planning requires dedicating a significant portion of your current paycheck to retirement savings. The result is you must work even harder to make up this deficit and thus have even less free time *now*. This failed strategy also assumes you'll make it to retirement with enough vigor to enjoy it.

Even assuming you do reach retirement healthy and wealthy enough to enjoy it, you will have been so programmed for a life of work that retirement is an alien environment that leaves you lost and unhappy. Enlightenment provides you with the clarity of mind to define your perfect day and then move incrementally toward it as your life progresses. By having this goal in mind, you will make the big decisions in life that move you toward a daily routine that is more in tune with your natural desires. This path of life results in the perfect day—one in which suffering is relieved. This is Lao Tzu's gift to the world. For a special few, he delivers life.

The Final Tuning

> For a thing which retains its substance but has lost the magic touch of life is but a ghost (of reality).
>
> —*The Wisdom of Laotse,* 18

To put the process of enlightenment into focus, let's use the analogy of a small magnet orbiting around a larger one. The large magnet represents the absolute reality of the Tao; the smaller magnet represents the human animal with all its hopes, desires, and limitations. If the smaller magnet orbits closer to the larger magnet, it is influenced by a stronger magnetic field and consequently holds a more stable orbit. This decreasing orbit is analogous to an individual learning basic Taoist principles (moving toward the Tao); the results are realistic desires and expectations that add stability to one's life. Alternatively, the farther away the small magnet is when it circles around the larger one, the weaker the magnetic attraction and the less stable the orbit. At some point, the smaller magnet's

Enlightenment

centrifugal force will spin it off into oblivion. Similarly, by embracing society's fantasies and unrealistic expectations, we accelerate the instabilities in our own lives until all hope is lost.

This analogy carries further implications. We must recognize that the smaller magnet's mass can never draw the larger magnet. The large magnet is immovable, ambivalent toward the small one. This is also true with reality and man. We cannot create reality or even budge it—we can only get closer or farther from it. Reality is immovable, unchangeable. Inevitably, any attempt to distort reality just moves your orbit farther away from the Tao until its pull is lost and your soul doomed.

Enlightenment is a quest to move as close as possible to the larger magnet of the Great Ultimate. In the path through life, there are only two choices: you can move closer to reality, or you can move toward a world of fantasy. The choice is difficult, for all of society will urge you to move away from the Tao. It will be a tussle between societal forces pushing you away from the large magnet of reality and your willpower to move closer. Society will use confusion to push you away from your natural instincts. By blinding your sight and numbing your sensitivity to the magnetic pull of the Great Ultimate, society destabilizes your orbit until you spin out of control.

Our body is formed in the nine-month process of gestation. At some point, a soul or spirit force joins the physical form, and the embryo becomes a sentient being. That soul or spirit is invisible energy that originated from the Great Ultimate (which we've represented here as a large magnet). At the time of death, the soul returns to its origin. Since the enlightened Taoist has cultivated the balance between mind and body, the soul is better prepared to function when the body is discarded. If one's stay on earth is dedicated only to the physical aspects of life (eating, drinking, working), then the soul is lost without its physical form. On the other hand, if one's life is dedicated only to mental pursuits, then there is no clarification of reality through physical interaction and this person, too, has a confused mental outlook. In both cases, without a balance between mind and body, confusion is likely, both here on earth and on the trip afterward.

Further, as individuals disregard or ignore their inevitable mortality, they sever the tether with the Tao. The Taoist understanding of death gives value to life today. By clearly viewing the reality of daily life and embracing the inevitability of death, we tune our soul to the functioning cosmos. Our small magnet moves closer to the larger one, making the soul's final leap a small one. Taoism provides us with the tools to live a content life in our physical form and simultaneously prepares us for the final journey. Chuang Tzu writes,

> **He who clearly apprehends the scheme of existence does not rejoice over life, nor repine at death; for he knows that external limits are not final.**
>
> —*The Wisdom of Laotse*, 52

CHAPTER 2

Dealing with Western Confusion

And then when [social] Sages appeared,
straining for humanity and limping with justice,
doubt and confusion entered men's minds.

—*The Wisdom of Laotse*, 120

Confusion is universal. Once man became a social animal, creating rules of behavior to support society's values, he opened the door to confusion and suffering.

History documents that the rise and fall of the world's great societies is a direct function of the proliferation of values that contradict reality. Initially, societies built by the sword possessed values grounded in reality out of necessity. The reality of the battlefield and its effect on the warrior society made such societies pragmatic to the core. But as success and its resulting security was realized, values grew more esoteric. As a result, civilizations weakened and ultimately collapsed.

As a testament to man's inventiveness, each society develops its own unique brand of values and confusion. America is now at the peak of its life cycle. The rough-and-ready American culture of the past, built on the efforts of focused immigrants, has now metamorphosed into a culture of secure and comfortable weaklings. As our original toughness declined, the culture of weakness and fantasy grew.

This chapter focuses on American confusion as the representation of modern Western thought in general. As the Western world is shaped by the values of the Vatican, Washington, D.C., and Hollywood, America—with all of its greatness—has institutionalized confusion. By understanding these harmful values, you can inoculate yourself against them, particularly their blurring effect on your clear vision of the world. These values are your enemy. Understanding your enemy is the first rule of combat.

American confusion has constructed an obstacle course that you must conquer in your quest for spirituality. It represents a test of your character and will determine the ultimate outcome of your soul.

Let's define the ten major principles of confusion in America and how to deal with them.

Confusion #1: Mind over Body

> Therefore the Sage:
> Provides for the belly and not for the eye.
> Hence, he rejects the one and accepts the other.
>
> —*The Wisdom of Laotse*, 90

Taoist philosophy uses nature as a model for reality. This is a reflection of its shamanistic heritage, which Lao Tzu codified into a pragmatic philosophical system. At the core of man's natural existence is his body. While we think of our body as a permanent fixture—because it's always there when we wake up in the morning—it is in fact not very strong and definitely temporary.

Think of the physical body as an engine in a car. When the car is brand-new, its engine works well. After a hundred thousand miles of wear and tear, the engine will require frequent repairs and a constant supply of oil. As the mileage continues to climb, the engine wears out and ultimately self-destructs. Frequent tune-ups and oil changes will extend the engine's life, but they cost the owner considerable time and aggravation.

Similarly, it takes tremendous energy to keep the human body in good condition. We must exercise, watch our diet, and guard against the diseases that attack our immune system. Yet no matter how hard we try to protect our body from injury or disease, it will degrade with time. A simple, invisible virus can destroy the healthiest body in a short time. The body is only a temporary vessel, requiring food, exercise, and endless care. For the duration of our lives, we must tend to our body like the engine in our car.

To reinforce the concept of its temporary nature, think of the human body as a water bag floating down the river of life. Any sharp object in the river can puncture and rip apart the bag, destroying it forever. There are millions of obstacles in life that can puncture our water bag. Even the smallest hole will ultimately allow its essence to leak out and lead to its destruction. Having a body as fragile as a water bag is a burden, demanding that we navigate the river of life with care and diligence.

Our physical bodies, however, do not differentiate us from other living creatures within the animal kingdom. Our distinct body shape alone does not define the human creature. Animals too confront the same obstacles in the river of life, and like us, they must protect their water bags from death and destruction.

What, then, separates mankind from these animals? Both animals and humans require food, fight for shelter, and try to take care of their bodies. The answer most often given is that, unlike animals, human beings have a "soul." Unfortunately, that answer gives birth to more questions. Just what, exactly, is the soul? And how do we know that animals lack souls?

Great philosophers and sociologists have argued these points for millennia and still provide no answer. While most people believe that something akin to a soul or a spirit exists, few can articulate its essence. What we agree on is that, in the physical world, the manifestation of our soul or spirit is our body as it writes and speaks

Dealing with Western Confusion

our thoughts. Our body arrives in this world at birth and is the vessel containing our soul.

Homo sapiens are the superior species: we control other animals, build sophisticated social structures, produce art and literature, and develop modern technology for the mastery of our environment. On the one hand, we are of the animal kingdom and as such possess a body that needs food, shelter, and constant care. On the other hand, we are spiritual creatures who write poetry, philosophize, and build technology for our comfort. So what portion of the human creature is animal and what portion spiritual or intellectual?

Think of the spiritual or intellectual component of human beings as our "segment of God." It is this segment of God that differentiates us from the animal kingdom. While quantification is impossible, it certainly represents less than 10 percent of our existence—and maybe a lot less than 10 percent.

Since we are mostly animal (let's say over 90 percent), it is illogical to think of ourselves as superspiritual and unbelievably pure. That 10 percent does not render us separate from the animal kingdom. Yet, we do not live or behave as animals do. It seems this little segment of God both differentiates us and creates complications in our understanding of our place in the world. Animals' lives do not have the complications ours do. The behaviors and instincts of animals are predictable and routine, their lives simplistic and easy to define. Our lives, although 90 percent animal, are different, unpredictable, and complicated. So it turns out that our 10 percent segment of God is also the source of much of our confusion.

It is impossible for humans to be purely animal. We understand—through our intellect, our ability to communicate, and our capacity to rationalize—that there is an element transcending the body. But as long as we comprehend that our segment of God is less than 10 percent of our existence and acknowledge that we are vulnerable to diseases of the body and desires of the mind, then our picture of ourselves becomes clearer. Only in our imagination can we dream of spirits or angels divorced from the physical realm. It is our bodily existence that keeps us grounded in the material world.

Comprehending our place in the world results in philosophical principles and daily action that balances the mind and body. Unfortunately, such understanding is rare. In most universities and high-tech companies throughout the world, you will find professors and intellectuals who disregard their bodies. These people believe their bodies are simply extensions of their minds; the mind is everything. Usually they are overweight or extraordinarily thin. They are unconcerned with food or diet; they care little about their external appearance. If you speak to them about exercise, they are proud to proclaim they are not "health freaks" but rather "creatures of the mind and intellect."

This elevation of the brain over the body is contrary to reality. Imagine these intellectuals deprived of food and water for two days. Imagine them suffering from a week of severe diarrhea or a painful toothache. These "creatures of intellect" would cry like babies, caring little about Hegel's philosophy, computer programming, or astrophysics.

Dealing with Western Confusion

This attitude of "mind over body" breeds confusion regarding the necessity of having a body. This in turn disturbs our clear understanding of reality, as our minds mean little without functioning bodies. Think of how helpless and useless the human brain would be in a glass jar; it's obvious the brain is nothing without the body. The mind needs the body and the body needs the mind. The connection represents the necessary balance of mind and body.

The body has been called "the temple of the mind." The body is the housing for our brain. We cannot live in a filthy house with broken windows and holes in the roof. Nor can a house stand on a crumbling foundation. We care for the house in which we live, fixing the roof when it leaks, reinforcing the foundation, and replacing the windows' broken glass. The same is true with our body. We cannot regard our body as an abstract extension of our mind. It is one of the most important parts of our existence.

For a student of the Tao, enlightenment requires developing a healthy bridge between body and mind. This is one of the most important and pragmatic ways to eliminate confusion and suffering. A sound body reflects a sound mind and vice versa. Unfortunately, most Americans do not realize this—as evidenced by the fact that many of them are obese.

The same confusion is found in people at the other end of the spectrum—those who believe their body is the sole essence of their existence. Bodybuilders and health freaks who spend all of their time and energy on their physique are equally out of balance. They focus solely on the body, and the lack of mental exercise creates a beautiful body with a hollow skull.

Return to our analogy of the body as a house: theirs is in excellent shape, the windows are in place, the roof doesn't leak, the foundation is strong. Unfortunately, no one is home. Only a breeze rustles through the attic. Their lack of mind-body balance is as severe as the intellectuals'. Again, the confusion of physical and mental reality breeds anguish and pain.

Many Taoist temples contain a statue of the God of Longevity. He symbolizes the importance of the body's well-being, and Taoists pray to him for a healthy body. His place of importance in the temple provides an explicit and definitive message to the congregation: "Take care of your body in order to house a healthy mind."

It is interesting to note that the Taoist religion—one of the most mystical of all the world's theologies—places great emphasis on the temporal body. There is no confusion allowed on this point. To train as a Taoist, you begin by developing your body with martial arts and chi quong. This is subsequently combined with mental development through meditation and instruction in Lao Tzu's philosophy. But physical training is always the starting point for the young Taoist student's classical training.

Confusion #2: The Family Unit

The tiger loves his cub.

—*The Wisdom of Laotse,* 67

As creatures born into this world, we are dependent on those around us—especially within the family unit—to teach us how to deal with reality and survive. Unfortunately,

Dealing with Western Confusion

modern American society has practically destroyed the traditions and values of the classic family unit. In the past, tradition required that the father pass the family's values and the infrastructure of their livelihood on to his son. As an example, one born into a farming family would, at an early age, be educated and involved in the family's farming business. From the beginning, the father, mother, and older siblings would teach the traditions of the family's way of life and how to survive through a knowledge of farming. A child learned the life of farming and all that it meant: respect for the land, the value of manual labor, the rearing of animals as livestock. When the child grew to adulthood, he would continue on in the traditional lifestyle of his family. As such, the reality of daily life on the farm formed a common bond among the members of the family.

By contrast, today's children have little involvement in their parents' professions. In many cases, these children do not believe in their parents' basic values. They go off to college, often far away from home. They frequently pursue professional and personal goals that are completely opposed to those of their parents. If the child of a doctor becomes a rock musician, what do these individuals have in common? Further, the "generation gap" of parents who are twenty to forty years older than their children accentuates their differing philosophies and expectations of life. At most, they share the annual Thanksgiving dinner and perhaps a religious holiday like Christmas. Differences become greater over time, in some cases manifesting in antagonism and hostility. This animosity is born of each generation's differing perceptions of reality.

The loss of a working family lifestyle has important implications in the development of children's values. In the prototypical preindustrial family, grandparents lived with their children and played a major role in rearing their grandchildren. When the grandparents passed away, the youngsters learned about one of life's most important lessons—the "circle of life." By observing the death of a beloved elder, the mortality of human existence became a real and emotional experience. The cycle of life and death was not relegated to an intellectual understanding of a distant relative who expired two thousand miles away, but in a truly heartfelt loss. The modern family, with relatives communicating primarily by telephone, does not have the emotional connections necessary to make the circle of life an ingrained concept—one of life's most important principles of existence.

With the loss of the family unit as a child's source of knowledge of how to survive and prosper in life, the role of instruction and education falls to the learning institutions established by modern society. Long ago in China, when the agrarian society evolved into a more complex economy, parents could send their children to spiritual teachers. These teachers, such as the monks of a Taoist temple, would instruct young children in how to perceive reality and survive.

Modern America has no such institution, as personal teachers are available only for children with severe learning disabilities. Children are sent to community-based schools, then off to college to learn a set educational curriculum. Courses are mostly technical and scientific and do little to assist the youth in understanding reality or living in today's

Dealing with Western Confusion

complex society. Much of the knowledge learned in college is never used again. When was the last time you employed calculus or organic chemistry in your daily life?

Further, the teaching institutions in America have become so ineffective that many young adults lack the basic skills their parents acquired. Today, many high school graduates do not have a working knowledge of geography, mathematics, world history, or even basic grammar skills. The family unit's diminished role has resulted in the abdication of the parents' responsibility to train their offspring. Now, the job is left to ill-trained teachers and unmotivated educational systems.

In the wild, animal parents teach their offspring the basic elements of survival. Birds teach their young to fly. Carnivores teach their young to hunt. All animals teach their young how to live and survive. Nature has programmed this instructional role of parenthood to be the elders' primary responsibility.

What type of training do American youths get today? Modern American lifestyles make it difficult for parents to spend the time necessary to train their children in the ways of the world. The average family has two wage earners; both the father and mother are forced to work many hours. They return home after a long day and have neither the time nor the energy to educate their youngsters. In such an environment, it is impossible for parents to transfer their knowledge to their children.

There is also little opportunity for children who want to become apprentices in the professions of their parents. One of the major differences between today's society and that of the past is that the professional skills of parents now tend to be technical in nature. Generations ago, it was not difficult for a farmer to transfer the knowledge of farming to his children. From birth, a child was part of daily activities that the family undertook to sustain their livelihood. No such apprenticeship is possible when a parent has a high-tech career. Even the most advanced child is unable to sit alongside his father and assist him in writing intricate computer software programs.

America's technology-based society and the resultant lack of parenting time have resulted in a schism between the lives of adults and children. The child attends school and has his life. The parents work in their professions and have theirs. In today's society, parents cannot do the job that the parent in the animal kingdom performs automatically.

The fact that most spouses spend so much of their day in separate professional environments not only separates parents from children, but also separates one parent from the other. This helps explain why the majority of marriages now end in divorce. Commonality of experience begets a commonality of interests and values. Unfortunately, modern society forces children to spend most of their time in schools while parents pass the day in different jobs. The home has turned into a mere hotel where some guests are called "parents" and others "children."

With parents unable, unwilling, or incapable of teaching their offspring, it becomes the role of institutions to perform this vital function. Schools and churches are society's institutions of instruction. While they are marginally capable of teaching reading, writing, and arithmetic, they fail in teaching children to see the world clearly and to deal with reality. Ideally, schools would teach the former and churches

Dealing with Western Confusion

would teach the latter. This was partly the impetus for the separation between church and state in America, as specified by our country's founders in the Constitution. Schools (the state) taught the three Rs and churches (religion) taught children how to view the world.

While declining test scores demonstrate the failure of schools in their mission, it is the failure of traditional religious institutions to provide a clear vision of the world that is most damaging. Ironically, America's declining test scores cause public consternation, while there is no similar concern over sending children out into the world without the capability of dealing with life's challenges. Religious institutions sermonize on "faith" and the values of universal love but are mute regarding reality and survival.

This is akin to neglecting to provide a young army recruit with basic instruction in fighting. Such a recruit would be thrown in the trenches and told to learn from his own mistakes. What would his chance of survival be?

So it is in life as in war. How can we allow our children to learn from institutions that don't instruct them in survival? The mistakes made every day through a lack of proper instruction can be as deadly as those made on the battlefield. Once we understand that life is a battle, we realize that learning by mistakes is suicidal folly. Without parents or institutions doing their jobs, society sends its kids into battle not knowing how to aim a gun. The result is a metaphorical massacre.

Western mistakes about educating children are born out of a misunderstanding of the obligations between parent and child, resulting in confusion and suffering.

In most societies, the expectation is that children will respect, love, and repay parents for the time and energy expended to raise them. However, in all cases, there will come a time when our children will no longer need us. They will almost vanish from our lives. Parents often expect their children to respect them in later years, perhaps even providing financial and material support. However, this comes to pass only infrequently.

How legitimate are these desires and expectations concerning our children? First of all, children never ask to be brought into the world. The birth of a child is the total responsibility of the parents. As parents, we bring children into this world from an unknown source; years later, they will leave this world in death to an unknown destination. Children are never asked whether they want to come to this world, just as they are not later asked if they are ready to leave. Parents alone are responsible for creating their children and are therefore solely responsible for raising them.

People have different reasons for having children. Some, unfortunately, have no reason at all. In many cases, parents have children merely for the sake of having children or because their peers do. For a good Catholic, desire has nothing to do with it; it is the Catholic's duty to have children, regardless of the cost.

Sadly, families are too often overburdened with the financial and emotional pressures of raising children. In today's society, it is a tremendous financial and moral responsibility to raise even one child. Child rearing takes a significant amount of time, and proper education requires a substantial amount of money.

Dealing with Western Confusion

For those couples with the desire, resources, and time: go ahead and have four or five children! Such families are the exception, however. Most people lack the resources and time and are unable to educate their children properly with the survival skills necessary to thrive in our competitive society.

Responsible parents will spend lots of time, energy, and financial resources to raise their children. It is only natural that they expect something in return for these efforts. In truth, however, raising children is a poor investment.

With each passing year, the schism between parent and child grows wider, as the child spends less and less time at home. Parents, who have spent the best years of their adult life making sacrifices for their children, are loath to accept this ever-widening gap. Their expectations are out of sync with their children's natural course of growth. The result is confusion and suffering.

Parents schooled in the Tao accept that children will grow and leave the nest. There will be no return on their investment. By accepting this inevitability and letting go of unreasonable expectations, parents can eliminate this source of confusion and suffering. On the other hand, children should understand that at some point they will no longer require a connection to their parents. They will no longer desire to be under their parents' control. Neither will they owe their parents a debt of obligation; they have their own path to follow. This understanding eliminates the guilt that poisons our children and destroys their lives as they pointlessly endeavor to please their parents. Chuang Tzu was clear when he wrote,

> Your children and grandchildren are not possessed by you; they are the thrown-off skins (as of snakes or cicadas) lent to you by the universe.
>
> —*The Wisdom of Laotse,* 95

The model for Taoists is nature. By looking to nature, we see the mistakes of our society. The parent-child relationship is a perfect example. Animals give birth to their offspring, train (educate) them to survive, and then let them go. The offspring do not return later during periods of hardship and mooch off their parents. Parents don't chase down their children in search of support in old age.

The natural path of a child is birth, instruction, and then departure. Our society has lost this clarity. We give birth to the child, then leave true teaching to mass-production education factories (schools and churches) that don't even attempt to talk about reality and survival. Later, the parent-child relationship disintegrates into a futile attempt to extend its duration artificially, and the result of such unrealistic expectations is anguish and heartache.

While the Taoist perspective is a bitter pill—as it tells parents their "investment" in children is a poor one—it is also a wake-up call regarding moral obligation. Parents drag a soul into this world without its permission. In doing so, they incur a duty to train that child in the ways of life and then release him. Children not adequately trained by their parents would be as unable to cope with the harsh realities of life as baby birds that weren't trained to fly.

A similar dilemma exists among all members of the family. If you are lucky, there is a natural bond between you and your family, characterized by open communication. If the lines of communication between parent and child or husband and wife are not natural but forced by social structure and artificial values, the result will be a strained and difficult relationship. When we are forced to do something—whether by guilt, social values, or simple necessity—our endeavors will usually not succeed.

What we must do and what we want to do are separate and distinct. We happily pursue those things we want and our heart is committed to this pursuit, even if the endeavor requires much time and money. But we only grudgingly perform those endeavors forced on us, and the result is generally misery or failure.

Each of us has our own path. If this path takes us away from our family because of incompatibility, then we must walk away from any forced "family values" and be on our own. While there may be financial obligations for such a decision—particularly if one is the head of the household—if carefully considered, it is a justifiable action when done to avoid confusion and suffering.

Confusion #3: Engines of Hypocrisy

The learned is not necessarily wise, and the good talker is not necessarily clever.

—*The Wisdom of Laotse,* 312

There are only two types of sages in this world. The first one is the "classical sage" who resides in the mountains and to whom people travel to gain enlightenment. Such sages are not interested in bringing their knowledge to the masses. They have no interest in manipulation and control. They simply wish to fulfill their own spirituality and perhaps help a few select students do the same. By contrast, there exists a second, far more common type of sage: the "social sage." Such sages have no interest in spirituality, but instead want to bring their ideology to the masses for personal gain, reputation, power, and wealth.

Throughout history, social sages of all societies have created their "engines of hypocrisy." The hypocrisy of the ruling institutions, under the direction of social sages, manipulates and controls the masses. In clarifying our vision of the world, we must understand Western hypocrisy and how to deal with it. Hypocrisy consists of untruths offered (consciously or unconsciously) to persuade people to take imprudent action. Hypocrisy arises either from individuals creating their own false thoughts or from using others' false thoughts and words to persuade themselves to take unwise actions.

Hypocrisy has three possible causes. First, it can originate from sheer ignorance. When an individual is knowingly ignorant of the facts and still fights for some idea or principle, he is hypocritical.

Second, hypocrisy occurs when people use statements they know to be untrue for personal gain, making promises they have no intention of keeping. This form of manipulation has been prevalent throughout history. Individuals and groups have used hypocrisy to further their ambitions, fooling large segments of the population with their lies and false promises. Politicians and dictators are prime examples of such behavior.

Dealing with Western Confusion

The third cause of hypocrisy is idealism. Certain idealists, whether philosophers or politicians, attempt to bring about change in society based on ideals founded not on reality but on their own pet principles. The danger of such idealism is its attempt to manifest hypothetical concepts in the real world. When these ideals, based on expectations and desires of the mind, conflict with the real values of nature, the consequences are often catastrophic. The idealists attempt to bring a world of fantasy into reality, and chaos is born. Examples include the reign of Hitler, whose ideal of a "super race" resulted in worldwide death and destruction. Or Lenin and Stalin's Marxist experiment, which promised a socialized utopia and instead yielded 40 million deaths and an unworkable economic system that ultimately collapsed.

There are three engines of hypocrisy in America today: religion, education, and politics. These institutions spread confusion by promulgating values—the antithesis of enlightenment. In an irony that only a true Taoist can appreciate, the institutions that people rely on for survival principles and values actually give a dose of the opposite. These supposed institutions of clarification are actually sources of confusion.

Let's return to our analogy of enlightenment being akin to cleaning your car's windshield so you can see reality clearly. People rely on religion, education, and politics for clarification just as they use a car wash to clean their automobiles. In this analogy, however, instead of driving away from the car wash with clean cars, they return to the road with windshields still too dirty to see through. This occurs every day, with people leaving religious institutions, schools, and political forums blind to the world's realities.

Hypocrisy in Religion

> As an agent of man, it is easy to be false, but not as an agent of God.
>
> —*The Wisdom of Laotse,* 121

Religion holds a place of great importance in American life. The Pledge of Allegiance states that we are "one nation, under God, indivisible, with liberty and justice for all." With our constitutionally mandated separation of church and state, organized religion is the sole institution for teaching various creeds to the populace. As in most Western cultures, the Judeo-Christian faiths predominate here, espousing principles they contend are the word of God. The role of priests, ministers, and rabbis is to teach their congregations the governing principles of life as transmitted by God through his messengers—Christ, Moses, and others.

As skeptical Taoists, we should apply our test of a good teacher to Judeo-Christian teachings, checking for hypocrisy. We do not want our clear vision blurred by a charlatan's words. We must apply the same method for verifying the legitimacy of Taoism to any other religious belief system we wish to examine.

The most important criterion of an institution is whether its principles can be demonstrated in reality. Taoists want "earned faith" not "blind faith." Blind faith offers us no mechanism to validate what our priest tells us. Religious institutions counter this argument by proclaiming that they preach the word of God—and God's word must not be challenged.

However, God has never appeared before a congregation to speak his teachings. So the purported "word of God"

Dealing with Western Confusion

depends entirely on its sources—the Bible, the Koran, and the Torah. No matter how we view these "holy" words—the fundamental source for all of the principles espoused by Western clergy—they were written by mortal men. While Moses appeared before the Israelites and relayed the commandments of God, the Israelites themselves never saw or heard directly from God. In Christianity, God sent his only son to earth, yet mortals wrote the words of the New Testament. Both the Old and the New Testament have the perfect alibi for claiming their religious principles are God-given without having God appear. We should view with skepticism mortals who purport to speak the words or thoughts of God. Moses came down from Mount Sinai and claimed to present the words of God to the masses. Four apostles wrote the Gospels and stated that their words were in fact those of Jesus. Ultimately, there is no proof—just blind faith that these works represent God's word.

Since the sources of Judeo-Christian teachings cannot be verified, the Taoist next checks to see if their philosophical systems can be explained with consistent principles. Consistency is an important test to determine whether a system is true or merely a hodgepodge of unrelated (and often hypocritical) principles.

In the days before printing, the Bible was handwritten over and over again by mortals. Each transcriber brought to the task his own intelligence and emotions, as well as his own notion of the way of the world and the meaning of God's word. Each was thus tempted to put his own interpretation into his translation of the Bible.

This partly explains why all of the great sages and prophets of Judeo-Christian theology constantly bicker among themselves regarding the correct interpretation of God's word. Each religion has volumes and volumes of rules, regulations, and explanations. Conflicting branches (sects) have their own interpretations of the Torah and the Bible. These interpretations vary, and inconsistent principles run rampant. Each sect's followers—with blind, unquestioning faith—wage wars to validate their beliefs.

It is clear that the Judeo-Christian faiths lack the consistency of principles that illustrate a cohesive system. It is conceivable that the original words of God, passed down through two thousand years, possessed wisdom that has since been lost through mankind's tinkering. But there is no way to know. There are too many contradictions. Sorting through these contradictory principles would be futile.

Thus, the predominant religions in America fail on two counts: unverifiable sources and extraordinary lack of consistency. There is, however, one last test. A good Taoist master demonstrates, via genuine, witnessed applications, the manifestation of Taoism. Do Judeo-Christian principles also work in the real world? Let's play heretic and check out some Judeo-Christian teachings in life.

Because any philosophical system must be integrated, the failure of a couple of key principles represents the failure of the entire system. Of all their tenets, the power of love is the topic preached by most Judeo-Christian sects. An underlying theme of these religions is that universal love can be found through their respective teachings. Unfortunately, the principles born out of this belief don't work in the real world.

Dealing with Western Confusion

If you "turn the other cheek" during a mugging, you simply get hit on the other cheek. If you rely on man's loving charity to survive, you starve. More wars have been fought by Christian and Jewish soldiers in the name of religion than for any other cause—an odd and hypocritical brand of universal love. Love by slaughter. "Love thy neighbor" is a beautiful theory; unfortunately, it only works when your neighbor stays on his side of the fence, his dog doesn't defecate on your grass, and he doesn't paint his house purple. Otherwise, love is quickly forgotten.

The principles stated in the Ten Commandments work only in a fantasy world of peace, love, and abundant resources. Would you not steal from a rich man to feed your starving children? Would a husband not seek revenge against his wife's rapist? Yet these acts, justifiable in the eyes of most, are contrary to the Ten Commandments. How can seemingly natural behavior conflict with the purported laws of God?

It is clear that religious dogma is out of sync with reality. The principles of nature—bestowed by God—clearly apply to man, for we are mostly animal and thus not apart and distinct from nature. And these intrinsic principles tell us that Western religions have unrealistic ideals. As such, they don't work.

So Judeo-Christianity fails on three counts: unverifiable sources; logical inconsistencies; and unrealistic, unworkable principles.

Given that Western religions teach values and principles with no grounding in reality, blatantly against the interests of their congregations, what could be their goals? Consider that religious institutions are massive organizations, rivaling governments in size, wealth, and power. Is it possible they are nothing more than another controlling instrument for the ruling elite?

If one examines various interpretations of the Torah and the New Testament through history, it becomes evident they were often changed to meet the needs of the controlling class. One would expect the word of God to be immutable over time. A viable explanation for changing tenets is that they have been twisted to serve the needs of the prevailing social and political structures. Indeed, religious and political institutions have long been in lockstep for mutual gain. World leaders have consistently formed partnerships with popes and rabbis, supporting their own well-being at the expense of their constituents. Readers of history can find entertaining examples in medieval Europe and, closer to home, in America during Prohibition.

The most remarkable aspect of Western religions' hypocrisy is its blatancy. Observe religious leaders in their gilded attire and ornate palaces telling the poor how to live. "Have more and more children," they preach, "and by all means keep donating to the local church." Watch ministers collect donations from struggling parishioners in exchange for inane preachings each Sunday. Celibate priests live such an unnatural lifestyle that they molest children as an outlet for their sexual urges. The heads of these institutions preach that the body is the temple of the mind, yet they almost uniformly have unhealthy physiques.

Hold a convention of typical clergy, and try to imagine a more dysfunctional and confused group. America takes its spiritual guidance from teachers who have no passion for life. Some may not be "bad guys" per se, but they are uniformly confused—hypocritical to the core.

Most religious leaders deserve as little respect as the conniving politician. This is the unfortunate reality of organized religion's hypocrisy. It is not pretty, not pleasant to think about. But it is reality. Don't fall victim to their confusion.

Hypocrisy in the Schools

> **Petty knowledge is injurious to one's character, and petty conduct is injurious to Tao.**
>
> — *The Wisdom of Laotse,* 94

America's school system, like religious institutions, violates the trust bestowed by its constituents. The system designated to teach our young how to survive in the world has had its mission twisted and is now used to indoctrinate our children in the dysfunctional values of America.

In the twelve years of schooling that represents basic education in America, only a small segment of instruction is useful in adult life. The essentials—reading, writing, and arithmetic—are important, but certainly shouldn't require twelve full years to master.

Instead, the bulk of time is spent teaching subjects for which we have no use. How much of your public school instruction do you remember, and how has it helped you in everyday life? For example, many of us are taught foreign languages that we will never speak outside the classroom.

What is the benefit of studying the French language for two years unless you plan to live in Paris (in which case, two years would be woefully insufficient to learn to speak, read, and write the language fluently)? Communities develop curricula and thus dictate how our children are prepared for adult life. Yet, even with twelve long years of study to accomplish their goals, our schools insufficiently prepare kids for the real world. Unlike animals, humans are taught a staggering amount of unnecessary information. Schools have expanded their basic mission to include teaching social values and theories without benefit.

Worse still, the values taught in our schools are actually dysfunctional. Political correctness currently tops the educator's social agenda. As such, the grading system places great emphasis on achieving straight As. The lesson for children is that one's self-worth is tied to besting one's fellow students. Even more hypocritically, our schools stress cooperation on one hand while encouraging children to work diligently to outscore their classmates on the other hand.

In the ultimate hypocrisy, the school system that presumably prepares our youth for life does exactly the opposite. The artificial world of modern education has evolved into an institution dedicated to programming the community's values of confusion.

Schools teach society's values through a combination of two methods. Explicit programming systematically exposes children to community values, and unintentional programming occurs as a consequence of confused educators teaching confused children. Explicit programming includes the Pledge of Allegiance (fostering patriotism) and

Dealing with Western Confusion

prayer in private schools (reinforcing Judeo-Christian values). Unintentional programming includes naming a prom queen (reinforcing the power of physical beauty—unattainable for most girls) and cheering the football hero (reinforcing physical prowess—unattainable for most boys). Modern schools have increasingly become value factories.

As schools teach children how to think and behave according to current social values, they also teach the value of hypocrisy. When a child learns that success is tied to embracing dysfunctional social beliefs, schools subconsciously teach that hypocrisy is the way of life. They instruct our youth in hypocritical ways of behaving and viewing the world. The "new curriculum" stresses positive self-worth, allowing poor work habits, incorrect grammar, and faulty mathematics as long as children feel good about themselves. Such a curriculum results in a whole generation of children without discipline. It permits broadly defined "disorders" to excuse children's lack of attentiveness and willingness to learn. The true lessons learned by students are that accomplishments are unnecessary, bad behavior is acceptable, and society will absolve them of responsibility. That these students ultimately grow into underachievers, criminals, and welfare recipients should come as no surprise. We hypocritically profess to prepare our students for the world, when in fact we merely prepare them for failure. In effect, the three Rs are really the three Rs plus an H—for "hypocrisy."

Corrupting our young with hypocrisy is bad. Failing to provide them with the tools with which to fight life's struggle is damning. Parents must accept the blame for hypocrisy as well, because they knowingly send their children to schools to learn values that are the opposite of those needed to survive and prosper.

Hypocrisy in Politics

> In my opinion, the doctrines of humanity and justice and the paths of right and wrong are so confused that it is impossible to know their contentions.
>
> —*The Wisdom of Laotse,* 260

Politics is the business of creating and reinforcing values used to control the masses. These values support a social structure—institutions and customs—that the population is expected to embrace. Does the American political system promulgate legitimate values and concepts? Let's use the now familiar three-prong test to check for hypocrisy: (1) look to see if the politicians practice what they preach, (2) see whether their value system is logically consistent, and (3) determine if their political principles work in the real world.

Politicians are famous for saying one thing and doing another. Even the naive American citizenry is skeptical when it comes to politicians. This political hypocrisy is best observed in the lifestyle of American presidents. Part of the role of presidents in our democracy is to lead by example—to do otherwise would be hypocritical. Because the president is charged with reinforcing society's values by enforcing its laws, it is assumed he should abide by those values and laws. In essence, the president is America's role model.

Dealing with Western Confusion

Reality fails to meet our expectations, however. Many presidents have lived lives of rampant hypocrisy. The gaps between their words and actions have been large and well documented. For example, some presidents have dodged the draft but later, as commanders-in-chief of the armed forces, ordered soldiers into combat. They've talked about the dangers of narcotics and led America's War on Drugs yet have admitted to smoking marijuana in college. They've preached the value of a strong family unit yet engaged in sexual relations with office workers, models, and movie stars. They've extolled the merits of physical fitness yet had flabby, overweight bodies.

And it gets no better if we look to our legislators. Not only do their personal transgressions rival the president's, but these representatives of the common man have little in common with their constituents. Almost one-half of our senators are millionaires. They do not live day to day wondering how they will feed their families or pay their bills. Limousines take them from one spacious office to another, and they often own two large homes—one in their home state and one in Washington, D.C. They fly first-class and have large expense accounts. They have personal lawyers, secretaries, accountants, and advisers, all working to make their life easier. Special-interest groups curry favor, providing heaps of campaign cash. Job security is almost guaranteed, as the vast majority win reelection. And when legislators leave public office, prestigious jobs await them—if they choose to turn down the $80,000 appearance fees on the corporate dinner circuit.

At one time, legislators were working businessmen,

serving a part-time position in office out of civic duty before returning to their homes and businesses. When they spoke about how government could help (or hurt) the citizenry, their words were born of experience. For today's legislators, born of wealth and luxury, arguing that they understand the common life is the height of hypocrisy.

Thus, political leaders fail the first of our three tests for hypocrisy—they certainly don't practice what they preach.

> **In regard to man's desires or interests, if we say that a thing is good or bad because it is either good or bad according to our individual (subjective) standards, then there is nothing which is not good, nothing which is not bad.**
>
> —*The Wisdom of Laotse,* 51

The greatest cause of confusion for Americans is the lack of consistency in our country's social values. With hypocritical politicians at the helm, popular values are continually changed to meet political agendas.

For example, look at the early twentieth century in America. In 1919, Congress, urged by a zealous and hypocritical religious movement, passed a constitutional amendment that prohibited the sale and consumption of alcohol. Social convention dictated that it was unhealthy, impure, and criminal to consume alcohol. After a decade of law enforcement apprehending and convicting anyone associated with alcohol, the political structure reversed course and legalized alcohol in 1933. What was legal became illegal and then legal once again.

Dealing with Western Confusion

Such hypocrisy confuses the population. When social values change like the tides, the populace must blindly follow and "buy into" the hypocrisy. The common man is slave to a system controlled by ruling politicians; he is at their mercy. As Chuang Tzu noted,

> **Steal a hook and you hang as a crook; steal a kingdom and you are made a duke.**
>
> —*The Wisdom of Laotse,* 124

America is not unique in its inconsistently fluctuating social values. An even more dramatic example of an entire population held captive to hypocrisy is the Russian revolution of 1917. The revolution destroyed the social and religious values of the Czar's Russia, ushering in Communism. For seventy-five years, this new leadership oppressed and massacred anyone who stood in the way of the prevailing social beliefs. Stalin alone ordered the murder of millions (especially those with any religious affiliations) in his quest for a perfect Communist society.

Then in 1991, the Soviet Union crumbled under the weight of its unrealistic theories and failed economic policies. In Russia today, religions are back and capitalism is king. The Russian leadership has declared the old Communist values hypocritical and has instituted new values, which are similar to those of seventy-five years ago.

How can one realistically expect the human mind to adapt so quickly? The citizenry ultimately finds it easier to embrace the hypocrisy of the day blindly—the fewer questions asked, the better. Politicians, with their ever-shifting values, destroy our clear view of reality. The victim is the common man, confused and forced merely to bend with the changing political winds.

Western civilization's greatest example of rapidly changing social values is Germany between the First and Second World Wars. Prior to World War I, Germany was at the height of civilization and civility. Known for its arts, literature, and philosophy, it was a tolerant country that sheltered exiled victims of other nations. After the First World War, however, Adolf Hitler's Third Reich rose to power. The previous social values of civility were replaced by new values based on the goals of Nazi leaders. The result was history's largest global war and the destruction and annihilation of those who did not meet Hitler's Aryan ideals. Yet Hitler's social values, born of his psychotic mind and ungrounded in reality, would soon disappear after the defeat of Nazi Germany. And, as if the Nazi experiment had never occurred, Germans were expected to reembrace the values and morals of their past.

When America's founders—learned men who had to fight for independence from a tyrannical English king—gathered to prescribe a government for a new nation, they made a wise and remarkable decision. Noting a historical tendency to pervert governmental power for personal gain, they created a constitutional system of "checks and balances": three separate branches of government, each with the power to overrule the others.

This arrangement has minimized the inherent excesses of power that political systems foster. In essence, the competing branches of government have different and often competing goals, which helps manage both tyranny and corruption. Sadly, it's not foolproof. Loyal Japanese Americans were illegally jailed during World War II. Federal income tax, when created in the early 1900s, exempted 90 percent of the population and was not to exceed 7 percent of income; today, most Americans pay taxes at rates of more than 40 percent. We spend billions on our War on Drugs, while giving billions in aid to the foreign governments that support narcotics trafficking. Meddlesome, intrusive legislation robs us of our personal liberties. Our politicians maintain a spending deficit amounting to billions of dollars and robbing our country of future prosperity. The list is nearly infinite, but one theme prevails: although gentler than the version found in Soviet Russia or Nazi Germany, hypocrisy marches on in American politics. So, the political system fails the second of our three tests—it has no logical consistency.

> **I think one who knows how to govern the empire should not do so.**
>
> —*The Wisdom of Laotse,* 162

Our final check of American political hypocrisy is to examine whether the prevailing beliefs and values work for the average citizen in the real world. Our politicians are, theoretically, in office for one reason: to serve us, to make our lives safer and more prosperous. They are, in effect, responsible for making the American dream accessible to our citizens. To weigh their successfulness, we should determine whether they accomplish these missions. In short, do they enable everyone to achieve the American dream?

What best represents the American dream? Owning one's own land and home. This is the apex of our social—and political—values; home ownership has long been the litmus test for determining success in America. There is no gauge more often discussed by mass media, politicians, and our peers.

We need only look at our tax laws to see the importance our government places on home ownership. Home ownership has long been a stable oasis of tax reduction for the average American. The message from our politicians is clear: nothing is more important than acquiring and maintaining a home, and the bigger, the better.

We begin with a little house and a small mortgage, triumphant in our achievement. However, as our success and prosperity increases, we buy a bigger house, then perhaps another. With each successive home, we acquire a larger mortgage. As our home's size increases, it becomes necessary for both spouses to work, and our family never enjoys the tangible result of prosperity. In pursuit of the American dream, life becomes more difficult. Bigger houses, bigger mortgages, less free time, and a vicious cycle of keeping up with the neighbors.

Yet why is it necessary to have larger houses, bigger cars, and fancier clothes? Is it necessary for a family of four to live in a six-bedroom house with a pool and a Mercedes? Why not live in a two- or three-bedroom house with no mortgage, free of debt, just like the house most families start with?

The American social structure makes it unpopular to live a modest lifestyle. Success in America is demonstrated by owning expensive things. To support this image, the family

Dealing with Western Confusion

must work harder and longer, sacrificing free time. Life becomes more difficult, more filled with stress and frustration. The irony is that owning a large house, fancy cars, and fine clothes gives the desired image of success and the easy life; in reality, such a life is usually harder and more stressful. The hypocrisy is clear.

Besides the large home, what else do American politicians trumpet and support? If you examine any election campaign from the past ten years, one of the most popular topics is the American family. Indeed, our politicians wear "family values" like a badge of honor. Through speeches, debates, and legislature, they stress the notion that a good American is part of a family with many children.

Is there a concrete manifestation of our politicians' stated beliefs? Here once again, it is clear what social values they support. Our tax laws benefit families with lots of kids. The more children, the more tax deductions. The message is clear: having children is a good thing.

While there is nothing wrong with children per se, we might ask why we need children so badly. Why can't a family consist of just a husband and wife living in love and peace with each other? Ever since societies were formed, they urged their citizens to procreate. Their goal? More soldiers and more taxpayers. The implicit message was that, in return for raising children, society would reward you.

But nothing could be further from the truth. Children require tremendous energy and resources. They need food, shelter, schooling, peer-approved clothing, computers, and entertainment. Kids also require an emotional investment, replete with the many stresses encountered in meeting their needs. Parents must work harder and longer, and in doing so, forfeit the time to live their own lives.

Parents frequently say they are lonely and without purpose once their children leave home. They do not know what to do with their lives without the incessant demands of raising their children within the framework of the social structure. Sadly, they are so shallow they do not know what to do with their free time. Like so many others in American society, they are frightened by the thought of managing themselves during their free time; raising children has long been the single focus or purpose for their lives, a way to avoid this free-time crisis.

If this is truly the reason for rearing children, then parents have created an empty and primitive life for themselves, devoid of spirituality. They pursue meaningless activities to kill time. They always need someone or something outside their own body and soul for entertainment. Many Americans are on an endless treadmill of fulfilling the wishes and desires of their children, only to discover later in life that they have wasted their precious youth and time for little reward. All of this is at the urging of hypocritical social values and beliefs.

Contrary to social convention, not everyone needs a large home or scores of children. Everyone does not need a Mercedes and a gold Rolex. Each person has his own path and need not follow stereotypes dictated by the social structure. Quietly ask yourself if you truly need those things that popular values force on you.

Despite the fact that home ownership and procreation are two of life's major decisions, they are made with the least amount of thought. Even to question whether one wants to own a home or rear children is taboo in American society.

Surely both can be rewarding experiences, but only for people with adequate resources and temperament.

As one Greek philosopher used to say to his students while leading them through a well-stocked market, "Now you can see, my students, how many wonderful things I can live happily without." In ancient Greece, society's push for material possessions overshadowed the necessities of living a happy life. And so it is in America today. This helps us understand why Chuang Tzu cautioned that for every social sage, a great thief appears. His message was that politicians (social sages) who create the social structure's values are nothing more than big thieves. It is a warning to be on guard for hypocritical politicians who manipulate social values for their own gain. Ultimately, it is the people who pay, because the political belief system fails our final test—it doesn't work in real life.

Confusion #4: Money and the Work Ethic

> **I have heard that to have no money is called poverty, but to know the truth and not be able to follow it is called a disease. I am poor but not sick.**
>
> —*The Wisdom of Laotse,* 177

Work has always been necessary to survive. Viewed as one of life's unpleasant necessities, it was needed to acquire food, shelter, warmth, and security. It was the drudgery of daily existence—pulling you out of bed each morning, requiring sweat, and resulting in sore muscles. There was no mistaking "work" and "play": work was nasty, unhealthy, and demeaning, reserved for the lower classes. Only the social elite enjoyed dancing and luxurious finery; the lower class rubbed their blistered feet and picked splinters from their swollen palms.

Then came the Industrial Revolution. The old rules of feudal order—whether European or Asian—became vestiges of the past. In their stead came the ascendance of a new breed of worker: capable managers to oversee the factories, distribution centers, and engines of commerce. *Work* changed from being a dirty word of the illiterate to an anthem of the capable. Driven by economic necessity, it became a noble virtue. Ability replaced brawn. And the institutions of society took notice.

Through a change in the values promulgated by government and organized religion, work became a socially desirable trait. The "work ethic" was born. Whether driven by the hammer of communism or the allure of capitalism, work's image was transformed. It became accepted as a test of good character. Once the yoke of serfdom, it became a badge of honor. Working and its rewards became the goal in life. A good man worked two jobs—a great man worked three.

Appealing to man's unbounded vanity, society created symbols of success. The goal of any man of substance was to achieve tangible displays of self-worth: fine clothes, big houses, a large family, and all of the trappings of money. Life's purpose was to work for these symbols; acquiring the images of success became the measure of the man. The common class, once the feudal lord's slaves, became slaves to money. Encouraged by the brainwashing of society's institutions—including the church (promoting the Protestant work ethic), government (giving tax deductions for investing), and

Dealing with Western Confusion

Hollywood (equating material success with self-worth)—the population became a collection of voluntary slaves.

In modern America, the seductive power of money has expanded, its worship driving the emergence of two-income families. When the woman enters the work force as well, the quest for a bigger house and a fancy car come at the expense of a closer family. Workdays, traditionally nine-to-five, are typically much longer. Getting the next promotion outweighs the value of free time. Financial institutions create binding obligations that appeal to the Siren call of money: thirty-year mortgages, five-year auto loans, and retirement plans. The work ethic and its twin, the "money chase," sacrifice free time to acquire more material possessions. Instead of living within a budget—enabling him to spend a modicum of free time enjoying life—the common man follows the herd. He trades up to a bigger home or a newer auto, paying not only with his money but his life.

This single-minded focus on money and its accompanying symbols of success has hidden consequences as well, furthering the voluntary enslavement of the typical American. By constantly working and worrying about money, the common man doesn't have time to think. Work cannot coexist with reflection on life's priorities. The typical American returns home each day, comatose with fatigue, hoping only to enjoy on average five hours of mindless TV viewing. Life slips away, unencumbered by philosophizing on one's place in the universe. There is a comforting numbness.

Society applauds the work-driven lifestyle. The hardworking couple is heroic; the couple that takes time off, enjoys good food and good wine, and relishes less work is society's parasite. In America, anyone who devotes himself to not working is labeled a lazy bum. Ironically, several hundred years ago, not working was the ideal life of aristocracy. Now it is reviled.

The Taoist strives to enjoy daily life, viewing the work ethic as another social disease designed to shepherd the herd. For the Taoist, America offers a great opportunity. In this affluent country, a focused professional can earn a decent living and use the earnings to "purchase" free time. Time is more precious than money, too valuable to waste. Realizing this, you recapture your soul from the robot world, the collection of slaves marching bleary-eyed to the office each morning.

Confusion #5: Fate and the Futility of Planning

> Make not your mind a clearinghouse of plans and strategy.
>
> —*The Wisdom of Laotse*, 110

A child's physical substance is born from the union of man and woman, yin and yang. The child's spiritual substance is born of the Great Ultimate, or God. This spiritual substance can be thought of as a separate soul with its own fate on earth. As your body and soul flow through life, your path intersects other paths. When these paths intersect naturally, they flow easily and clearly together. However, when we attempt to force a union outside our path's natural course, using the power of social values and persuasion, we create confusion and misery.

Each individual's fate is unique unto itself. The soul we receive is ours, and there is no changing it, ever. Our soul may

Dealing with Western Confusion

be disturbed by our education, family upbringing, and environment, but it will never lose its core essence. As students of the Tao, we work to understand our physical body and its nonphysical soul. By doing so and remaining sensitive to the world around us, we interact with our fate's influences more effectively. We thus navigate life's waters more successfully, moderately guiding our fate to flow with the universe.

Let's explore the concept of fate, or "karma" as Hindus and Buddhists label it. There is much confusion and little clarity concerning this concept. Some believe fate cannot be changed, that we are born with a separate soul imprinted with a predetermined future. However, if we believe in the predestination of fate, then we eliminate any responsibility for navigating through life. In effect, we should sit down in the middle of the room and wait for fate to take its course. Life's empirical evidence indicates the contrary: we have at least some control over our destiny. If we chose not to eat, we would starve; if we jumped off a bridge, we would die. Closely examined, therefore, predestination seems preposterous.

Other schools of fate believe that nothing is predestined and that we as humans are in total control. They believe we determine the direction of our own path. Unfortunately, this logic fails too, because we humans are "mortal and mortal unexpectedly." We cannot make great plans for the future because we know nothing about tomorrow. We could be hit by a car, fall down the stairs, or develop a fatal disease. How much control do we exert over our fate when our life can end at any second?

In true Taoist fashion, a proper understanding of fate requires a balance between these two schools of thought. Just as we cannot control when we enter this world, we also cannot

The Truth of Tao

control when we depart. Nor, on the other hand, has the Great Ultimate constructed a path so primitive that every step is predetermined.

Instead, Taoist sages explain fate—the following of one's path—as a series of multiple tests. Each test may have one or more questions, and each question may have several answers. An individual's challenge is to find the right answer. If he fails, he cannot move forward, but rather will stay in the same place and not develop. Graver still, sometimes the wrong answer is fatal.

Just as we are all responsible for our own actions, we are also responsible for our individual fates. If our actions flow in concert with the currents of our universe, we will be successful. Not only will our souls develop, but we will also lead a happier life. The consequences are real and tangible; it's not an esoteric exercise. How, then, can you sense the direction of your predestined paths? First, you must understand your limitations, the environment around you, and the social structure within which you live. If you use your knowledge and experience, aware of your weaknesses and limitations, then your expectations are correct and you navigate life successfully. You will "pass" the tests that fate deals you.

If you go beyond your limitations and develop unrealistic expectations, then you will make one mistake after another, failing your tests. These mistakes will grow exponentially until they fall on you like an avalanche. Your fate will be disturbed, your body and soul doomed.

That is why you must be careful with your decisions in life. The past is a prologue to the future. Each test of fate is critical, and decisions must not be made lightheartedly. Some decisions may be difficult, requiring extraordinary effort and carrying painful consequences. You must meet reality with the attitude of a warrior and not flunk your personal tests of enlightenment.

An enlightened view of reality is required to follow your path. You must be free of confusion, not following the path prescribed by society. You must understand that your composition includes a small "segment of God"; as such, you are part of the animal kingdom, yet slightly separate from it. You must understand how to interpret your desires and maintain your body (the temple of your mind). You must view your relationships with your parents and your children clearly. Finally, you must take the proper actions when required. If your training does not reflect reality and prepare you for such actions, you will surely fail. When you understand these things, then you avoid confusion and live in accordance with the Tao.

Confusion #6: It's Never Too Late

> **Human life is limited, but knowledge is limitless. To drive the limited in pursuit of the limitless is fatal;** . . .
>
> —*The Wisdom of Laotse*, 174

According to the Taoist's concept of fate, life challenges you with many multiple-choice tests as you progress through its stages. Make too many bad choices, and you move farther off your path until recovery is impossible. You must take life's decisions seriously. Some appear mundane yet carry catastrophic outcomes. Fate is a harsh mistress, not to be trifled with.

Your actions have definite consequences. So, too, do your thoughts and words. But time carries the most dramatic of all consequences: time gone is irrevocable, irretrievable. There is no second chance to relive an hour gone by.

In the fantasy world of American thought, the passage of time is trivial—it's never too late to do anything. Start a new career at forty-five, have a first child at fifty; start martial arts at fifty-five; sky dive at sixty; immigrate at sixty-five; sail solo across the Atlantic at seventy. According to this philosophy—promulgated by mass media, particularly television—it doesn't matter how many mistakes you make in life, it's never too late. Time is irrelevant. Anywhere, anyplace, anytime.

Yet we know there is a time to be born and a time to die. Observing nature, we see that the four seasons follow an unchanging progression. With each rotation of the earth, day transforms to night and back again to day. There is a correct time for everything. And since we are part of nature, so it is a part of us. At each point in our life's path, there is a proper place to be and little recourse if we miss it. If a twenty-five-year-old acts like a five-year-old, the psychiatric ward is not far away.

A classic American archetype is the forty-year-old man who, experiencing a midlife crisis, decides to change his entire life and career. For the sake of illustration, let's say our man is a stockbroker who suddenly desires to become a dentist. Although his desire is remotely feasible, there are numerous problems. How could he support his family during his six to eight years of dentistry training? And once he graduates, how will he build a practice? Would you trust your teeth to a fifty-year-old dentist who has twenty years of experience or to a

Dealing with Western Confusion

fifty-year-old stockbroker newly graduated from dental school? Sadly, the fifty-year-old graduate could never compete with professionals with many years of experience. Failure is likely for our new dentist; his lofty plans are doomed. Soon suffering will replace ill-conceived hope.

With few exceptions, it is important to be in the right place at the right time. Popular convention will try to convince you that there are no negative consequences to missed opportunities. Nothing could be further from the truth. As a student of the Tao, you must train yourself to understand the timing of your physical and mental stages and then synchronize your actions with society's forces. This is a core concept in your spiritual development. Indeed, timing is everything.

Confusion #7: Unrealistic Expectations

> **He who knows where to stop**
> **May be exempt from danger.**
>
> —*The Wisdom of Laotse*, 172

The hard-core pragmatism of this country's builders forged the greatest superpower in history. Security and prosperity in America stemmed from tough immigrants; they sacrificed everything to make a modest living, wasting no time with grandiose plans.

Today America's young people, raised in a prosperous environment, harbor a disturbing popular myth: "The sky's the limit." Taught in schools and reinforced by television, this myth instructs us that any dream is possible: think positively and you will become whatever you want; there are no limits to your imagination or your goals. It is a mythology designed to produce failure, misery, and suffering.

Nature's limits manifest themselves in concrete ways, often with devastating consequences. Physical limitations are the easiest to comprehend. Take, for example, the novice weight lifter who tries to bench-press three hundred pounds and ends up trapped, a steel barbell on his neck. Even if the weight lifter was psyched, pumped, and confident enough to press the weight, gravity had a different idea.

There are countless other examples illustrating this point. The middle-aged mountain climber overreaches his limits and gets stuck on Mount Everest, perishing with eight others. The amateur pilot overestimates his piloting skill and flies into bad weather, precipitating a fatal crash. The thirty-year-old marathoner runs fifty to seventy miles a week, acquiring a bad back, destroyed knees, and fallen arches. The young girl uses diet drugs to emulate the models in fashion magazines. In all these cases, exceeding physical limits yields dramatic and costly consequences.

This is one reason that practicing Taoists perform martial arts. Dealing with physical contact reminds them that there are personal limits imposed by corporeal reality.

Hit a chunk of wood with your hand before you are ready, and your hand will break. Strike a target with *nunchaku* before developing the correct motion and strong ligaments, and you'll likely destroy your face with the ricochet. Attack a bigger, stronger student with poor technique, and pain is certain. The constant pain and humiliation of realistic martial arts training reinforces that the sky isn't the limit—your aching body is.

Dealing with Western Confusion

American confusion extends beyond the physical and into the intellectual arena of life. Many pursue professions for which they lack the mental ability or talent to succeed: starving artists have only modest talent; "actors" spend their lives waiting tables and bartending, awaiting their big break; computer programmers with little mathematical ability waste years of fruitless training; idealistic entrepreneurs lack even a modicum of business sense; terrific salesmen with no management savvy fail after being promoted to supervisor. The list is endless. Everywhere the limitless power of the human mind to embrace improbable futures causes people to overreach their abilities.

Understanding the concept of limits is vital to becoming an enlightened and spiritual person. So how does the Taoist identify his personal limitations, particularly since certain abilities increase with correct training and experience?

The answer lies in recognizing that we naturally overestimate our abilities. Our human nature deceives us into believing that we are handsome, witty, talented, and wise, even if we are ugly, dull, untalented, and stupid. By recognizing this flawed self-perception, we can construct a "challenge" process to test our actual limits. In this process, we don't trust our self-defined limits, but instead check them out in safe, incremental steps. For example, the experienced weight lifter increases his lifts by ten-pound increments (and always with a spotter waiting to help). The dieting girl getting ready for bikini season loses only one or two pounds a week over a three-month span, not ten pounds over the weekend. The amateur pilot gradually increases his flying distances as experience dictates. The budding computer hobbyist takes a nighttime course in programming before changing his career path. Each of us has strengths and weaknesses; only through constant testing in doable increments can we progress safely. This is the spiritual path.

Limitations surround us in millions of ways. Our birthplace, material wealth, and physical and mental abilities all work to limit our reach. Contentment is only possible if we recognize our limits and act within them. In Asia, some monks walk with their heads bowed, donning hats designed to restrict sight to a three-foot range. This is a reminder that suffering is eliminated by keeping our sight (and our expectations) directly before us, one small step away. This practical advice means that the sky is not the limit; rather, our maximum reach is the length of our outstretched arm—three feet, not three miles. Overextended expectations are a leading cause of confusion and suffering. We can avoid them by realistically assessing our natural limits.

Confusion #8: The Power of Positive Thinking

> Surely, the earth is vast and great, yet what man can put to use is only where his feet rest.
>
> —*The Wisdom of Laotse*, 88

The power of positive thinking is another highly promoted principle with no basis in reality. You can stand in front of a five-hundred-pound barbell and think positively that you can lift it. Despite all your mental conviction, you are more likely to suffer a hernia than budge the barbell. The unrealistic weight lifter is a victim of today's American culture, which teaches that, with positive thinking, everything is possible and will turn out all right. It implies that you need not work very hard; positive thinking alone will make your dreams come true.

Thinking positively is akin to dreaming positively. Dreaming positively is quite acceptable, however, if you understand that positive dreams are still only dreams, with no bearing on reality. Yet it is distinctly American to believe that the world of dreams and reality are intertwined.

Positive thinking backed up by no action is an exercise in fantasy and is best left to dreamers. If, however, you think positively and act positively (seeing the tangible results of your actions), this combination of thinking and doing will work positively. It is a paradigm that achieves successful results. Positive thinking without action possesses no value and merely obscures your vision of the Tao.

Confusion #9: Universal Love

> And then when [social] Sages appeared, straining for humanity and limping with justice, doubt and confusion entered men's minds.
>
> —*The Wisdom of Laotse*, 120

Our social institutions bombard Americans with messages reinforcing the power of love. *Love* is a word used by clergy, spiritual teachers, gurus, politicians, and demagogues. Entire religions, philosophies, political slogans, communes, and even popular rock concerts are built around the banner of universal love. Love has been reduced to greeting card images, often accompanied by pictures of smiling children, cuddly puppies, and bouquets of roses. Yet, what is love? Has anyone defined it? The practicing Taoist needs a concrete definition for such a central concept. Otherwise, confusion manifests and the path to enlightenment becomes obscured.

Despite Taoists being warriors in life (with a skeptical view toward all that is intangible), Taoism has a romantic core that embraces the concept of love but defines it in a distinctly concrete way. Taoists understand that *love* is a beautiful word encompassing acceptance, devotion, and compassion; when we truly love someone, it is our natural desire to take care of them. Unfortunately, this beautiful concept has been abused and raped by society's manipulators— religious institutions, politicians, and New Age gurus, for example—to control their followers. They preach that love is the answer to many of life's problems. They explain that through love we will become enlightened and find contentment in this world. Mass media, with television in the lead, promulgate this belief. Yet nothing could be further from the truth.

Taoists view love as one of the most natural and simple feelings. It is an integral part of the human character, an emotion we experience from the moment we are born and take our first breath. The mother gazing on her suckling child understands this connection.

Natural love is akin to breathing. No one teaches us to breathe because the act is a natural instinct. Similarly, natural love is an emotion that is not forced. Love goes to

Dealing with Western Confusion

the core of a person's essence. No rationalization is needed; it is inscrutable because it is based in the spontaneity of the soul. It is uncontrived, simple, from the heart.

This Taoist concept of instinctual love is opposed to the love taught in churches. Since love is a natural function like breathing, why is it necessary to go to social institutions like the church to learn how to love? Consider the absurdity. Do we go to a school of breathing? Why should we need others to teach us something we already know, something totally natural for us? Is there an ulterior motive behind the church teaching universal love?

The Taoist becomes suspicious when an institution blabbers about principles regarding emotions that should be instinctual. It is a definite clue that the institution—political or religious—is setting us up for manipulation, usually to our detriment. On observing someone preaching love, a student of the Tao immediately sees a large, red DANGER sign. Lessons purporting to teach us concepts that should be natural teach us something artificial instead. Institutions, particularly the church, teach us artificial love. And artificial love removes us from the ultimate reality of true love, which can be experienced on a daily basis.

Universal love is the most absurd notion in the collection of artificial loves, a bizarre tenet underlying many of the great faiths. In this paradigm, if all of mankind simply embraces universal love, then the planet becomes a better place, a world without conflict and wars.

This is nice in theory, but unfortunately, it has no basis in reality. Is it possible to love the whole world, filled with its billions of strangers? Just how natural is it to love total strangers? Love is built on subjective individual feelings expressed to a small and select group of people. Love is personal and private. It is a feeling that cannot be transmitted to the whole world.

Universal love is thus an abstract notion, an easy shield suppressing genuine emotions. It is easy to hide such artificial love, for it is a false emotion not involving the heart. It is axiomatic: the bigger the proponent of universal love, the worse the friend. Artificial love and true love cannot coexist— a universal lover equals a lousy friend and an unreliable partner. Preachers of universal love seek to spread to others their inability to express natural love. Or worse, their charade of universal love is more calculated, meant to manipulate others for their own monetary gain.

As Taoists, we know words are cheap. Without action, words are simply the movement of air across vocal cords. Words supported by actions enable the student to assess the veracity of the lesson. Words without action often lead to confusion and manipulation. This means true love must incorporate concrete action. Therefore, professors of universal love's power must manifest its ideals; otherwise, they abet another empty and destructive social value.

For example, many charitable organizations raise money to build shelters for the thousands of homeless people in large American cities. The contributors to these noble efforts feel good about themselves for giving a little bit of money to such a worthy cause. By giving tax-deductible donations, they feel pride and self-satisfaction, as if they are great patrons of the poor. True patrons of the poor, having embraced universal love toward strangers, could take a homeless person

Dealing with Western Confusion

into their household and eliminate the homeless problem overnight. Yet few charitable families embracing the idea of universal love deign to shelter even one homeless person. Words are cheap and substantive actions expensive for practitioners of universal love. It is much easier to talk about love and compassion than to put these emotions into action. Universal love fails the test: it lacks any tangible action to back its theoretical origins.

Why is universal love—such a compelling and desirable notion—impossible to realize in the real world? What limiting factor prevents universal love from flourishing and peace on earth from presiding?

Our limitations prevent us from loving the whole world as intensely as we love individuals. As Chuang Tzu wrote,

> **Isn't it abstruse to talk of love for all mankind? Impartiality implies the recognition of partiality (for individuals).**
>
> —*The Wisdom of Laotse*, 316

Chuang Tzu's axiom defines not only human existence but also all phenomena. Since natural love entails a concrete connection with specific individuals, we cannot naturally love a nebulous, abstract group of strangers. We can either love the world or love specific individuals. We cannot love both. Or, to paraphrase Chuang Tzu, if we are partial to the world then we must be impartial to individuals with whom we wish to be close. By embracing universal love, we sacrifice the ability to love individuals.

When we read about striking Russian mine workers who have had no salary for more than eight months, we feel compassion toward these people. But it is compassion in its most abstract form. How could we compare our feelings toward distant Russian mine workers with our feelings of love toward our own children? The emotions toward our children are natural. The abstract feelings of compassion we may feel toward the rest of the world are, for the most part, meaningless.

Thus, the Taoist must understand the concept of "healthy egocentrism." It is healthy to love yourself and the select individuals you consider your loved ones. This small group forms a cocoon. The Taoist experiences natural love for this cocoon, reinforced with action. And since we all have limited time and resources, the cocoon remains small by necessity.

This means the Taoist views the world outside the cocoon with ambivalence. The man of Tao maintains a state of cease-fire with those outside his cocoon until such time as war erupts. Similarly, the rest of the world really doesn't care about us. We understand and accept this.

Healthy egocentrism is how we should avoid hypocritical and unnatural expressions of love, reserving our natural love for a special few and letting the rest of the world deal with the hypocrites of artificial love.

Confusion #10: Avoid Conflict at All Cost

> . . . he can sit still like a corpse or
> spring into action like a dragon, . . .
>
> —*The Wisdom of Laotse*, 61

Since we now comprehend the principles of love, it is important to understand its opposite: conflict. Love is compassion, devotion, a protective instinct toward the

Dealing with Western Confusion

object of one's affection. Conflict has the single-minded goal of destroying the object of one's ire. Love and conflict cannot coexist; they are mutually exclusive.

If two people truly love each other, there cannot be hostility, anger, or hate. The classical American "stormy relationship" is a farce. For the Taoist, love and conflict are black and white—there is no gray. They are diametrically opposed notions, and to believe otherwise explains the many loveless marriages throughout this country.

The Taoist is alert to symptoms of degrading relationships with friends and loved ones. His sensitivity is enhanced, tuned to the precursors of conflict. Likewise, the Taoist constantly looks for positive symptoms that reinforce his compassion toward loved ones.

These positive and negative symptoms often manifest at times of stress. For example, observe your supposed lifelong friend when you lose your job and suffer financially. Does he lend you money or offer other concrete help? When you are sick, does your spouse support your weakened state with soothing comfort? Life deals many challenges and much stress and conflict. During those periods, you can gauge the true feelings of those around you by observing their actions.

Just as modern American lifestyles reduce your passion for life by not recognizing the value of absolute love, they have also created generations of Americans who are unappreciative of conflict's role in life. Life is a war. Interference in your life's path can cause suffering and even death.

This interference with your life's path can be as direct and physical as a knife-wielding attacker; it can also be slightly less immediate, as when a fellow worker attempts to steal your job. Your reaction in either case affects your well-being, as do the actions of those around you.

It has become distinctly American to avoid conflict at all costs. We hide our aversion under the mask of social politeness or a professed disdain for direct confrontation, but in reality, we are fast becoming a nation of wimps. Confrontation of any kind is to be avoided; when avoidance is impossible, it must be embraced with passion.

You cannot politely deter an attacker. You must respond aggressively, seeking to destroy him with maximum harm. Going to war in a polite fashion resulted in the prolonged, pointless fighting in Vietnam. A business that embraces passive coexistence with its competition is a step away from bankruptcy. Conflict requires a passionate, unrelenting response. This response must be cultivated; your goal is to destroy your enemy with as much enthusiasm as you display in caring for your loved ones.

Avoiding conflict at all costs is a coward's principle. The lack of passion to fight finds its twin in the lack of passion to love. A master warrior is a sensitive person.

An interesting result of embracing the coward's way is that those who wish to do harm sense your fear. It is a proven theory of victimology that an attitude of avoiding conflict actually invites trouble. The old lady who strides down the street with an upright posture, alert eyes, and a brisk step will be passed over as a target. The dazed, 140-pound wimp with untied shoes, computer manuals in hand, and eyes darting in fear will probably be mugged. Just as a lion identifies its prey by searching out the herd's weak or sickly members, so too do human predators seek out the weak or cowardly to victimize.

An attitude of avoiding conflict is not the Taoist way. Enlightenment includes learning to deal with conflict head-on. A paradox of the Tao is that the more you train and prepare for conflict—mentally and physically—the less likely it is to appear. Or, as the Romans stated, "To live in peace, prepare for war."

Conclusion

> Without clarity, the Heavens would shake, . . .
>
> —*The Wisdom of Laotse,* 204

From a historical perspective, America is arguably the best nation in the world, currently enjoying its finest hour. With economic prosperity and unparalleled national security, the United States provides most citizens with a safe environment and the means to support themselves. Even more remarkable, the freedoms afforded by our unique constitutional government allow individuals to lead almost any lifestyle (as long as they do so quietly). Unfortunately, many Americans have been beguiled by the dysfunctional values of this society and become enslaved robots. Using motivations like pride, greed, and cowardice, the social elite have created a land of the walking dead. And, in the gentle world of modern America, reality's harsh forces are ameliorated, unable to slap society's victims out of their trance.

As the American Taoist attempts to shrug off the influences of society, he finds he must unflinchingly address his confusion. This requires abandoning cherished beliefs, learned since childhood, through a brutal process of self-sacrifice and perseverance. Such a journey requires a special individual who has both sensitivity and courage. And that rare individual needs a rare master—a confluence of time and place that only the gods can effect.

Lao Tzu performed an amazing feat. He developed—from his vantage point twenty-five hundred years ago—a philosophy that instructs Americans how to operate in a world of "chaos, suffering, and absurdity." Somehow this ancient sage accomplished the impossible: linking tangible with intangible, physical with nonphysical, and nature with society, this wise old man implores us from across the centuries to rediscover our natural soul. His message is in sync with our national heritage, reflecting the values of the original American persona: tough Irish immigrants, practical Yankees, and swaggering cowboys. He reminds us that life is so short that our passion must be recaptured from the clergy and politicians who sap our essence and turn us into zombies. He challenges us to look life squarely in the eyes and act.

Like a cell key given to a prisoner, Lao Tzu's truths allow the American Taoist to escape the prison of false values. His eighty-one poems in the Tao Te Ching unlock the secrets to contentment. They are as relevant today as they were in 600 B.C. These tools are defined in a structured philosophical system that passes the tests of simplicity, consistency, and practicality. Most important, the Old Master was a prophet with no ulterior motives. He wrote the five thousand words of the Tao Te Ching and disappeared.

Dealing with Western Confusion

If you choose to use Lao Tzu's principles to find contentment, you commit yourself to a deeply personal process of enlightenment. Under the guidance of a master, the student's confusion is stripped away layer by layer, as the body and mind develop sensitivity to the Tao's forces. This ability—to see things as they truly are—is the prerequisite for passing the tests that life will throw at you. Clear vision yields correct action.

America's confusion is pervasive but not unique. All societies through history have used different brands of confusion; this confusion, crucial to the societies' development, eventually metamorphosed into structures that led to their collapse.

Similarly, American society is a necessary evil; it is the foundation of our stable government and its functioning economic system. Its strength enables us to build superhighways stretching from coast to coast, construct buildings rising to the clouds, replace decayed heart valves, operate billion-dollar banks, fly to the moon, supply supermarkets with fresh food, and provide all the trappings of modern life.

To accomplish this feat, we have created laws and regulations supported by the cultural norms. Mass media, particularly television, wittingly and unwittingly conspire with clergy, educators, and politicians to breed confusion, furthering support of the system. The majority of Americans blindly and unquestioningly accepts institutional hypocrisy, even though it becomes blatantly clear when explained. The brainwashing by church, state, and Hollywood has been successful. The trained Taoist learns to recognize these promulgators of false values, inoculating himself to their deleterious effects. He wisely disguises his disdain for this environment, camouflaging it to avoid the wrath of an aroused herd of unthinking men.

Lao Tzu's use of poetry to explain his profound system—combined with his desire to make the teachings understandable only through the instruction of a master—has led to many distorted versions of his philosophy. Consequently, the typical American's interpretation of the Tao is a mixture of illogical New Age trash that bears no resemblance to his actual teachings.

Contrary to Taoism's pragmatic core, Americans place Lao Tzu's teachings in a category filled with exotic and esoteric ideas. Nothing could be further from the truth. Rather, Taoism is ironically the most "American" of all of the world's religions. It embraces capitalism, for example, since that economic system is fundamentally consistent with the Taoist view of natural self-interest. The country's founders had a powerful distrust of centralized governmental authority, which is consistent with Taoist thinking. The constitutional right to bear arms reflects the Taoist view that personal protection is primarily one's own responsibility and shouldn't be left to others. Even the pragmatism of Taoist sciences (demonstrated in their ancient use of herbal medicine, discovery of gun powder, and development of precise astronomical charts) would be appreciated by Thomas Jefferson, Thomas Edison, Henry Ford, and other American innovators.

This ancient Chinese philosophy calls for Americans to rediscover the core of what made this country great. While America's ultimate fate (like that of great civilizations

Dealing with Western Confusion

throughout history) is probably doomed, there is hope for those few individuals who can grasp Lao Tzu's concepts. They can carve out a truly content life and live in peace.

For that rare American willing to venture out from modern civilization's stifling shroud, there is a philosophy with principles that once typified America's best: self-awareness, self-preservation, and self-reliance. Mystically formulated thousands of years ago, it may well be your home.

CHAPTER 3

Dealing with Eastern Confusion

People who abnormally develop humanity . . . make the world noisy with their discussions and cause it to follow impractical doctrines.

—*The Wisdom of Laotse*, 59

Why Do We Need This Chapter?

Some readers may ask why *The Truth of Tao* includes a chapter explaining the basic tenets of Buddhism and Confucianism. Indeed, Lao Tzu warns that effort spent in extraneous mental explorations wastes energy and opens the door to confusion; it is enough of a challenge to comprehend fully the profound teachings of Taoism, let alone try to understand other belief systems. Further, Taoists care little about "converting" others to their way of thinking, only wishing to explain Lao Tzu's principles to interested parties and then leave them to their own devices. Stated succinctly: Taoists don't preach, they explain.

Despite these concerns, it is necessary to delve into Buddhism and Confucianism for three basic reasons. First, Taoism, Buddhism, and Confucianism concurrently dominated ancient China and have influenced each other over the past two millennia. Significantly, Buddhist and Confucian beliefs contributed to the mutation of *classical* Taoism into *popular* Taoism, which has little in common with the original postulates of Lao Tzu. Popular Taoism borrowed heavily from Buddhist and Confucian principles to create a superficial philosophy designed for the masses and contributed to the loss of much of Taoism's original teachings. For example, some Taoist sects have embraced Confucian principles that honor certain aspects of social convention (anathema to classical Taoists); other Taoist sects have borrowed Buddhist vegetarianism; and in their religious mythologies, Taoism and Buddhism share the Legend of the Eight Immortals and the Goddess of Mercy. Thus, it is helpful to identify those doctrines that have transformed some of classical Taoism's core principles into non-Taoist notions.

The second reason for discussing Buddhism and Confucianism is that comparing their philosophical principles to Taoism clarifies basic concepts. Comparative analysis is a traditional method of studying phenomena by

Dealing with Eastern Confusion

looking at the stark contrasts between them. This is similar to the Taoist principle of opposites (yin and yang). For example, to understand "hot," one must first experience "cold." Comparing Buddhism and Confucianism to Taoism eliminates ambiguity and sharpens one's overall appreciation of classical Taoist principles.

The third reason for including an analysis of Buddhism and Confucianism gets to *The Truth of Tao's* central purpose: to explain unambiguously the philosophy and religion of the Tao to Americans. The American reader who invests time in reading this book has probably found traditional Judeo-Christian beliefs lacking in some way, and the allure of Eastern philosophies offers hope. Yet a concise explanation of these seemingly related philosophies does not exist.

Thousands of books and essays have been written about Taoism, Buddhism, and Confucianism. Unfortunately they do not give simple, clear, and succinct explanations of each religion's principles. All the truly great books written about these religions are intended for scholars, an audience already familiar with the material and thus able to comprehend the texts. These lofty, academic discourses create confusion by offering conflicting interpretations and abstract notions. New Age texts confuse the issue further with principles bearing no resemblance to any classical teachings. *The Truth of Tao* fills this void by explaining relevant core principles in simple terms so that esoteric notions do not beguile the American reader.

The sages of Taoism, Confucianism, and Buddhism were all born within a fifty-year period. It is believed that Buddha was born around 560 B.C., Confucius around 551 B.C., and Lao Tzu around 571 B.C. While each proclaimed they were not gods themselves, the birth of these three great teachers signified an unusual change in the rhythm of the universe. Their impact on the lives of the people throughout Asia cannot be overestimated.

While Western studies of Eastern belief systems traditionally categorize them as similar philosophical teachings, nothing could be further from the truth. Their differences are as great as those between night and day, heaven and earth. Fundamentally, Taoism stands alone among the three in its dedication to cultivating one's individual nature against society's tidal force. Buddhism and Confucianism, on the other hand, work to reinforce the connection between the goals of their respective societies and those of the individual. In the comparative analysis that follows, the reader should note the uniqueness of Taoism's central theme: fighting for a clear vision of reality against the confusions promulgated by social values—even those prescribed by other Eastern philosophies.

Buddhism

When a man is born, sorrow comes with it.

—The Wisdom of Laotse, 247

Buddhism originated, not in China, but in India almost twenty-five hundred years ago. It was introduced to China approximately four hundred years later and spread rapidly, becoming one of the country's three major religions. There are no "official" religions under the Communist regime controlling today's People's Republic of China, yet Buddhist temples still exist and function throughout the country.

Dealing with Eastern Confusion

Prince Siddhartha (Buddha), a nobleman born into a wealthy Brahmin family, founded Buddhism. While his legend has been greatly embellished over time, it is instructive as to the origins of this important religion and philosophical system.

The legend begins between the sixth and fifth century B.C. with young Prince Siddhartha living a luxurious life, guarded from all suffering and pain. Once, on a trip outside the shelter of the palace grounds, he came upon an aged man and learned of the afflictions associated with growing old. On his next trip, he met a sick man and discovered disease. On a third trip, he saw a dead body and learned about death. Siddhartha realized that he had been sheltered from the realities of life and set out to travel into the real world and search for life's truths.

At the age of twenty-nine, the prince left his palace, wife, and newborn son to find enlightenment. During his journeys throughout India, he joined several religious groups and learned meditation and yoga. One group with whom Siddhartha purportedly lived was the "Ascetics." The Ascetics believed that by depriving themselves of food and water—torturing themselves—they would achieve enlightenment. After days without food and water, however, Siddhartha understood enlightenment had nothing to do with self-deprivation. He left the Ascetics and continued on his travels.

In the sixth year of his journey, Siddhartha stopped to rest under a banyan tree, determined to become enlightened. Following a period of deep meditation, he came to understand the "Four Noble Truths." These truths are the cornerstone of Buddhism and form the basis of his teachings.

Later in his life, pilgrims would come to Buddha and ask him if he were a god or an angel. He would answer, "I am just a man, but I am an awakened one." His message was that in a world full of people sleepwalking through life, he was aware of or awakened to the world's truths.

Pilgrims would also ask about the existence of supreme powers, the afterlife, and immortality. Buddha would never answer. For this reason, he was given the title of the "Silent One." While silence on religion's major concepts frustrated Buddha's students, he believed that such concepts were beyond the comprehension of mortal men, including himself. Buddha's teachings were therefore practical. He adhered to his goal of simply teaching how to relieve suffering.

Despite Buddha's repeated denial that he was either a god or a messenger of God, on his death his teachings became the basis for the religion of Buddhism. Thus, nearly everything he had denied in his lifetime, including his promotion to the status of a god, was later embraced by his followers. Buddhist statues were created, with attendant rituals and ceremonies. Today Buddhism is an endless series of ceremonies, worship, and rituals, all honoring a man who wished for nothing of the sort. A layer of inconsequential ceremonial performances has masked the core beliefs of this teacher.

The Four Noble Truths

Buddha's enlightenment resulted in his realization of the Four Noble Truths. According to Buddha, the highest form of suffering stems from ignorance of these truths. Buddha clearly states that his tenets represent the only correct path in life. There is no ambiguity; in classical Buddhism, only the teachings of Buddha lead to spiritual freedom.

The First Noble Truth is that man's existence is full of conflict, sorrow, and suffering. This point is embraced by almost all religions throughout the world: suffering is a constant of the human condition, be it mental, physical, or spiritual. Few can dispute that existence on earth entails this burden.

The Second Noble Truth explains why man suffers. The answer is simple: we have desires that cannot be completely satisfied. These desires can be material wants, the appetite for power, the quest for knowledge, the longing for wealth, or the need to reach spiritual goals. They can be as simple as hunger for food and the need for true love. They can be as natural as the urge to have a healthy body and companionship. While it is possible to satisfy some of our desires, it is impossible to satisfy all of them at once. We are therefore left in a state of continual suffering.

The logical progression of the first two truths yields the Third Noble Truth. This truth states that since we cannot satisfy all of our desires, we must free ourselves from any desires at all. This is Buddha's recipe to free us of our suffering: to rid ourselves of desires is to rid ourselves of suffering and to be emancipated.

The Fourth Noble Truth defines the way to obtain enlightenment, or the "Noble Eightfold Path." The prior noble truths teach us that ridding ourselves of desires makes us free. We must remove ourselves from the material world and instead follow reality's natural course. Thus, following a path without desires leads to enlightenment or nirvana. Nirvana, according to Buddha, is the extinction of all desires.

Paramount and central to these desires is the desire to exist. Therefore, Buddha prescribes eliminating this most fundamental desire. When this is achieved, all other desires will be eliminated, since all desires logically relate to living or existing. Buddha's teachings advocate mental detachment from the desire to exist while we are physically alive. Achieving this mental death leads to nirvana.

The Noble Eightfold Path

Buddha teaches eight principles, dubbed the Noble Eightfold Path, to rid us of desires and lead us to spiritual freedom. These principles represent a logical progression of how a classical Buddhist should conduct his life to obtain spiritual enlightenment: right view, right thought, right speech, right action, right mode of living, right endeavor, right mindfulness, and right concentration. Buddha was adamant that his Eightfold Path was the only means to achieve enlightenment. There was no questioning the Silent One on the reasoning behind his method. It was to be followed blindly.

The first principle of the classical Buddhist Eightfold Path is to see things clearly. We must have Buddha's vision of the world as it truly exists before we can begin correct training. The second principle is to think like Buddha and possess his priorities, which logically follow from his view of the world. As we are confronted with choices in life, clear sight and an understanding of priorities enable us to choose the Buddhist course of action. The third principle is Buddha's prescription to speak and express ourselves. If we can clarify our thoughts, we can express these thoughts with similar clarity. The reverse is also true, as clear speech fortifies clear thoughts. Think of the ancient Roman saying, "He who thinks clearly, speaks clearly." The fourth and fifth principles prescribe the Buddhist way to act and the associated lifestyle. Here, *lifestyle* means living or residing in a Buddhist community, one with a common set of values and prescribed behavior. Because of Buddha's understanding of human nature, he placed significant emphasis on an individual's correct behavior within the social structure of the Buddhist community. He dictated that everyone living together in such a community must behave identically, helping each other understand his teachings and reinforcing correct behavior.

The sixth principle is identification of one's correct work. We need to determine what occupation best fits our skills and abilities. We may be adept at business, construction, child rearing, or creating art. Whatever our occupation, it must be performed in conjunction with meditation and yoga exercises.

The seventh principle is Buddha's specification of the correct attitude or mindset required to understand his teachings. Buddha placed much emphasis on dedication, focus, and concentration in absorbing his teachings. Once we choose to be Buddhists, we must apply our willpower and self-control to achieve the desired result. The eighth principle is Buddha's way of thinking, which he believed stemmed from correct behavior. With proper focus, willpower, and thought, the way of Buddha becomes automatic. It truly becomes part of our nature, eliminating the preconceived notions that we harbor.

The principles outlined in the Eightfold Path progress logically, each building on the ideas preceding it. They are clearly intertwined, focusing our thoughts to achieve Buddha's goal. By dogmatically following his teachings, we are pulled along step by step until we reach the point where Buddha wants us to be.

Buddhism and Its Effect on Society

Buddhism's extraordinary success throughout India and Asia was primarily due to the support of the region's ruling classes. Had Buddha's teachings and theology been contrary to the philosophy of the elite, Buddhism would have been outlawed and relegated to an underground movement. Support was demonstrated by the material gifts he received, including a park from King Bimbisara and a monastery from a Savatthi banker. Buddha took great care to ensure that his teachings would not conflict with the beliefs of the authorities. For instance, while Buddha said that the "door of eternity" was open for everyone who listened and believed, he did not want to infuriate the aristocracy of India. Therefore, he did not allow the likes of servants and soldiers in the service of the maharajas to join his monasteries. He also prohibited slaves and debtors so as not to circumvent the ownership rights of the ruling classes. Despite Buddha's professed love of humanity, he excluded the infirm (such as lepers and those suffering from tuberculosis and epilepsy). Overall, it is clear that Buddha offered membership in his communities only to those who would not cause trouble for the ruling class or bring undue hardship to fellow Buddhists.

Dealing with Eastern Confusion

During Buddhism's founding years, there was a strong system of social castes established by the rulers of India. For thousands of years, the rich and powerful used this caste structure to control the general population. Buddha's greatest supporters were the "untouchables," the lowest rung on the ladder of this social hierarchy. These unfortunates lived in abject poverty, filled with frustration and on the edge of revolt. The ruling classes were well aware of the danger inherent in overseeing an enormous sea of people at the brink of rebellion. When the Buddhist philosophy was born, promulgating principles of peaceful and passive coexistence, the aristocracy allowed it to flourish. Why? Because it was quickly recognized as their best means to contain an angry lower class.

Thus, the caste system broke down, replaced with a religious philosophy that essentially became the world's first official welfare system. Buddha accomplished this remarkable feat by training an entire segment of the population to give up their place within the caste system and become society's beggars and parasites. He then convinced the remainder of society to support these beggars. In reward for this astonishing feat, the ruling class anointed Buddhism as society's officially recognized religion.

Buddha's model society was essentially a military organization. Buddha demanded a pledge of allegiance from his followers and established a plethora of rules and regulations dictating the way monks were expected to live. For example, monks could eat only once a day, their diet consisting of small portions of rice and bread without meat or other protein sources. Monks were not allowed much sleep and were often forced to meditate through the night. Their lives were characterized by sexual abstinence and long hours of silence; their days were filled with an overwhelming array of activities, leaving little time for rest or contemplation. As Buddha said, "Laziness brings about evil desires."

Buddha analyzed humanity and determined that most people would rather be followers than leaders. He believed the masses seeking relief from suffering would prefer a militaristic structure at the sacrifice of individuality. This phenomenon can still be observed in modern times: soldiers and prisoners often become confused and uncomfortable when they try to leave behind their structured lives and adjust to a civilian lifestyle. The transition to a strict Buddhist society was virtually seamless for the lower classes, who gladly left behind their previous lives of despair. This may partly explain why Buddhism, while successful throughout India and central Asia, never gained a strong foothold in Western cultures.

By creating a social welfare system, Buddha's impact on society was immense. For millions of untouchables destined to a life of misery, the life in a Buddhist monastery offered hope. Life in the temple not only assured them of some small measure of sustenance, but also gave them a degree of respect and dignity.

The Taoist View of Buddhism

> Of the five vices, the vice of the mind is the worst.
>
> —*The Wisdom of Laotse,* 142

On initial review, Buddhism appears to be a rational, logical, and useful philosophical system. After all, the social structure created by Buddha took in millions of destitute people and gave them a means of survival. While a classical Taoist must recognize the positive sociological results of Buddhism, a critical examination of the philosophy demonstrates fundamental problems that must be addressed and not overlooked. Contrasting Buddha's solution to mankind's suffering with Lao Tzu's approach is a valuable exercise.

Buddhism's first problem goes to the heart of the Taoist view of life. A Taoist uses nature as his absolute model of life's correct path; philosophical principles must be consistent with the observed reality of the natural world. Buddha, by contrast, advocated a life that contradicted natural human existence. He offered a life with limited food and drink, no sexual relations, and constant sleep deprivation. In essence, he took a healthy man and made him one of the walking dead.

While this technique is clearly successful in eliminating most of a man's desires, it also results in the death of his natural instincts. The process kills the goal. A classical Taoist therefore views Buddhist philosophy—dedicated to the premature death of the body—as an affront to the soul of the individual. It is also an unequivocal violation of the laws of nature and, in all likelihood, a violation of the laws of the gods.

Despite some contradictory sects (like Shaolin temple) that embrace martial arts, classical Buddhism advocates a philosophy that embraces passivity as a means to coexist in the world. Ideally, the world would respect a peaceful individual's demeanor and not interfere with his path. Realistically, however, the immutable laws of nature dictate our world, and they do not respect a pacifist's point of view. Weak animals that are unable to fight are the first victims on the African plains, just as nonviolent pedestrians are the first crime victims on the streets of New York.

Perhaps most damning to this philosophy is the realization that passivity is a rare luxury, suitable only when times are easy. In times of conflict—whether fighting a physical disease in the body or fending off an aggressor on the street—a pacifist's path is exclusively reserved for those lacking courage. Life's correct path requires a constant fight: mental, physical, and spiritual. Buddhism's physical and mental retreat behind the walls of a monastery has little real-world validity.

Classical Taoism addresses the danger posed when society interacts with the individual. A Taoist acquires an array of tools to offset the destructive influences of society, allowing his physical being and attendant soul to survive within it. Buddhism similarly recognizes the dangers of society, particularly its propensity to foster unattainable desires. Unlike Taoism, however, Buddhism's solution is to hide behind monastery walls and beg for financial support from the society it fears and disdains. The hypocrisy of running from society while being dependent on it is a philosophical paradox that Buddha chose not to address. Lao Tzu teaches us that hypocrisy is the predecessor of confusion and that Buddhism's way of life is akin to that of a parasite—taking material sustenance from the body of a society it condemns as materialistic.

Buddha created a mandatory model of society designed for monks cloistered within a Buddhist temple. While this prescription may be appropriate for this small group, it offers no solution for the layman. Buddha's philosophy, designed to relieve mankind's suffering, excludes the majority of the population. Laypersons who venerated Buddha followed only those aspects of his teachings that were relevant to them and provided material support to the ascetic Buddhists. Classical Buddhism offers no hope for the majority of the world—its solutions apply to a few robed monks living sheltered lives and leeching off of the surrounding community.

Taoism teaches there must be a balance between the male and female in life. For this reason, the famous Taoist yin/yang symbol represents equal portions of female (black) and male (white). This female/male balance is a prerequisite for adherence to the laws of nature; a happy, healthy male animal needs a female and vice versa.

By contrast, Buddha was clear in his disdain of the female. After abandoning his wife and child, he founded Buddhist monasteries that initially barred women. Only after relenting to immense pressure from friends and fellow monks did he recant and permit the ordination of women as nuns. Even then, he authored eight special rules that subjugated nuns to monks, and he sourly predicted that ordaining nuns would halve the life span of his teachings. Buddha forbade his monks from having sexual relations with women. While a monk must bow to any senior monk, Buddha mandated that "a nun 'even of a hundred years' standing' shall bow down before a monk ordained 'even a day.'"* Clearly, a woman embracing Buddhism subjugates herself to the male, which is as illogical as day subjugating to night or hot subjugating to cold. Buddhism's blatant disdain of women is yet another symptom of an unnatural philosophy, one that contradicts Lao Tzu's warning to "embrace the female."

Since Buddha provided a philosophy of confusing signals and contradictions, the American Buddhist is left with a conundrum. How can one be free of desires in today's materialistic world? Most Americans won't quit their jobs, give away their possessions, abandon their families, and head to a monastery. American Buddhists claim they gain a sense of enlightenment and fulfillment by attending Buddhist services, meditating before statues of Buddha, and practicing yoga. Essentially, American Buddhists have adopted Buddhism's interesting and exotic ceremonies as its religious core; they have not absorbed Buddha's original teachings to relieve them from the suffering of modern life. Consequently, they have chosen a path that guarantees continued confusion and frustration, coupled with a false sense of self-satisfaction. Sadly, American Buddhism merely complicates life and proliferates confusion, ultimately leading to chaos, absurdity, and more suffering. Buddha's teachings have no relevance to modern Western life, and twisting his philosophy to fit modern lifestyles perverts his prescribed path. Only undesirable consequences can result.

---

* Kate Wheeler, "Bowing Not Scraping," *Tricycle: The Buddhist Review*, Winter 1993, 27.

Confucianism

> Those who seek to satisfy the mind of man by hampering it with ceremonies and music and affecting humanity and justice have lost the original nature of man.
>
> —*The Wisdom of Laotse,* 58

Confucianism has its roots in China more than two millennia ago. Its influence over the Chinese grew quickly, both numerically and geographically, and still stretches far and wide, overshadowing Taoism. Even in today's Communist Chinese regime, the structure and order that Confucius proposed are evident.

Much like Buddhism, Confucianism has enjoyed a robust exchange of philosophical and theological concepts with popular Taoism. Although often grouped with the major historical religions, Confucianism differs by not being an organized religion. However, for more than two thousand years, its ethical values have shaped the rules of conduct for human interaction and indelibly marked the development of government, society, education, and family within East Asia. Despite the link with popular Taoism, one should understand that Confucianism and classical Taoism have little common ground: Chuang Tzu's Lao Tzu translations ridicule Confucian principles.

The name *Confucius* was coined by the Western world, a Latin form of "K'ung Fu-tzu." While little is known about Confucius, we do know that he was born in 551 B.C. in Ch'u-fu in the small feudal state of Lu (now Shanyung

Province). After childhood, he served in minor government posts. His mastery of the six arts—ritual, music, archery, chariot driving, calligraphy, and arithmetic—and his familiarity with poetry and history enabled him to start a teaching career in his thirties. In his late forties and early fifties, Confucius served first as a magistrate, then as an assistant minister of public works, and eventually as minister of justice in the state of Lu.

From his writings completed as an older man, it is clear that young Confucius always had a sense of direction in his life, as well as abundant confidence and self-esteem. His desire was to become a politician offering a clearly defined structure to the world. After observing rampant corruption in the government, he came to believe he alone was capable of producing a social structure that would be workable, effective, and useful for the masses.

By the age of fifty, Confucius found the opportunity to implement his system. Within five years of establishing a Confucian order in the province of Lu, he was able to control the citizens under his jurisdiction. He did this by using the law in ways he felt were fairer and more just. At fifty-six, when he realized his superiors were uninterested in his politics, Confucius left the country to find another feudal state to which he could render his service. Despite his political frustration, he was accompanied by an expanding circle of students during this self-imposed exile of almost twelve years. His reputation grew, and at the age of sixty-seven, he returned home to teach and preserve his cherished teachings in writing. He died at the age of seventy-three.

Immediately following his death—just as with Prince Siddhartha and Buddhism—the legend of Confucius grew larger than the man himself. The ruling class of China embraced Confucian techniques of manipulation with enthusiasm, just as India's rulers supported Buddhism. As a result, Confucianism became the accepted philosophy and system of ethical beliefs for more than two millennia.

Confucius and His Mandate

The philosophy of Confucius was born out of the accelerating chaos of Chinese society between 600 and 500 B.C. During this period, China lacked a centralized government, and the Chou dynasty was in a steep decline. With the weakening of the rulers, anarchy was on the rise as countless civil wars broke out between warlords and local kings. Nearly constant treaty violations and shifting alliances between warlords resulted in armies moving through regions and mercilessly preying on civilians. This brutal subjugation of the populace totally disrupted farming and brought commerce to a standstill. Onerous taxes imposed by these unchecked warlords destroyed any initiative to rebuild commercial enterprises. The economy was weakened, and famine was imminent. China was on the brink of turmoil, its future uncertain.

As a historian, Confucius was aware of the prosperity that had flourished for thousands of years before the current anarchy. He yearned for a return to a "golden age" in which people lived naturally and society prospered. This golden age was a fictitious creation of Chinese philosophers, a hypothetical and allegorical period during which the Yellow Emperor brought harmony, wisdom, and peaceful coexistence to the citizens. Confucius believed his mission was to restore the values and social structure of this utopian age; if he could create an efficient administration using these ancient values, order would return and the civil strife plaguing China would end. Confucius believed creating an ethical government would ensure order throughout the provinces and end the ceaseless factional fighting.

Confucius's concept involved using the power of social values to build a centralized government. He attempted to replace the undesirable natural values with his artificial ones. By teaching and reinforcing a set of artificial values, he could transform the populace into voluntary robots—slaves to the social order. The social structure envisioned by Confucius could suppress mankind's natural instincts and violent behavior to the benefit of all.

The most important element in Confucius's system of control was the creation of powerful educational institutions that were used to disseminate social values. Education has two distinct purposes. The first is to teach or train students in a broad range of subjects with the intent of transferring information. The student then filters this information and—using free will—believes and understands what he chooses. The second purpose of education is to subject students to a constant stream of propagandized information with the intent of establishing control. Mass education is similar to boot camp: the primary intent is not to teach cadets the rules of combat but rather to create loyal soldiers.

Confucius focused on this "secondary" purpose of education: propaganda. His solution to China's terrible condition was to use education as a tool to enslave the population and disseminate his values. Confucius believed his values reflected the will of the ancients and that his mandate would save China. Education was his weapon of choice to accomplish that goal.

The Five Relationships

While Taoism uses nature as its reference for the principles possessed by the ancients, Confucius manufactured a social structure composed of rules dictating individual behavior. One of his most important sets of rules is "the Five Relationships," which describe five levels of interpersonal relationships so that every member of society will understand his place within the community's social fabric.

The first relationship is between older and younger friends; it is the role of the older friend to dominate and oversee the younger friend. The next relationship is between husband and wife; the man is the master of the relationship, and the role of the woman is to obey her husband. The next relationship is between older and younger brothers; the older brother dominates and teaches the younger one. In the parent-child relationship, the father oversees and teaches his son. In the last relationship, the family unit is under the control of the local government's authority. The strength of these relationships always derives from the obedience of the junior member to the senior member.

Confucius believed this strong system of obedience, respect, dignity, and filial piety would be the key to restoring and maintaining social order. At its heart, Confucius's system treated the family unit as a microcosm of the social hierarchy and the basis for control of society as a whole. By defining the order among brother, son, wife, and husband, the five relationships ensured that family units would obey the local administrator or emperor and complete the circle of authority. It is easy to understand how a strong degree of control within the family unit was a logical precursor to overall social control through government oversight. Citizens trained since birth to display obedience to their superiors grew into adults who complied with the wishes of their rulers. Since Confucian philosophy said the emperor was an emissary from the higher powers, the family unit's obedience to governmental authorities was tantamount to following God's will.

The Five Keys

To ensure that the Chinese adhered to his rules of order, Confucius created five critical principles to be used by society's institutions in training people and establishing desired traditions. Confucius hoped social order could be maintained without the use of force and in a manner that created happier citizens. His method was a combination of teaching social values to all members of society (including children), then reinforcing those values through a strong sense of tradition. This method was dubbed the "Five Keys," or "Five Virtues."

Jen. *Jen*, the first key, is the original goodness residing in everyone, the basic virtue with which everyone is born. Through a system of cultivation, one can nurture this goodness to become a logical and rational member of society. If left uncultivated, however, jen will wither and die. Confucius believed that if citizens learned good and proper values, this original goodness would flower into the adoption of values that would benefit all mankind. Confucius believed the educational system—as well as other traditional systems of training—was the proper conduit through which to transmit these values. In essence, the people could be taught en masse how to cultivate their jen.

Confucius believed cultivating the values of natural goodness developed a sense of humanity, compassion, and understanding of one's fellow man. Jen would manifest itself in softness and gentleness—qualities one typically associates with aristocratic gentlemen. This state of "gentlemanliness" includes a specific mindset as well as continuous cultivation of the arts, literature, music, poetry, and philosophy. Striving to become a gentleman cultivates jen and creates an individual of sophistication and culture.

Confucius taught that a good man deserves to be treated well by others. A community composed of gentlemen would be a society of people faithful to duty and country who were filled with compassion to all and harbored no evil intentions.

Chun-tzu. The second key, *chun-tzu*, is the spiritual essence of a man represented by the manners of a perfect gentleman. Confucius was extremely concerned with the ritualistic aspects of behavior and the practice of rituals themselves, because he believed rituals were the foundation of tradition.

Confucius viewed the manners of proper citizens as critical elements that separated rational men from emotionally driven animals. Manners constitute ritualistic behavior *and* a code of moral attitudes. Gentlemanly manners are a mechanism used to control the undesirable or violent behavior better left to beasts.

The violence inherent in animalistic behavior can be avoided by rational human beings. The key is to understand chun-tzu: develop a compassionate attitude and foster logical, nonviolent reactions to all conflicts. When confronted with any violent situation and an irrational, emotional, and violent aggressor, a man possessing chun-tzu will respond with rational arguments, exhibiting education, politeness, and logic. The principle of chun-tzu mirrors the ethic of "treat others as you would have them treat you."

Li. The principles of *li*, the third Confucian key, are the means by which one disseminates proper manners throughout society. It is not enough to possess gentlemanly manners; one must transmit them to fellow citizens by example. As the gentleman cultivates his chun-tzu through proper behavior, he becomes a role model for others. If everyone around the gentleman copies this good behavior, they too will cultivate their chun-tzu. In doing so, they will set a good example for others. This chain reaction of proper, gentlemanly behavior will eventually propagate throughout the world, counteracting chaos and violence. Thus, living without conflict, chaos, and violence—and serving as a model to others while doing so—creates an entire society characterized by harmony, peace, and good moral values.

There is a second, better-known facet to the principle of li: the famous Confucian principle of the "middle way," or "Golden Mean." The middle way dictates that an appropriate understanding of gentlemanly behavior results in an abhorrence of excess. The gentleman avoids excess because reason cautions against the harm that stems from extremes. In the Confucian model of controlling emotions, one should experience neither too much happiness nor too much sorrow. Anger and hate are especially to be avoided. By following the principle of the middle way, one better cultivates chun-tzu. The example set by gentlemen—in accordance with li—would be a low-reaction, softer model of behavior. Harmony is achieved by adopting the middle way throughout one's life. A life without excesses is the core of Confucianism. The doctrine of li comprises an entire volume of Confucius's Five Canons.

Li carries powerful implications in the Confucian prescription for a perfect society. If li creates a constant stream of well-behaved role models, the Five Relationships are perpetuated throughout society. For example, each successive generation of a family would be obedient to the previous one; the younger generation could be controlled because of their respect toward their elders. Similarly, a family's respect for the local government—and, by extension, the emperor—would create a perfect society. The effect is to create a pseudomilitaristic society, one whose chain of command is voluntarily enforced by the principle of li and by the traditional institutions of education.

Te. In modern terms, this principle translates to the power of positive suggestion. *Te* is the logical progression of jen, chun-tzu, and li; Confucius instructs that the power of positive suggestion allows mankind to achieve harmony. It is the ultimate power of moral example.

Unlike dictators who use violence to build their ideal societies, Confucius offered a much more sophisticated and subtle method of controlling the masses. The power of te reinforces Confucian values, forging a single, unifying system for a well-behaved, controllable society.

Wen. The fifth key is the principle of *wen*. While the previous four keys deal with building a stable society without resorting to physical force, the fifth key deals with the arts. Often thought to be one of the more fascinating and intellectual principles of Confucianism, wen demonstrates Confucius's idealistic attitude toward human nature. He believed humans innately possessed artistic abilities in music, poetry, philosophy, and the visual arts. By participating in all these arts, the human character would be complete and flourish. Wen centers around the Confucian belief that art acts as a unifying force for all of its principles. Man's appreciation of art segregates him from the animal kingdom; cultivating this appreciation further distances man from beast and establishes his unique stature in the universe. This appreciation cements man's position as the leading force in nature.

The Taoist View of Confucianism

> Not to allow the human and the divine to be confused, therein was what distinguished the pure man.
>
> —*The Wisdom of Laotse*, 45

In examining Confucianism critically, it must be acknowledged that Confucius was trying to restore order to a society locked in violent conflict. In this sense, the chaos of human existence was somewhat improved. However, it is the mission of any philosophical system to provide a clear picture of the world and to present principles that function in everyday life. With the ultimate objective of helping man live a happier and healthier life, Confucianism fails in many ways.

The divergence between classical Taoism and Confucianism begins with Confucius's reliance on the immutable power of man's rationality. Confucius believed that by educating the populace in the Five Relationships and Five Keys, rational man would behave appropriately. To the critical Taoist, the evidence from the world around us belies the logic of this approach. If rationality were part of man's natural core, why was Confucius's prescribed manipulation necessary in the first place? And how could such chaos and violence emerge in China if man's innate rationality would naturally keep such behavior in check?

Despite the romantic desire for mankind to possess a buried core of "good" values, the Taoist's clear review of history—a history that Confucius lamented—proves otherwise. Throughout history, as in Confucius's China, chaos, absurdity, and suffering has been brought about by deeply rooted *irrational* behavior. This was not an aberration waiting to be snuffed out by Confucian propaganda; it is the essence of being human.

A key part of the human condition includes an emotional component that defies logic. Confucius built a masterful mechanism to suppress those natural human emotions. He built a society of well-behaved robots without resorting to violence. But to the Taoist in search of a path rooted in the naturalness of the individual, Confucian dictates are frightening. Their goal is akin to trying to force a lion to become a lamb or a tiger to become an antelope.

Even though Confucius uses the peaceful propaganda tool of education, as opposed to more forceful methods of subjugation, a Taoist views Confucianism as an enemy who uses deception to achieve his goals. For a man of Tao, Confucian rulers who obscure reality are as dangerous as Nazi storm troopers invading his home. At the same time, Confucianists are infinitely more seductive, rendering them even more menacing. A classical Taoist therefore views the fight for natural values—waged against the tide of Confucian tradition—as a battle for his soul.

Another problem with Confucianism is its internal contradiction. As previously discussed, the critical Taoist vigilantly watches for hypocrisy as a symptom of deeper faults. Unfortunately, Confucianism fails on this count too. Confucius wanted to relieve the suffering of the population as a whole, but he created a society of robots controlled by the ruling elite. This enslavement benefited a small group of rulers, and Confucianism flourished in China because it was accepted and reinforced by the ruling class it benefited. The rulers appreciated its amazing success in controlling a vast empire through manipulation.

The fact is, despite thousands of years' exposure to the teachings of Confucianism, the Chinese have continued to suffer crime, violence, and debasement. Even success in the most basic of its goals has eluded Confucianism. Its emphasis on education, for example, did nothing to teach the common man the basic skills of reading and writing;

until the last century, most of the population was illiterate. In this respect, as in countless others, China has remained unchanged under Confucianism. Despite its grandiose claims, this philosophy was nothing more than a means of control for the good of the ruling class—a big lie that has lasted for more than two millennia.

The gentle facade of Confucianism masks its darker aspects, which have been used in modern times to support brutally repressive regimes. For almost eighty years, for example, three generations of Russians were controlled by a Soviet system characterized by its use of Confucian techniques, including education, propaganda, and regulations. Although the Soviet revolutionaries never consciously mimicked the Confucian system, they used its principles to control society.

Using one of Confucius's most important concepts, the Soviets subjected citizens to systematic education and widespread media-driven propaganda designed to convince the populace that the Communist government and social structure were the best in the world. There are also remarkable similarities between the values taught by Confucius and those taught by Soviets as delineated in *The Code of the Builder of Communism*. This text states that every man is a brother, comrade, and friend, and that one must "treat and love your fellow man as you would treat yourself"—an accurate paraphrase of Confucius's writings. The Soviet people were also taught that their first duty belonged to the social structure, with personal well-being a distant second—a prescription for citizenry remarkably similar to Confucius's Five Relationships.

While Confucius taught that everyone is born with original goodness, the Soviets instructed that the value of fairness would restore prosperity to the masses. Confucius preached that adherence to his system of order would cause the economy to flourish and the citizens to find happiness; the Soviets did the same during the 1917 revolution, promising prosperity and happiness by redistributing wealth "to each according to their need." The Soviet use of propaganda rivaled the Confucian use of education; the Soviets tirelessly dispensed values to all strata of society, beginning of course with the family unit. They placed such great importance on the use of "education" that Lenin, while developing his strategy for the Russian Revolution, diverted precious funds from the purchase of weapons to the construction and operation of propaganda trains. He slyly realized, as had Confucius, that the revolution's success would depend on winning the hearts and minds of the populace.

Ultimately, the Soviets' scientific atheism, with its usurpation of God's supremacy, resulted in the system's demise. Soviet doctrine was built on the theory that the rational core of man did not need God. Consequently, religious institutions were dismantled, and government replaced God as the highest authority. This switch had an unforeseen effect, however: citizens held the government accountable for their well-being. There was no "will of God" to blame for bad times; the government bore the brunt of periods of discontent and despair. As a result, the financial crisis of the 1980s led to the collapse of the Soviet system. Confucius was more careful in his social design, avoiding any discussion of religion.

Dealing with Eastern Confusion

The Soviet comparison not only demonstrates how Confucian ideals can build a social structure detrimental to its citizens, but is also a lesson for the student of Tao. While Confucianism has lasted thousands of years, the Soviet system collapsed after only eighty. The governmental usurpation of religion is but one reason; the use of physical subjugation is another. Confucius understood that although rulers could obtain rapid results through the use of force, the more subtle approach of teaching social values created an enduring structure. Understanding this, his methods avoided the brutal means of oppression (mass exterminations, secret police campaigns, and gulag internments, for example) favored by the Soviets. This historical comparison demonstrates that the subtle manipulation of minds has more power to control people than does physical force. In essence, the state's use of mental confusion is one of its most powerful tools. This is the reason that Lao Tzu and Chuang Tzu warned about the values promulgated by the mass media. Inevitably, the majority of those values work against the individual, resulting in more personal confusion and suffering.

Confucius advocated a philosophy encouraging gentlemanly behavior to promote coexistence. Ideally, the world would respect a gentleman and not interfere with his path. Further, a Confucian gentleman would act as a good example to his peers (li), spreading these behaviors throughout society like a virulent flu. Unfortunately, the world is ruled by the irrational laws of nature, which do not respect a gentleman's point of view. New York street criminals would quickly victimize a well-behaved gentleman. Human and animal predators alike identify easy victims by the outward appearance of softness and passivity. In times of conflict, a passive, gentlemanly approach is exclusively reserved for those who lack courage. The label *gentleman* has *gentle* as its root word because it reflects precisely this approach to life. Life demands constant fighting—mental, physical, and spiritual.

Confucianism's gentlemanly behavior is identical to Buddhism's retreat behind the walls of a monastery; both have little philosophical validity in the real world. A "gentlemanly" target is synonymous with an "easy" target. Reality has shown that nothing increases suffering more than becoming an easy target. Yet Confucianism makes this a virtue. To a Taoist, promoting the virtues of being an easy victim is the antithesis of teaching others how to live a better life. The life of a victim is one of a confused, directionless soul tossed about like a rudderless vessel. This is not the path to spirituality—it is the path to a living hell.

Confucius's formula for social order was predicated on constant reinforcement of the Five Relationships; this approach trained the populace to respect family elders and government officials. While fine in theory, the reality is less promising: dumb youngsters make dumb adults, and government officials have a predilection toward bureaucratic thinking and corruption. Once again, Confucius's hypothetical world of order and reason doesn't square with reality's ugly truth. Why should a clear-minded youth listen to a confused elder? Just because a person has white hair doesn't mean he's smart. Why should citizens blindly obey a corrupt ruler? How did Confucius's experience with rulers who built a society of turmoil allow him to recommend a social structure subservient to this same ruling class?

Dealing with Eastern Confusion

Even Confucius himself was compelled to resign from a government post because of disillusionment and dismay. Doesn't this illustrate a fundamental problem with a social hierarchy based on the artificial merits of seniority and governmental position? If Confucius couldn't tolerate such a system, why would he expect his followers to do so?

A Taoist observes his world with skepticism. Despite the fine-sounding words uttered by those around him, the Taoist constantly checks to see whether the deeds of others corroborate their professed friendship and caring. Only after observing a history of beneficial deeds does a Taoist entrust his loyalty. To the horror of a Confucianist, Taoists are especially suspicious of social convention, since it almost always enforces values that contradict one's self-interest. Values that Confucianists most respect are those that Taoists most loathe, and loyalties based on the Five Relationships lead to a life of bitter disappointment and constant suffering.

A delightful Confucian theory is the use of wen, or artistic development, to cultivate the buried goodness of man. Confucius believed pursuit of the arts would separate rational man from the baseness of animal nature. It was an essential element of his plan to relieve the suffering of the masses, yet in the Confucian society of China, almost no one had time to pursue anything except survival. An agrarian economy demanded twelve-hour days and seven-day weeks to earn enough to survive. Confucius's formula for goodness through the arts meant nothing to the hard-working masses. A clear reading of wen reveals that it was a betrayal of the common man. Confucius proclaimed from his academic perch that the vast majority of the population—those without the luxury of time to practice the arts—failed to meet his criteria for goodness. Either the height of hypocrisy or an unbelievable disconnection from reality allowed Confucius to promote the arts to a suffering society struggling to survive.

Finally, Confucius recommended the path of the middle way as one navigates through the challenges of life. While a classical Taoist acknowledges the benefit of avoiding excesses—as expressed in Lao Tzu's Three Treasures—the middle way has dangerous consequences if followed blindly. Life is such a constant battle, waged against an army of forces massed against the individual, that the middle way fails in spectacular fashion to prepare one for this war. Taoist temples feature gods and deities brandishing drawn weapons and attired in combat armor—a graphic depiction of the message that any competitive battle requires 100 percent effort, whether in the business world or a physical confrontation. There is no such thing as a gentle conflict; bring your armor because there is no fairness in combat.

The good guys don't always win because any confrontation requires a concentrated effort. The middle way is nothing more than the confused way, and it's often the way of a loser. Ask any professional athlete about the middle way's relevance to how he approaches competition. It is likely that he prepares with the polar opposite of Confucius's teachings: intensity and passion.

The challenges of life are so tough that finding one's path requires extraordinary dedication. In fighting for clarity in life, the serious student of Tao pursues a vision of the world that does not correspond with the values of the

Dealing with Eastern Confusion

common man. The middle way is an easier, intellectually safer ground where the common man joins the comforting confusion of society. Yet Confucius's middle way demands that one yield to the way of the robot. The classical Taoist kneels before armor-clad gods and asks for help in life's fiercest battle—the struggle to find his path, a path far removed from the one that Confucius built.

CHAPTER 4

The Principles of Tao

To be in harmony with men is the music of man,
and to be in harmony with God is the music of God.

—*The Wisdom of Laotse,* 196

The Diamond of the Tao

Taoism's Tao Te Ching is one of the most widely read and translated books of all time. However, most of these translations do not fulfill the promise of any bona fide philosophical discourse: to clarify the reader's view of reality and simultaneously provide guidance in operating within the parameters of a worldly existence. These non-functional translations are the natural consequence of their authors' limitations. Without exception, the writers are capable linguists untrained in philosophy. Think of a physician reading a foreign medical text translated by a linguistic scholar with no medical training. The words may be interpreted correctly, but the functionality of the text will be limited by the translator's lack of medical knowledge. The result will, at a minimum, lack important nuances and likely include outright errors. Philosophy, which is even more dependent on nuances and semantic construction, requires an expert to correctly blend linguistic translation with understandable explanations.

For the serious student of philosophy—seeking to clarify his picture of the world and develop realistic and practical principles—all philosophical systems, including Taoism, must pass a two-step test. The first test of a philosophy is whether there is a logical progression of concepts from one principle to the next (that is, there must be logical consistency among all aspects of the system). The second test is whether its principles can be applied to the real world and yield consistent, verifiable results; its teachings must reflect observed reality and not dwell in hypothetical creations of the mind. A valid philosophy must pass both tests to claim legitimacy.

As an example, a common misinterpretation of the Tao Te Ching's early chapters is the proclamation that nature is beautiful and that, consequently, man mimics nature by pursuing a pacifist's outlook. This interpretation fails the proposed test on two counts. First, it is internally inconsistent, as subsequent chapters of Lao Tzu's book clearly state that nature is unkind. Second, a consistent theme of human history is that—as in the animal kingdom where only the strong survive—mankind is cruel. There is no verifiable evidence that philosophical concepts based on a pastoral view of nature and life are workable in the real world. Thus, a common misinterpretation of the Tao Te Ching could not be further from true Taoism.

Why are there so many misinterpretations of the Tao Te Ching? How can a philosophy dedicated to eliminating confusion spawn hundreds of misinterpretations?

Certainly one source of confusion is that Lao Tzu chose to compose the Tao Te Ching's eighty-one poems in Mandarin Chinese. At the time, reading and writing in China were skills reserved for 1 percent of the population: priests, upper-class citizens, and aristocrats. Lao Tzu's beautiful poetic form and sophisticated language was intended exclusively for Chinese nobles and priests. During this period the *spoken* language of the nobility was entirely different from that of the common man; nobles could converse among themselves with little possibility of the common men around them understanding. This language barrier created more opportunities for misinterpretations as society's various channels of communication dispersed Lao Tzu's ideas.

While the Tao Te Ching's linguistic format acted as a barrier to understanding, Lao Tzu also purposely hid its meaning within the text. Lin Yutang's excellent translation, *The Wisdom of Laotse*, describes Lao Tzu as "the first philosopher of camouflage." Lin Yutang meant that not only did Lao Tzu write his book for the aristocracy and clergy of China, he also intended that the Tao Te Ching would be understood solely by those who could decipher and comprehend the meanings he placed in his poetry.

Lao Tzu camouflaged his thoughts and ideas within the text. But why?

To answer this question, we can examine the motivations of a philosopher and thinker of the Western world, Leonardo da Vinci. He went to great lengths to hide his scientific theories, thoughts, and philosophies. For example, his scientific manuscripts were written in mirror-image text so the unknowledgeable observer couldn't decipher his writings. He did this for fear that the ignorant population would incorrectly interpret or steal his ideas.

Perhaps Lao Tzu, too, believed that exposing his observations, theories, and beliefs to the masses would have dangerous consequences. The herd would never truly comprehend the philosophy's wisdom and could use their misinterpretations to the detriment of man. These great men, da Vinci and Lao Tzu, felt responsible for their bold ideas and were fearful that they could unleash the fire of chaos when the ignorant masses opened Pandora's box.

As a consequence of Lao Tzu's use of camouflage, the serious student of the Tao needs a reliable beacon to navigate through the text and discover its true meanings. He needs the tutelage of a Taoist master. Only with such instruction and guidance can he truly understand the meaning of Lao Tzu. Chuang Tzu tells us that no one can learn from a book alone:

> **Books are only words and words, of course, have a value. But the value of words lies in the meaning behind them.**
>
> —*The Wisdom of Laotse*, 257

It is impossible to learn anything of major consequence solely from reading a book. Think of any serious job or occupation. Would you want to fly in an airplane with a pilot who learned his skill from books alone? Would you want to undergo surgery under the scalpel of a surgeon who learned his technique exclusively from studying a medical textbook?

The limitations of book learning are severe, since even the best book cannot answer all of the student's questions. Interaction with a knowledgeable and experienced tutor is needed to clarify the student's thinking. Without the ability to engage in discourse, the student must guess at the answers to questions that arise throughout the learning process. And, for a topic as difficult and serious as clarifying one's picture of the world, relying solely on a book is a dangerous course. Guessing about Lao Tzu's meanings invariably results in misunderstandings and misapplications.

Given the limitations of book learning and the difficulty of deciphering Lao Tzu's camouflage, how is the student of Tao to use the Tao Te Ching? Lao Tzu's lovely collection of poems uses allegories and metaphors that tell us about life, nature, and God. Yet all of this information is hidden. On cursory review, the poetry appears to have no real purpose.

Fortunately, at the core of the Tao Te Ching is a *practical* guide to understanding reality and applying this knowledge to our advantage. To continue our analogy of the student pilot, his instruction manual is a valuable guide containing many facts, techniques, and warnings for the novice flyer. Even experienced pilots retain their flight manuals and use written checklists as reminders in their dangerous occupation. In a similar way, the Tao Te Ching is a book of reminders and warnings to help us navigate through life.

In explaining how to use the Tao Te Ching, it is helpful to draw a parallel to a multifaceted diamond. Each facet is cut in a clear, straight plane and connected to other facets at perfectly symmetric angles. The clean cuts and interconnections transform an unformed mineral into a priceless gem. Held in the palm of one's hand, the gem displays all of the myriad colors of the spectrum. So it is with the Tao Te Ching. Each part is like a facet of a diamond. Each part touches the others in a structure that reflects the wisdom of the universe. Like a diamond reflecting the colors of the sun and moon, the Tao Te Ching reflects the seen and unseen mysteries of life. But to understand the diamond of the Tao's reflections, the student needs a teacher who can enlighten him to this great book's secrets.

In understanding the allegorical "diamond of the Tao," we can view Lao Tzu's philosophy as a single, powerful system, not just a random collection of interesting principles. In essence, the Tao is like a diamond whose monolithic structure is composed of facets with different sizes, shapes, and angles, appropriately connected to maximize its brilliance. The Tao is a system from which we can understand how all phenomena—seen and unseen—are connected across the past, present, and future. It is the role of a master to roll the diamond around in his palm, display all of its facets, and explain their intertwined relationships. Without this guidance, we would miss the exact angles that display the magnificent glow and burst of color within the diamond.

Principles of Tao

Each facet of the diamond of the Tao represents a different philosophical principle. Each principle, like a facet of a diamond, is connected to other principles in a combination creating a beautiful and brilliant philosophical system. With each turn of the diamond of the Tao, the teacher exposes a new viewpoint of its principles, allowing the student to observe the individual facets and their interconnection. Lao Tzu's wonderful system helps us fulfill our spiritual mission and clarify our picture of the world through the brilliant focus of the diamond of the Tao.

Classical Taoist Principles

Those who possess my Tao are princes in this life and rulers in the hereafter.

—The Wisdom of Laotse, 240

It is the purpose of any legitimate philosophical system to provide practical benefits for its practitioners. Otherwise, the effort is nothing more than an intellectual exercise performed for entertainment. The student of Tao accrues such practical benefits by grasping a small number of core principles, for the entire philosophical system of Taoism consists of but a few interlocking tenets that are simple and yet profoundly practical. These principles are so powerful that they are applied to many aspects of Chinese life: philosophy, religion, medicine, science, art, politics, and martial arts. Modern Western arts and sciences are slowly recognizing that Taoist principles—used in a variety of applications, like alternative medicine—have powerful benefits, and these principles are being embraced by American and European practitioners.

To grasp the principles of Tao, it is first important to recognize that there are two basic branches of Taoism which offer dramatically different interpretations of Lao Tzu's teachings: *classical* Taoism and *popular* Taoism. It is helpful to understand that these two branches sometimes promulgate conflicting principles, since a student of the Tao may read contrasting and even contradictory interpretations of the same passage of the Tao Te Ching.

Classical Taoism, the subject of this book, believes one understands the principles of Tao by observing its manifestations (*teh*) through a visible model: nature. Using nature as a guide, classical Taoism outlines principles that help one survive life's daily struggles. Further, just as any religion's goal is to strengthen the communication between man and higher powers or deities, classical Taoism provides a simple, pragmatic means of strengthening this connection. Classical Taoist principles are simple, clear, and consistent.

In contrast to classical Taoism, popular Taoism represents a watered-down version of Lao Tzu's teachings by using the mystical (or unknown) source of Tao as its core. Unlike the classical Taoist's quest for understanding through the visible observation of nature, a popular Taoist's focus is on exotic ceremonies and rituals for enlightenment. Popular Taoist canons provide descriptions of long ceremonies that violate a true Taoist's rule of simplicity in communicating to the higher powers.

Popular Taoism, like all other popular religions, creates institutions whose motivations have little to do with true enlightenment; rather, they focus on expanding their own power and wealth. In that respect, popular Taoism is not different from Christianity, an institution of incredible wealth and power with the ironic mission of saving and serving the poor. Certainly popular Taoism exists on a far less grandiose scale than Christianity. However, it should be emphasized that popular Taoism, unlike other religions, does provide some small benefit to its congregation: it honestly represents life as a struggle, not a fantasy world of unrequited love awaiting realization.

Only classical Taoism, however, provides enlightenment by imparting to its students the Tao's core principles. It does this by explaining how its tenets' manifestations in the world serve as a pragmatic guide to navigate life's journey. Wise Lao Tzu foresaw that even his beloved Tao would be subjected to man's tendency to create an unworkable popular (but appealing) version when he warned,

> **The prophets are the flowering of Tao**
> **And the origin of folly.**
> **Therefore the noble man dwells in the heavy (base),**
> **And not in the thinning (end).**
> **He dwells in the fruit,**
> **And not in the flowering (expression).**
>
> —*The Wisdom of Laotse,* 199

Oneness

> What he saw as One was One, and what he saw as not One was also One. In that he saw the unity, he was of God; in that he saw the distinctions, he was of man.
>
> —*The Wisdom of Laotse,* 45

A practicing Taoist clarifies his perception of the world by understanding a set of underlying principles that guide the operation of all phenomena. By using these principles, an individual can eliminate the confusion that causes mental and physical anguish. Central to this philosophy is a holistic view of reality that recognizes the inherent duality of nature. Lao Tzu's brilliant simplification of the world's operation begins with the recognition that opposites exist in any active system and that they must coexist in balance to create an indivisible oneness. Whereas a confused person emphasizes one over the other, Lao Tzu emphasizes that

> Only the truly intelligent understand this principle of the levelling of all things into One. . . .
>
> —*The Wisdom of Laotse,* 244

Opposites permeate everything. In Newtonian physics, any action causes an equal and opposite reaction; in the ancient religions, the creation of good results in evil; for a healthy mental outlook on life, a passion for living is realized by embracing death. This basic principle of oneness and relative opposites is one of the Taoist's most powerful tools to understand what is happening around him and deduce the best course of action.

Yin and Yang

> **The yin and yang principles act on one another, affect one another and keep one another in place.**
>
> —*The Wisdom of Laotse,* 148

For three thousand years, the yin/yang principle—depicted in the familiar circular symbol—has been known throughout the world. It is worn on bracelets, appears on clothing, and is used in corporate logos. Yet few can clearly explain its meaning, which is central to Taoist philosophy.

The black and white of the yin/yang symbol represent the polar opposites of all the universe's phenomena; for example, life and death, male and female, hot and cold, thinking and not thinking, action and inaction. The symbol is half white and half black, each side representing a polar opposite. Note, too, that the symbol is neither predominantly white nor predominantly black, but equal proportions of each. This is meant to represent the natural proportions of our universe. For example, both day and night are required for life on earth to thrive. Twenty-four hours of daylight would overheat and dry out the planet, and plant life would turn brown and die. Likewise, twenty-four hours of night would turn vegetation rotten. Both day and night are required in roughly equal proportions for the harmony of life on earth. Similar examples of conflicting yet complementary opposites are observable at every turn throughout nature. The symbol also contains a rotating pattern between the two colors, suggesting the continuous exchange or movement from black to white and from white to black. These natural manifestations of the yin/yang principle illustrate how opposites must exist in balance for harmony to be achieved. In Chinese medicine, the balance of yin/yang forces is the most important of healing principles. For a student of the Tao, understanding the balance of yin/yang forces in his life is central to understanding his path. Lao Tzu writes,

> **Being and non-being interdepend in growth;**
> **Difficult and easy interdepend in completion;**
> **Long and short interdepend in contrast;**
> **High and low interdepend in position;**
> **Tones and voice interdepend in harmony;**
> **Front and behind interdepend in company.**
>
> —*The Wisdom of Laotse,* 47

The yin/yang symbol illustrates another important philosophical concept. Notice that there is a concrete line between the white and black sides of the symbol, a definite contour distinguishing the two colors. This clarity of color symbolizes the need for clarity in all aspects of a Taoist's life. Gray isn't found in the yin/yang symbol.

Principles of Tao

Clarity requires that the Taoist do nothing halfway; to paraphrase an old adage, one shouldn't try to sit on two chairs. In becoming a spiritual person, a clear, purposeful understanding of what is happening is required so that appropriate action can be taken. Caution is required when black and white mix.

Unfortunately, confusion will invariably arise as the Taoist is presented with new situations during life's daily struggles. Periods of confusion can be expected in life, in much the same way that each day transitions through twilight into night. It is the goal of the Taoist, however, to keep his twilight—his period of confusion—as short as possible. As in nature, twilight does not last all day.

Imagine someone driving a car when a fog bank suddenly appears. His vision is obscured; driving is suddenly perilous. The driver must pass through this fog as quickly as possible, maintaining extreme caution and vigilance. The driver finds no comfort in the fog and only wants it to end. Similarly, it is important for the individual fighting life's confusing periods to seek clarity and not relish unclear states.

Many people embrace confusion, chasing the fog. They fear decision making because it carries responsibility for action. For these people, the line between yin and yang is blurred, and they remain passive in dangerous periods. It is the goal of a spiritual person to gain clarity, not tolerating the middle road.

It is equally important for the Taoist to distinguish clarity from purity. A clear vision of the world and decisive navigation throughout life should not be based on unrealistic expectations of purity. The futility of searching for absolute purity is illustrated by the small white dot in the black area and the small black dot in the white area of the yin/yang symbol.

For example, one has no trouble distinguishing day from night, and yet there is not pure darkness at night—there is still some light from the moon and stars. Similarly, when an accomplished artist paints a leaf, he mixes in a little brown and yellow paint with the green to achieve a natural, lifelike appearance; a child painting the same leaf would use pure green, which appears artificial and unnatural.

The Taoist understands that the inclusion of opposites is necessary for most phenomena to function correctly. A professional athlete knows muscles grow only if intense physical training is followed by a period of relaxation—otherwise overtraining results in weakened muscles. A military officer cultivates tactics and strategies for aggressive attack, but also understands how to hide and take cover. Lao Tzu emphasized the inclusion of a small component of opposites, warning that the male part of any phenomenon should "embrace the female." Clearly, the natural path does not seek unrealistic purity, but rather a blending of opposites.

In recognizing and following a spiritual path, the Taoist accepts a significant life challenge. Clarity requires constant vigilance and effort. There can be no "halfways." The man of Tao understands that grasping the fundamentals and nuances of one's daily profession requires a deep commitment. To the Taoist, a half-skilled professional should not exist. One either embraces a profession or does not claim professionalism. There is no middle ground. A Taoist professional is a clear-thinking individual who forms and executes unambiguous commitments.

Religious beliefs must be clear and unambiguous. Many people make religion a mere nicety, with little understanding of the consequences of their beliefs. If one asked typical Americans to explain their religion, the responses would be a scattered collection of faith-based dogma with no validated connection to the real world. It must not be so. Religious beliefs must be clear and grounded in reality, for there is no room for confusion in a topic dedicated to clarifying one's picture of reality.

Life and Death

> **Things live and die and change their forms, without knowing the root from which they come.**
>
> —*The Wisdom of Laotse*, 68

The phenomenon of life and death is addressed by understanding yin and yang. Death is all around us. Fear of death is the most basic and primal of fears. One observes death stealing away friends and loved ones by illness, accident, or old age. *National Geographic* broadcasts images of animals suffering brutal, violent deaths at the hands of predators. How can one deal with so pervasive and horrible a fear? How can a student of Tao use the principle of yin/yang to more fully understand this inseparable part of nature?

A Taoist's yin/yang view of life begins by recognizing that life is a circle with living as its *visible* component and death as its *invisible* counterpart. We can only see and experience the visible component of the life/death cycle and are left to wonder about the fate of our intangible component once the physical body ceases to function. Where does the invisible part of our existence, sometimes called the soul, go when we die?

To find these answers, we must apply the Tao's yin/yang principle of opposites. Worrying about the afterlife is as illogical as worrying about our prelife origin. Do we know what entered the world first—our body, mind, or spirit? We only see our physical manifestations which emerged from our mother's womb, but it stands to reason that our souls, too, came from *somewhere*. But from where? And do our souls have prior experiences that assist their new embodiments?

> **Remove its bondage, slip off its skin-carcass, and curling up, where shall the soul of man go and the body go with it? Is it perhaps on the great journey home?**
>
> —*The Wisdom of Laotse*, 237

Unfortunately, there are no answers for mortals. We come from the darkness of the cosmos—a darkness impenetrable to our eyes. We can only understand that our souls came from nothing and return to their unknown origin after death. All else is a mystery. We can know nothing more. Yet that realization alone is powerful, for it forces us to acknowledge that we are nothing more than guests on this planet. Perhaps the visible part of our life/death cycle is better or worse than its invisible part. Does the soul learn on each visit? We came from nothingness and return to its embrace. Chuang Tzu encourages us to find comfort in this view:

> **To have been cast in this human form is to us already a source of joy. How much greater joy beyond our conception to know that that which is now in human form may undergo countless transitions, with only the infinite to look forward to? Therefore it is that the Sage rejoices in that which can never be lost, but endures always.**
>
> —*The Wisdom of Laotse*, 98

Reversion

> **When something reaches a limit, then it reverses its direction; when the end is reached, the beginning begins.**
>
> —*The Wisdom of Laotse*, 148

Another pragmatic principle of yin/yang is how opposites bring about balance to any phenomenon. This understanding provides the Taoist with an important tool as he sorts through life's options and navigates a spiritual path.

On many occasions, we are confronted with a difficult decision that requires a choice among many options. Often these choices are critically important, yet we find it difficult to articulate the desired outcome. Facing such a quandary, the practicing Taoist looks to the principle of opposites for an answer.

A peculiar characteristic of human nature is our ability to describe what we do *not* want. By articulating the undesired potential consequences of decisions, we find it easy to recognize the desired choice. The process of understanding the negative, or black, side of a choice leads us to the desired, or white, side.

This principle of reversion can be applied to the most fundamental of questions, such as "What do you want out of life?" Most people's confusion renders them unable to answer this central question. In a sense, this is not surprising, for it is difficult to answer such a spiritual question without a teacher and his attendant wisdom as a guide. Using the principle of opposites, however, we can formulate our own answer. We begin by exploring the opposite side of the question: what do we *not* want from life? The answer to this question is easy. Most of us would say we don't want to be poor, unhappy, or unhealthy. This implies that we wish to have the opposite: adequate finances, health, and happiness. And that answers our perplexing question. The principle of reversion narrows the range of options and allows us to view our target more clearly.

The phenomenon of thinking from opposites—yin to yang and yang to yin—brings us to oneness. All things are perceived as one, part of the same rotation—like life and death, hot and cold. The Tao is a diamond viewed from different facets. This perception of oneness creates harmony, allowing us to view life as an endless, seamless cycle. Such is the natural manifestation, or teh, of the higher powers. It is a principle that ultimately leads to unifying the possible and impossible, dream and reality.

Inaction

> Therefore the perfect man does nothing, the great Sage takes no action. In doing this, he follows the pattern of the universe.
>
> —*The Wisdom of Laotse*, 68

One of the most important principles of Taoism is the principle of inaction, or *wu wei*. Unfortunately, the true meaning of wu wei has been misinterpreted for thousands of years, resulting in vast confusion. The source of this principle and its attendant confusion is one of Lao Tzu's most famous poems in which he introduces and describes wu wei. Most translations of the Tao Te Ching interpret *wei* as "to act" and *wu wei* as "not to act" or "inaction." The translation by Lin Yutang, however, was more accurate, interpreting *wei* as "to interfere" and *wu wei* as "not to interfere." Correctly read, then, the Taoist principle of inaction is really a principle of *noninterference*.

The misinterpretation of inaction is not merely semantics; it carries important consequences to the practitioner of Taoism. By embracing an incorrect principle, the confused individual in turn embraces a false view of the world. As a result, he behaves incorrectly in facing life's challenges. Sadder still, this incorrect interpretation of Lao Tzu is what most people find appealing. To them, when Lao Tzu writes, "By doing nothing everything is done" (p. 229), he appears to promise that their lives will be okay if they literally avoid acting. The common man finds this comforting, for it eliminates the necessity of having to fight for anything. In the minds of the masses, Lao Tzu's principle of inaction is an excuse to avoid confrontation. Their confused view of the world—propagandized by social and religious institutions—perceives that all of mankind's interactions can be managed through rational discourse and passivity. Action merely invites unwanted confrontation. The allure of this nonsensical interpretation is powerful: don't act because it creates problems.

Further, in the minds of weak men, inaction is a means to avoid responsibility. Here, the interpretation of "rest in inaction" is philosophically extended to place the responsibility for getting things done on *others*: other people, other forces, other natural occurrences, other gods, and other circumstances. In short, anything or anyone besides oneself.

The consequences of this belief are insidious. The lazy, fearful, and ineffectual man abdicates responsibility, giving evidence once again to the weakness of human nature. In this confused state, a man need not take responsibility as a male. A woman need not take responsibility as a female. This loss of individual responsibility leads to the loss of naturalness—the Taoist's model of reality. As we make our way down life's path, we are ultimately held accountable for what we have chosen to do and not do. This is such a central concept to Taoism that for thousands of years the entrances of classical Taoist temples have been inscribed with the words "Every man is responsible for his actions."

Words are cheap, actions expensive. The fool who follows the path of inaction chooses to believe words that fly in the face of reality. The confused man hiding behind this misinterpretation gives testament to the shallowness of human nature.

The confused interpretation of the principle of inaction is remarkable, for it is without any real-world application. How can an entire philosophical system be created around an approach that in essence says, "Just sit around and everything will work out by itself"? How could such an inane concept be treated seriously? No sane person could agree that food, money, shelter, and companionship will magically appear through inaction. On the contrary, it takes a lot of action to pay your bills, maintain your health, keep loved ones happy, and fight off an uninvited home invader. Or—to use nature as a model—imagine an African gazelle that, on seeing a stalking lion, simply lies placid in the grass. Would you expect the gazelle to live a long and fruitful life?

This misinterpretation of inaction is a contrivance of sheltered intellectuals and clergy who have never been forced to take risks. Wallowing in their self-satisfaction, they represent prototypical losers who smugly look down on those who are struggling to deal with life by taking action—sometimes winning and sometimes failing, but who at least take action within the limits of their abilities.

In opting for an existence of perpetual inaction, the confused individual removes himself from the rotation of life. Taoism views life as a cycle of movement, a wheel of constant change and applied energy. The student of inaction advocates no movement, no change, and no energy. And, removed from the pattern of life, the nonacting individual can expect no benefit from his philosophy. Instead, he can expect only constant hardship and misfortune. Nonmoving water becomes stagnant. Nonmoving blood leads to gangrene. The slovenly animal has an unhealthy physique.

Society treats the idle person as lazy on the job and lousy in relationships. The man of inaction will find money unavailable. In short, the disciple of inaction—by smugly placing himself outside the cycle of life—has doomed himself to spiritual and physical suicide. His vision of the world is wholly inconsistent with reality. Lin Yutang said it well in his translation:

> **It has also become clear that as we live in the human world, total abstention from activities is impossible, and so one comes to the resultant attitude of a mild passivity and indulgent quietness as the wisest mode of life.**
>
> —*The Wisdom of Laotse*, 194

The student of the Tao examines both sides of any phenomenon to learn its true meaning and application. This exploration of opposites is one of the most important teachings of the yin/yang principle. As portrayed in the diagram, the circle of nature requires that opposites must interact to create balance and harmony: day and night, life and death, summer and winter. This rotation—defined as the reversion principle—can be applied to discern the true use of inaction. Therefore, we must examine the correlation of inaction and action to identify inaction's core application: how does inaction's peace, tranquility, and stillness relate to action's struggle, movement, and fighting?

The Coiled Spring Phenomenon

> In his quietness he shares the same character with *yin*; in his activity the same energy with *yang*.
>
> —*The Wisdom of Laotse*, 273

Think of a coiled spring, still and unmoving, where potential energy is stored in its compressed position. Only when it uncoils is its potential energy turned into movement. In essence, the spring's energy is conserved in its unmoving, compressed state until such time as it is called on to release its power. The utility of a spring derives from its powerful movement, which cannot exist without the compressed, still period. An uncoiled spring contains no power, no potential energy. If called on to move, it will fail, for its energy has been expended. This example serves as an analogy for one of Taoism's major life principles.

In applying the spring principle to life's challenges, one remembers that the goal of a spiritual man is to see the world clearly and operate within his limits in order to live a happier and healthier life. The Taoist further recognizes that life can end unexpectedly and thus knows he should live each day as if it were his last. This in turn means that the objective of Taoists is to create a daily routine that is comfortable and enjoyable. In cultivating a way of life that brings enjoyment, the Taoist finds his place in the world. In essence, the Taoist who creates a comfortable daily routine has succeeded in achieving harmony with the world around him.

While creating a comfortable daily routine sounds like a reasonable and modest goal, it actually takes a tremendous amount of dedication and effort. It is an arduous task to acquire life's necessities, deal with the people around us, keep our bodies healthy, and eke out some time for leisure. It takes all of Taoism's principles to clearly understand how to prioritize our time and make the necessary trade-offs to achieve contentment. It requires correct expectations and an understanding of limits. It becomes the Taoist's ongoing test to conserve energy when dealing with issues that do not contribute to the desired outcome. The clear-thinking Taoist understands what he needs to achieve his comfortable daily life. He is not swayed by outside influences and wastes none of his precious energy on extraneous activities that do not help him realize his comfortable existence. He is like a coiled spring, filled with potential energy. He uncoils and expends this energy only in efforts that directly contribute to a perfect daily routine.

Unfortunately, when asked to describe their vision of a perfect daily routine, one without work or family obligations, most people have no answer. This is a sad testament to the modern human condition. Such people are lost souls, bound by the constraints of social convention. Their lives embody the routine of the walking dead. They expend their energies on the inanities hailed by the social structure and have none left for the passions of life. For these people, Taoism offers no solace—they are the doomed masses, wasting energy and donning blinders as they tread life's path.

Noninterference

> He responds only when moved, acts only when he is urged, and rises to action only when he is compelled to do so.
>
> —*The Wisdom of Laotse,* 273

Given that the spring principle encourages the Taoist to conserve energy, when is it correct to expend energy? In answering this question, we must reach into wu wei's deepest philosophical level. The answer, in typical Taoist fashion, is simple yet profound: action is required when any force attempts to remove the man of Tao from his daily routine.

The interference of outside factors in a Taoist's daily life causes him to exert concentrated effort to maintain his routine. The maintenance of a good routine requires constant innovation, creativity, and aggression. Importantly, because he has conserved energy, he has the power to overcome the interference. It is inaction that gives the Taoist strength to thwart interference in his pursuit of happiness.

Wu wei's noninterference is the method for achieving harmony in life. It is the principle that instructs the Taoist to act only when the outside world interferes with his desired routine. In essence, the Taoist walks down his life's path, relaxed but vigilant to the commotion around him. It is only when something jumps into his path, blocking his way, that he takes action. Conversely, the Taoist has no desire to interfere with others as they pursue their individual, albeit confused paths. Wu wei instructs us to "live and let live" until interference requires corrective action. The translation of Lao Tzu's "By doing nothing everything is done" should properly be "Don't interfere and everything is achievable." The principle of inaction is really the principle of noninterference.

Interference with one's daily routine comes about in two ways: physical and mental. Physical interference can be as brutal and direct as an assault by a knife-wielding criminal or as slow and insidious as an infectious disease's attack against one's immune system. The clear-thinking Taoist must prepare for these forms of interference through training in the combat martial arts and maintaining a healthy body via exercise and diet. In both cases, there is clear, unambiguous interference with one's path and an equally unambiguous remedy.

It is the mental aspect of wu wei, however, that seems to require more clarification, for it is less tangible and obvious.

It is difficult for man to understand his correct path because his original nature has been lost. This is not just a modern phenomenon. Lao Tzu lamented the loss of man's original nature twenty-five hundred years ago. Lao Tzu explained that the mechanism for this loss was the false values promulgated by the leaders of society. More specifically, these false values were the unending quest for money, fame, and power by society's most elite: political leaders, clergy, the rich, the famous, and all others who commanded the respect of society.

In today's America, probably the greatest of all societies, there is an incredible emphasis on the value of work and material possessions. To the Taoist, work is the means to a good life—nothing more. While professional pride is okay, there must be a clear recognition that work *is* work and not a form of fun. Work is a means to make money, allowing one to afford a perfect daily routine. Since time is at a premium, there is contention between time for work and time to enjoy life. Americans place an absurd value on the perfect vacation—comprising only two weeks of each year—because their daily lives are such a mess. Vacation time is akin to a brief parole from prison. Chuang Tzu observed this same dynamic in ancient China:

> **The common men sacrifice their lives for profit; the scholars sacrifice their lives for fame; the noblemen sacrifice their lives for their families; . . . All these people have different professions and their reputations vary, but in suffering injury to their original nature, they are alike.**
>
> —*The Wisdom of Laotse,* 91–92

The American preoccupation with work is symptomatic of a deeper mental disease. The constant running around to meet the demands of work and family leave the stressed American with little time for contemplation. Such lack of thought is a voluntary "dumbing down." The endless pursuit of money enables one to avoid thinking about life's path. Like an opiate, work delivers a drug-induced numbness. The priority to acquire a bigger house and more expensive cars is a trap that Americans find appealing. Instead of using an increased salary to buy time, the American buys a bigger mortgage.

A spiritual person recognizes that work is required to achieve a comfortable routine. Money is therefore a necessity, but not the goal. The man of Tao understands his occupation will inevitably be a source of interference with his daily routine and must therefore be carefully managed.

While the unending quest for material wealth is an obvious source of interference with one's path, Lao Tzu warns of an even greater threat: humanity and justice.

Humanity and Justice

> On the decline of the great Tao,
> The doctrines of "humanity" and "justice"
> arose.
>
> —*The Wisdom of Laotse,* 119

Lao Tzu warns us to be vigilant against the values of humanity and justice. They are the mechanism by which society interferes with an individual's original nature, manipulating the common man to behave in ways that reinforce society's structure at his expense. The values of humanity and justice replace an individual's own desires and needs, inevitably resulting in actions contrary to his self-interest. These seemingly benign values, like love, honor, and patriotism, are wickedly subtle and powerful. They enable society to achieve its goal of control—and ruin one's life.

How can values that are so blatantly against the individual's self-interest become so pervasive? Shouldn't these fraudulent social values, which inevitably lead to an unhappy life, fail immediately on introduction? What is Taoism's explanation for such absurdity?

Chuang Tzu answers,

Then came confusion between joy and anger, fraud between the simple and the cunning, recrimination between the virtuous and the evil-minded, . . .

—*The Wisdom of Laotse,* 126

Lao Tzu's disciple explains that the values of humanity and justice cause so much confusion that they can flourish, leading an individual to act against his own interests. These social values sound so incredibly wonderful. Unfortunately, they don't work in real life and are a certain prescription for confusion and suffering. How can Christianity claim to exalt the Ten Commandments when Christians have continued to kill each other for thousands of years? How can a good Christian, trying to follow his Bible's doctrines, turn his cheek against the blow of an attacker, only to receive another blow again and again? How can a man work hard all his life and faithfully pay his taxes, only to spend his twilight years forgotten and malnourished in a nursing home? Such disconnections between society's values of humanity and justice and life's brutal realities cause confusion. When such false expectations are not borne out in the real world, it is akin to having an inaccurate road map. A clear view of reality is impossible, and navigation through life is seriously impaired.

Chuang Tzu further elaborates by explaining that the values of humanity and justice are brought to us by social sages. He declares that the laws of the Sages preserve their thieves' lives. Chuang Tzu warns that society is a cunning thief who steals from the citizenry, its voluntary victims. The social sages have long convinced us that a big family, big house, and big car represent a winning scorecard in the game of life. Politicians, religious leaders, and academicians propagandize setting priorities that serve their own interests rather than those of the individual. In the ultimate hypocrisy, social sages convince the masses to discard their natural instincts in an effort to protect the interests of the few at the top of the social hierarchy. In Chuang Tzu's words, these sages are the "sharp weapons of the world" (p. 124).

It is important when reading Lao Tzu and Chuang Tzu to distinguish between true sages and social sages. Both frequently use the term *sages* and it is up to the reader to infer which meaning should be applied. A true sage is a master with a clear vision of the world and how to operate within it; he has no interest in joining the hypocrisy of social life. By contrast, a social sage is a powerful manipulator who relishes his position as a leader of society and who uses humanity and justice to serve his own interests, usually the acquisition of wealth, fame, and power.

Further exacerbating the confusion for the individual under the spell of social sages is the constant change of social values. While the laws of nature are immutable, the artificial values of humanity and justice are in constant flux. Consistent with Taoism's principle of reversion, the stronger the hypocrisy of a society's values, the more violently and unexpectedly they will change. For example, Germany in the late 1800s was one of the most liberal and progressive countries in the world—within twenty years, it turned into a society of intolerance and terror. In 1917, the Russian government declared that religion and private ownership of property were illegal. Religion returned in 1990, and capitalism is now king. The Kennedy family included bootleggers and stock market manipulators during the 1920s, yet became a revered and beloved political dynasty that spawned congressmen, senators, and a president.

Such topsy-turvy shifts in values foster confusion among the commoners and breed anarchy and chaos as hypocrisy runs rampant. As Lao Tzu explained, "When [social] Sages arose, gangsters appeared" (p. 123). Blatant hypocrisy causes opposition to emerge, resulting in conscious acts of violent revolution or unconscious psychiatric disorders. Therefore Chuang Tzu encourages mankind to "discard humanity and justice, and the character of the people will arrive at Mystic Unity" (p. 125).

It is clear that eliminating confusion is the key prerequisite for determining correct action. We cannot live a happy and healthy life while we're confused. Confusion disables the means by which we determine when action is needed. Confusion also disrupts our ability to detect the forces interfering with our natural path. Often the sin of confusion does not even allow us to recognize our path. Confusion is like flying a plane without navigational instruments or driving a car through never-ending fog.

In the war between individual and communal values, clarity of thought will determine the ultimate outcome. Lao Tzu encourages us to "realize the simple self." To do so, we must peer through the fog and see undistorted reality.

So how are we to overcome the tidal wave of social values that bombard and blind us from birth? How does a student begin to transform himself from a confused tool of society to a clear-thinking man of Tao? Isn't attainment of the "simple self" virtually impossible in today's world?

Fortunately, Lao Tzu was clear about where to start:

> **And who recognizes sick-mindedness as sick-mindedness is not sick-minded.**
>
> —*The Wisdom of Laotse,* 297

By acknowledging which of your values have been dictated by society, you begin the journey toward amputating this major source of confusion. In recognizing which of your desires are natural and which have been implanted by a controlling society, you slowly realize your natural self. It sounds simple, yet requires incredibly disciplined thought. It is a path that leads you away from the grazing herd of common men. You have a choice: embrace the artificial love of society's humanity and the artificial laws of society's justice, or fight for your natural core.

To deal with your "sick-mindedness," remind yourself of your inescapable limitations. The principles of humanity and justice are built first on the belief that individuals can comprehend and repair the problems of the world, and second on the belief that the tool to perform this deed is an improved social order.

In reality, each man's inherent limitations make it impossible to do anything more than observe the reality that immediately affects his well-being. Society's lie, that one individual can improve the world, results in the controlling power of humanity and justice. By understanding that your limitations render you capable only of realizing your individual path, you discard false and irrelevant values. Even casual thoughts about improving the world by embracing social values are a mental disease. The Taoist knows his limitations require him to restrict his thoughts and actions to only those values that can improve his current situation. All other considerations are inconsequential or outright false.

In repairing your "sick-mindedness," it is vital to recognize that the values of humanity and justice are those of a thief dedicated to robbing you. Social sages, propagandizing values, act against your self-interest and only contribute to your confusion. These social sages work tirelessly to convince you to work two jobs, buy a bigger house, rear offspring, and fight distant wars until you drop. These respected politicians, teachers, religious leaders, and philosophers conspire to influence your mind to their advantage. Chuang Tzu acknowledges this fact:

> **Since good men are scarce and bad men are the majority, the good the [social] Sages do to the world is little and the evil great.**
>
> —*The Wisdom of Laotse,* 123

Ironically, a burglar who steals your television deservedly goes to jail, yet the greatest thieves—the social sages—steal fortunes and are revered by society. This realization, that the originators of humanity and justice are the bad guys, is an important key to eliminating the havoc they have wrought in your mind. By becoming a constructive cynic, you build a mental shield against the bombardment of the social sages' values.

The Truth of Tao

As your vision clears, a frightening realization occurs: the values of the vast majority of people around you are fundamentally absurd. Sadly, most people are unable and unwilling to listen to the flaws of their cherished, long-held beliefs. It is too difficult for them to abandon the comfort of their confusion for the brightness of clear vision. The common man doesn't want to hear critiques disclosing the hypocrisy of his revered social sages.

The true Taoist recognizes this and accordingly keeps his thoughts and opinions to himself. He disguises his recognition of the absurdity of social values by camouflaging his beliefs. He has no willingness to become the target of an enraged society and thus doesn't try to transform his confused community. Nothing can more quickly remove a Taoist from his comfortable daily routine than being labeled a demagogue. Any attempt to teach society natural values is an ill-fated act of confusion, destined to invite disaster. Camouflaging his disdain of humanity and justice's values is therefore an essential prerequisite to realizing his path.

The principle of using camouflage to disguise Taoism's unconventionality results from recognizing that society is not ready for the truth of Tao. Lao Tzu understood that most of society depends on the comforting confusion of humanity and justice; he also knew that, once mankind lost its natural instincts, only a rare group of Taoists could truly comprehend his teachings. He warned that teaching the common man to discard social values could backfire, resulting in anarchy.

The animal kingdom's natural order works because it has been unpolluted by man's misguided social engineering. It is too late for society's masses, however, because they can never recapture their lost core. Any altruistic attempt to impart the Taoist knowledge to the masses is thus akin to opening Pandora's box. Without his natural core to steer him, the common man becomes an unguided missile if the constraints of social values are removed. Lao Tzu encourages the man of Tao to focus his limited abilities on healing his own sick-mindedness and letting the common man wallow in his confused state.

The World and I

> The people of the world all have a purpose;
> I alone appear stubborn and uncouth.
> I alone differ from the other people,
> And value drawing sustenance from the Mother.
>
> —*The Wisdom of Laotse*, 129

In choosing an unconventional road far removed from society's values, the student of Tao undertakes a serious goal. It is akin to a robot breaking away from the enslavement of its masters. In many ways, it is a recognition that the world and its values are so distinctly different from the individual's that you are a stranger in your own land.

Lao Tzu recognized this and became one of the first philosophers to deal with the effects of an imperfect society on spiritual persons. While most philosophers developed recipes for life in their imaginary perfect worlds, Lao Tzu was much more pragmatic. He taught us instead how to deal with the imperfect society around us. This pragmatism begins with the harsh recognition that those around us—as polite and smiling as they appear—must be viewed with extreme caution. Their values are as dangerous as the venom of a snake, poisonous to our souls. They are unwitting accomplices to the theft of our original nature.

The Common Man and the Man of Tao

> . . . the highest teachings are not accepted by the minds of the common men, and the words of wisdom are not popular, because they are overshadowed by conventional teachings.
>
> —*The Wisdom of Laotse*, 130

It is general knowledge that thinkers from Plato to Nietzsche have clearly distinguished the common man from philosophers, understanding there were powerful differences between them that needed to be articulated and codified. While he used independent reasoning, Lao Tzu shared this belief, but in a much more egalitarian manner. While other philosophers placed themselves at the top of the social ladder, Lao Tzu's "philosopher" is any Taoist who achieves true spirituality, regardless of profession or social rank. His philosopher is anyone who stands outside social convention and sees things for what they truly are.

In Latin, "common man" translates to "vulgar man." This vulgar man, representing 99.9 percent of the population, reflects society's values. He has been molded from birth by the values of society, reared to perpetuate social goals at the expense of his own individuality. By contrast, the philosopher (or Taoist) fights society's brainwashing and clearly observes what's going on. With the detachment of a scientist, he investigates the dysfunctional effects of society on an individual. This analytic detachment makes a Taoist a de facto philosopher. Further, this detachment makes the Taoist less likely to be manipulated by the emotional strings pulled by a controlling society.

So who creates these social values followed by the common man? Social sages are the power behind the propaganda controlling society. Social sages or social philosophers prescribe seductive solutions to the challenges of life, leveraging the values of humanity and justice to achieve their own goals. They can be politicians, academicians, or religious leaders—anyone who is in a position to deceive an audience. Remarkably, the common man voluntarily follows their prescription for spiritual suicide.

Social sages are easy to detect. While the man of Tao has no desire to waste his limited energies on teaching the common man, social sages relish this role. They are in the business of teaching everyone to death. They love being arbitrators of values and passionately preach them. The common man listens dumbly to these pronouncements and blindly follows them to their unhappy ends. By contrast, the Taoist recognizes that it is a full-time job to teach himself the ways of life—he has neither the time nor energy to bother with the common man.

Lao Tzu was clear that the ancients "aimed not to enlighten the people, but to keep them ignorant" (p. 285). Chuang Tzu was even more direct, describing the social sages of twenty-five hundred years ago in a manner relevant to today's politicians:

> They know how to give a good speech and tell appropriate anecdotes in order to attract the crowd, but from the very beginning to the very end, they do not know what it is all about. They put on the proper garb and dress in the proper colors and put on a decorous appearance in order to make themselves popular, but refuse to admit that they are hypocrites. They mingle with the crowd, and declare themselves in agreement with what the public likes and dislikes, at the same time claiming that they are better than the common men.
>
> —*The Wisdom of Laotse,* 130

The Taoist of twenty-five hundred years ago and the modern-day American share a common trait: a sense of practicality. The prototypical American has always been a problem-solving machine, skeptical in all matters related to commerce and industry. Try to sell a Connecticut Yankee a horse in the 1700s or an automobile in the present, and all measures of tests and inspections would be used to ensure a shrewd purchase. Ironically, try to sell present-day Americans a New Age pseudoreligion or a solution to global warming, and practicality goes out the window. When it comes to worldwide issues, for some unknown reason, the practical American turns into an ignorant fool: the tough sell no longer requires proof and does not mandate clear explanations.

Principles of Tao

The Taoist of ancient China shared the modern American's sense of practicality and Yankee ingenuity, creating remarkable healing sciences, weapons, astronomical tools, and other innovations. Unlike Americans, however, Taoists also consistently demanded proof of any philosophical principles. So-called truths had to be proven, or they were deemed inconsequential. Today's global solutions and New Age philosophies—which Americans are so eager to embrace—would be seen by the Taoist as unprovable and therefore irrelevant.

The idea of avoiding global issues boils down to this: don't stick your nose where it doesn't belong. Chuang Tzu reinforced this warning by observing,

> **For all men strive to grasp what they do not know, while none strive to grasp what they already know;** . . .
>
> —*The Wisdom of Laotse*, 287

Chuang Tzu observed that common men have a predilection for bypassing their practical circuit breakers when it comes to the affairs of the world. Take a hard-nosed businessman and put him in the company of social sages blabbering about solutions to world hunger, social injustice in Africa, and the shrinking Amazon rain forest. In no time, he becomes an intellectual boob. The allure of big solutions to far-off problems elevates the common man above his daily hassles. He sees himself as the world's savior. His pride is reinforced. Because the consequences of these irrelevant global crusades are seemingly distant, there is apparently no risk to this behavior; at worst, it seems merely harmless charity. It is easy mental work that has no recognizable downside other than to open him up to the forces of confusion.

A foolproof test to identify dysfunctional people is to gauge their involvement in the big issues: social justice, religious causes, politics, and ecology. The more they espouse such causes, the messier their personal lives. It is the hypocrisy of human nature to focus on the problems of others when one cannot manage one's own.

This curious desire of the common man—to grapple with the world's unsolvable issues—provides social sages with a powerful tool of manipulation. They use pride as a mechanism to gain control over the people, making them work hard and think little. The ignorant masses are led to feel that their sacrifice contributes to the greater good. The common man with a miserable daily life salvages his pride by naively believing that his effort, no matter how insignificant, will impact the world's eternal problems.

It is perplexing and, at first, humorous to hear weak, confused people who are unable to articulate a clear vision of their surroundings engage in passionate discourse about issues of global and timeless dimensions. This comedy becomes tragic when social sages use this confusion to impart values that hurt the common man and better the social elite. While the cynic can argue that this suicidal course is a consequence of man's own stupidity, Lao Tzu was more forthcoming. He clearly warned mankind of this danger.

The Taoist will notice that, throughout history, "good" values belong to the aristocracy and "bad" values to the common man. For example, Confucius described a "good" man as a "gentleman" in clean clothes who enjoyed music and read books. Terrific for 1 percent of the population—the ruling aristocracy and wealthy merchants. It was irrelevant, however, to the 99 percent of the Chinese who were poor and forced to labor in the fields seven days a week just to survive. Even today, the "good" values of suburban American families—preached by religious leaders and politicians—have no relevance to poor, inner-city households. Similarly, the values of a Harvard-educated lawyer are incomprehensible to an uneducated bricklayer.

Much fun has been made in literature and theater of the absurdity of the aristocracy pretending to understand and attempting to behave like the common man. The reverse is equally farcical. Each group has its own definitions of good and bad, its own culture and value systems. Those at the top of the social pyramid, emulated and revered by the have-nots, constantly propagandize their values through society's communication channels.

By contrast, the teachings of the Tao transcend social strata and convention. The values of Taoism apply equally to the rich man and the poor man. Because the Tao is indifferent to social convention, there are no good values or bad values. There are only pragmatic principles that work. Of course, social sages will labor tirelessly to obscure these immutable principles:

> **Destruction of Tao and character in order to strive for humanity and justice—this is the error of the [social] Sages.**
>
> —*The Wisdom of Laotse,* 120

Social sages, representing the interests of society's controlling elite, propagandize unworkable principles. They are nothing more than philosophical pimps peddling confusion. Ironically, those at the top of the social pyramid can avoid the consequences of this confusion, since they are insulated and protected by wealth and power. Meanwhile, the unfortunate masses become traumatized victims, for they can ill afford this stupidity.

The man of Tao recognizes that values are unique to each socioeconomic group and that there is no way for one group to truly comprehend another's values. This manifests itself in each group's unique clothes, slang, music, and behaviors. "Good" behavior is thus defined by each person's immediate social clique. The construct "if I were you . . ." is therefore recognized as an absurd concept by the Taoist, because he is *not* you and therefore cannot intellectually appreciate your values.

Overall, this idea that there are no good or bad values is profound. It requires the Tao man to look beyond social convention and instead embrace those values that transcend such convention. A Taoist knows, for example, that there is indeed honor among thieves; while society may label a thief as "bad," the Taoist is less judgmental. A telling religious fact is that, for millennia, both law enforcement officers and criminals worshipped the same god in Taoist temples. By recognizing that society's values are nothing more than tools of manipulation wielded by the ruling class, the individual has more intellectual ammunition to fend off their controlling power and avoid the resulting confusion.

Knowledge and Chaos

> ... the knowledge which stops at what it does not know is the highest knowledge.
>
> —*The Wisdom of Laotse,* 54

One of Lao Tzu's most important philosophical concepts was his explanation of the process by which the common man lost his original nature and thereby became a creature of discontent. By understanding this process, the student of Tao can attempt to undo the harm that society has inflicted on his natural core and recapture his soul. Lao Tzu speaks of ancient times when mankind embraced its original nature and then describes the decline of Taoism:

> On the decline of the great Tao,
> The doctrines of "humanity" and "justice" arose.
> When knowledge and cleverness appeared,
> Great hypocrisy followed in its wake.
>
> —*The Wisdom of Laotse,* 119

Here we see that social sages espoused the values of humanity and justice to the herds of common men, laying the foundation for knowledge and cleverness. Knowledge and cleverness then progressed to the next stage of social disease, wherein hypocrisy became rampant and chaos ensued. Society lost its natural core thousands of years ago, and mankind became a sad collection of lost souls with no connection to its natural core.

A good example of the social "knowledge" that Lao Tzu warns us against is the classic "American dream." Modern American values define a typical life cycle for the American family, providing a collection of supposed requirements for happiness that actually breed the opposite—discontent. The work ethic and a life of consumption are pounded into the heads of youngsters by all members of society, led by social sages. Happiness requires a big home, an expensive automobile, hordes of children, religious piety, and long-term savings. These become the de facto criteria for happiness to which all citizens devote their lives, leading to their ultimate misery.

Let's see how the achievement of the American dream actually plays out over time. After a childhood of schooling, the typical eighteen-year-old devotes all his efforts to acquiring a college education at the cost of a small fortune. Marriage is expected to follow, with the young husband and wife both working full-time to afford the down payment on a "starter" home. The birth of a child is then prescribed by convention, despite the reality that—after a brief respite—the mother must jump back into her career so the family can afford a demanding mortgage and day-care expenses.

After several years, another child or two is added to the family (one child is not enough), requiring a larger house and a bigger mortgage. A second car is needed to shuttle the children to their various activities. Now in their late thirties, the couple's young years of life are lost. Middle age approaches. Careers require long hours—perhaps even occasional geographic relocations—in the chase for promotions and salary raises; as a result, any hope of establishing long-term friendships is impossible. A larger house and fancy car—with their attendant big monthly payments—are expected with each significant promotion to reflect the elevated social status.

Now in their forties, the couple divert excess cash to a savings plan to save for their children's college tuitions and their own eventual retirement. Meanwhile, the grind of mortgage payments, car payments, and all the rest continues. Finally, assuming fate doesn't deal the hard-working pair a fatal illness, the children graduate from college and the parents reach their sixtieth birthdays and, eventually, retirement.

Many couples will enter retirement deeply in debt, usually with decades left on their current home's mortgage and with loans still outstanding for their children's college tuitions. Just as traumatically, retirement hits the lifelong wage earner with an abundance of free time and no idea what to do with it. Before, days were filled with the demands of work and the needs of children. Now there are long, empty days to fill. Ultimately, the dream of retirement is shallow. Life's best years, the twenties through the fifties, are spent on the treadmill of making money. Bitterness and a feeling of loss replace excitement and hope when, too late, the average American discovers the American dream is a fraud.

The bitterness felt by some of the herd's intelligent members is recognition that a life spent in pursuit of this hollow dream is wasted. The prescribed course of life is too demanding, too hard, with only the unfulfilled promise of future rewards. The Tao teaches us that when any goal requires too much effort to achieve, it is probably not part of our natural path. While focused effort is required to achieve anything in life, incremental gains must be realized on a steady basis. The professional athlete, for example, gradually increases his speed and strength, expecting measurable improvement with each training cycle. He quickly distrusts a coach who accepts stalled or nonexistent progress while promising outstanding future gains. Yet the American dream, by comparison, requires less and less free time in the present for the allure of a promising retirement in the distant future. The confused souls who accept this bargain devote little money and effort to developing a comfortable daily routine. They acquire bigger houses, fancier cars, larger families, and improved social status rather than free time and comfort. They accept months of misery, placing tremendous importance on their ten allotted vacation days. If those two weeks are so greatly anticipated, it goes without saying that the other fifty weeks must be truly bad. It means that the American dream is an unnatural path that needs to be challenged.

 While sixty years of following an unnatural path results in the irrevocable loss of time and youth, its implications for the soul are even more grave. In fighting the natural desire to enjoy life each day and training yourself to live instead as society's robot, you place your passion for life in jeopardy. By constantly deferring your joys—a cherished hobby, a walk with a beloved dog, an afternoon reading a good book—these natural desires die off like a neglected flower. In essence, by voluntarily suppressing your natural desires over sixty years, you become a dried-up, lifeless shell—assuming you are lucky enough to survive to retirement. This is all too often

Principles of Tao

the tragic epilogue to a hardworking person's life: a retiree who has lost all ability to enjoy life. There is a real danger in embracing an unnatural path: it kills your natural love of life.

So how is the typical American fooled by society's sages into pursuing a lifetime of discontent? The answer to this question gets to the heart of the common man's confusion. It is here that the role of images becomes tantamount.

As any con man knows, the key to success in any scam is to replace a tangible asset (the target's money) with promises of future gains. The con man uses images and promises to fool his victim into parting with hard-earned cash. In a similar way, society fools the common man into parting with the best years of his life. These images—used in mass media advertising, preached by ministers and priests, and sprinkled throughout politicians' speeches—define the successful man as a hardworking careerist with a large family. The person who has carved out a modest lifestyle with little work and tons of free time is never upheld as a role model. No way! The "successful" man works ninety-hour weeks, supports five kids, and never takes a vacation. And even if he makes a lot of money, he won't work less. Instead, he'll buy a second home and perhaps a new Porsche—images of success that only deepen his entrenchment in the cult of consumption. Society has built a structure wherein success does not allow individuals to escape their bonds.

Lao Tzu's description of the decline of the Tao concludes with hypocrisy giving birth to chaos. He identifies society's sinister use of images to cheapen the value of words and foster confusion. The term *friend*, for example, is bandied about in today's society, yet *true* friendship has been lost, replaced by superficial relationships. Similarly, religious institutions preach universal "love" in a society where true love—even within the family—is a rare occurrence. Men are judged by the car they drive rather than the character they display. Clothes make the man. Vegetarians wear leather shoes. People communicate by e-mail instead of face-to-face. Politicians babble doublespeak and lie with a smile in sixty-second sound bites.

Everything is reduced to images and cheap words, enabling hypocrisy to flourish. This disconnection between reality and communication fools the mind into embracing anything that "sounds good." The person who follows another's teachings because they "make sense" is an unwitting fool—almost anything can make sense when a clever manipulator is doing the explaining. Reducing life's goals to images is a technique used by social sages to support their hypocrisy.

Society's use of hypocritical images leads the individual to voluntary enslavement. He is numbed and no longer asks basic questions: Do I really need a bigger house? Can I afford more children? Do I spend time with those with whom I share a common interest? The images promulgated by society's communication channels are powerful and pervasive, causing the common man to kill himself. In essence, when Lao Tzu warns us that "the farther one pursues knowledge, the less one knows" (p. 227), he is talking about the knowledge or ideas that society stuffs into our heads. The social knowledge accepted by the common man as his cherished beliefs is based on images rather than reality. They are hypocritical at their core and go against man's natural self-interest.

This understanding that there are two diametrically opposed sets of values operating in the world is important to the Taoist. One set of values is created by social sages and blindly followed by society; it operates to the detriment of the individual. The other set of values serves the best interests of the individual; these values are labeled as "selfish" or "egocentric" by society. By definition and practice the two sets of values are in conflict, sometimes dangerously so.

Society has little tolerance for those who step outside the prescribed enslavement of its structure. The persecution of those who don't follow society's herd is well documented throughout history. In many subtle ways, this pressure will be exerted against the man of Tao as he navigates around social convention and embraces his natural path to contentment. Understanding that society fears and abhors his unconfused life, the man of Tao uses camouflage to disguise his strategy. One definite benefit of American society is that, as long as you remain quiet in your beliefs (and pay your taxes), you will be left alone. Nevertheless, recognize that the values of society absolutely conflict with your individual values. Dealing with reality represents one of your greatest challenges in life.

So how does the individual deal with the incredible pressure of society and its social sages as he tries to realize his natural core and find contentment? Lao Tzu and Chuang Tzu answer that the Taoist must "banish wisdom, discard knowledge." In essence, the Taoist must train himself to identify and ignore social values. He must regularly challenge his wants and desires. He trains himself to ask important questions: "Do I really need a bigger house? Do I really need a better car? Is a better paying job worth the increased stress? Is a large family really the key to happiness?" This honest assessment makes the man of Tao a true philosopher. He does not accept social convention, but instead determines how his desires fit with his personal vision of contentment.

Throughout history, acquiring material things to achieve social status has been mankind's consistent folly. Since ancient times, the display of material wealth for the sake of impressing others has demonstrated the shallowness of man's character. To avoid this trap, the Taoist should ask, "Am I acquiring these things because I really want them, or because I am trying to impress others?"

For example, car manufacturers use the idea of buying a luxury car to impress others as a means to sell automobiles. Their advertisements show beautiful, happy people owning expensive cars. This psychological manipulation leads the common man to desire these cars in order to belong to that successful class of society. A logical examination, however, reveals this concept's absurdity. Why would you want to impress total strangers on the road? True friends wouldn't care what type of car you drive. And if your car did influence the people with whom you associate, what kind of friends would they be? Is the luxury car—which requires many months of salary to purchase—really worth it? On reflection, unless you are truly wealthy, it is not. This is an example of distinguishing between your genuine desires and those resulting from society's propaganda. When Lao Tzu instructs us to "banish learning," he is urging us to identify and eliminate all social "knowledge" so that we can focus our efforts on achieving a comfortable daily routine.

The Futility of Plans

> For if fulfilment means enslavement,
> how can it be regarded as fulfilment?
>
> —*The Wisdom of Laotse,* 91

Society fools the common man into voluntarily sacrificing a comfortable daily routine for nonstop work and stress. The primary tool for this manipulation is the promise of the future. Modern man, unlike the unspoiled natural world, engages in constant planning. Society is a vast collection of planners. The typical American is constantly planning retirement, vacations, children's education, pay raises, next week's weather, the stock market, and the next pound lost through dieting. Some people even plan their planning.

So what's wrong with planning? After all, we've been told again and again, "You've got to have a plan." Doesn't it make sense to figure out a plan and then focus on achieving its goals?

The problem is that planning implicitly assumes that we have enough time left on this planet to achieve the plan's promised rewards. For example, there is a fundamental flaw in planning for a wonderful retirement when there is no guarantee that you will live to enjoy it. The further assumption is that, once you make it to sixty-five or seventy, you will have the mental and physical capacity to enjoy the hypothetical "retirement."

When Lao Tzu wrote that "the vulgar are clever, self-assured" (p. 129), he meant that the common man believes he is so smart that his plans for the future will yield guaranteed results. Such smugness is an affront to the gods who brought his soul into this world, for why would a creature with no control over its birth be so cocky as to believe it controls life's journey and exit? While the herd pays lip service to how life can end at any moment, it does not truly embrace the concept. The common man, following the American dream, will sacrifice daily contentment for the sake of building toward a happier future—a future that may never come. Social sages leverage this predilection for planning to their own benefit. They offer master plans that coincide with your individual ones, convincing you to follow them voluntarily. These master plans promise hypothetical futures of fantasy, leading you to alter your daily action and consequently destroy any chance for a content life.

There is another problem with planning. Planning implies that you have control over the millions of variables involved in any real-world environment. Unexpected mortality, for example, is an enormous variable that is beyond your control. Reality consistently demonstrates planning's futility: strong businesses that go bankrupt within a year, fatal illnesses that suddenly strike healthy athletes, and personal relationships that change overnight. Reality is somewhat akin to war, with its competing forces that are unpredictable and violent. Planning in life is thus akin to what Carl von Clausewitz wrote about the "fog of war": detailed battle plans become obsolete as soon as the fighting commences.

The Tao man understands that planning involves reaching out through time and into an unknown future. Recognizing and dealing with this mental process involves one of the most important teachings of Taoism: the theory of fear. Understanding this theory begins by recognizing that time is one of the least understood phenomena. We attempt to define it conveniently by establishing artificial markers—seconds, minutes, hours, days—but real comprehension remains beyond our grasp. All we truly know is that our personal time begins with our birth—over which we had no control—and will end in our death, which is similarly beyond our control. The fear of death involves our speculation about the unknown future. The process of fear is thus composed of thoughts projected into the past and future.

Fear = Thoughts + Time

In other words, fear is the result of thinking about things over which we exert no control. Thus, if we limit our thoughts to only the present moment, we eliminate the fear of death.

Constant speculation about the future creates continuous mental turmoil. Social sages use this fear to manipulate the common man. They use the fear of old age, the fear of eternal damnation, the fear of poverty, the fear of loneliness, and the fear of ridicule to manipulate him into sacrificing a comfortable daily routine for an unknown future. Advertisers, politicians, and religious leaders exert incredible pressure to mold the common man into an ideal slave. While no centralized authority coordinates this "conspiracy" of society's elite, it is unbelievably powerful and pervasive. By living for today and devoting all of his resources toward achieving a comfortable daily routine, the man of Tao resists this pressure and stands apart from the vulgar masses. He does not allow irrational fear to dissuade him from living a content life.

The Individual Path

> . . . do not let the artificial submerge the natural. Do not for material purposes destroy your life. Do not sacrifice your character for fame. Guard carefully your nature and do not let it go astray. This is called returning to one's nature.
>
> —*The Wisdom of Laotse,* 163

The choice to follow an individual path is an obvious one, yet one that goes directly against the force of society. The herd of mankind unquestionably follows the pronouncements of social sages and acts against its own self-interest like cattle on the way to the slaughterhouse. This has been the way of society for thousands of years and will be the way for many more, as validated by Chuang Tzu's observation that the truly confused can never get out of their confusion. The herd will forever embrace the values of society; the Tao man will not.

Recognizing that social values oppose individual values makes the challenge clear. The man of Tao must work hard to recognize his own path and limitations. He will not involve himself in the ways of society, except to earn enough money to support a comfortable daily routine. The Taoist will use all of his training, both physical and mental, to resist the infection of social values. As Lao Tzu wrote,

> **My teachings are very easy to understand
> and very easy to practice,**

> But no one can understand them and no one can practice them.
>
> —*The Wisdom of Laotse*, 297

Taking Lao Tzu's simple principles and applying them in everyday life requires commitment. It takes all the facets of the Tao to deal properly with society. Society's values are alluringly compelling, and despite their glaring flaws, it is difficult to be a lone spot of reason in an insane world, constantly on guard and camouflaging your beliefs to avoid the wrath of those around you. Lao Tzu wrote,

> I alone differ from the other people,
> And value drawing sustenance from the Mother.
>
> —*The Wisdom of Laotse*, 129

This loneliness is the way of a true philosopher. Standing outside social convention and using reason to carve out a content life is the ultimate victory.

Nature Is Unkind

> Nature is unkind:
> It treats the creation like sacrificial straw-dogs.
> The Sage is unkind:
> He treats the people like sacrificial straw-dogs.
>
> —*The Wisdom of Laotse*, 63

One of the most pervasive causes of confusion is a fundamental misunderstanding of the motivations that drive the behavior of all of nature's creations—including man. An individual navigates through life with certain expectations of how he will be treated by those around him. He has a better chance to survive and prosper if his expectations are correct. If, instead, his expectations are unrealistic, he will face constant disappointment and place himself in harm's way. Furthermore, by not understanding the reality of nature and natural desires, this lost individual will become unsure of his own instincts. This condition is fatal: without an appreciation of his core desires, a life of contentment is impossible. Suffering becomes his constant companion.

Lao Tzu created some of his most powerful and poignant poetry in describing the action of nature; he wanted to avoid any confusion on this point. The Old Master wrote that "Nature is unkind" and that people are "sacrificial straw-dogs." Contrary to the teachings of Christ and Confucius, nature is *not* benevolent and man's natural desires are *not* correspondingly kind. Enlightenment requires the understanding that strangers, coworkers, business partners, and your mother-in-law will not make your life any easier unless it serves their own selfish interests.

Strangers should be viewed with extreme suspicion and with the expectation that they will bring trouble into one's life. For instance, a well-known stereotype has strangers to small towns or villages being watched closely and sometimes "invited" to leave. Nature's distrust and fear of the unknown goes to the core of man's survival instincts. Recognizing that nature is fundamentally unkind must be

Principles of Tao

accepted with the same clinical attitude as one accepts the existence of gravity. Nature's treatment of individuals as sacrificial beings may be a harsh lesson for the coddled American, but all of the preaching and sermonizing in the world will not change this reality.

Chuang Tzu wrote that one should "not permit likes and dislikes to disturb his internal economy, but rather falls in line with nature . . ." (p. 256). Accordingly, as the Taoist attempts to become more spiritual, he learns to follow nature's model. Man is a product of nature. Unfortunately, society—with all of its mighty machinery of communication—pushes him in the opposite direction.

The clergies of many religious organizations preach universal love and ask for donations. Politicians preach love of country and ask for taxes. Teachers preach love of knowledge and ask for salary increases. Businesses preach the love of the team and ask for overtime. All of society—neighbors, friends, politicians, television shows, and universities—sing the song of universal love. They expound how man, like nature, is kind. In the world of their twisted logic, lions sleep with lambs nestled in their bosoms, enemies are vanquished with logical argument, and strangers bring happy greetings from distant lands.

These unnatural expectations of kindness, promulgated by social institutions, breed confusion within the individual. When the confused American experiences the back-stabbing nature of business, reads of rapes in the park, and watches politicians send eighteen-year-old boys to die in irrelevant foreign wars, he wonders, "Where is universal love?" The bewildered soul listens to religious leaders preach that universal love is attainable by converting the masses—

one confused individual at a time—to a life of exuberant kindness. They convince the converted sucker to believe in universal love and encourage him to set an example for others—regardless of the consequences to himself—until peace on earth prevails. The plan is for love to spread like a bad flu until mankind universally sniffles. Yet their strategy has a two-thousand-year history of failure. Unfortunately, man's true nature repels this contagion and defeats the virus of love. Sadly, the species is inoculated against kindness toward all.

How do we know that the values of universal love are fundamentally doomed at their formulation? Perhaps the best evidence is that the rules of whom and what to love change with time and geography. This is an important point, because nature is constant and immutable; the sky is blue, lions eat gazelles, rocks don't breathe, and fire is hot. And no matter how much intellectual persuasion we exert, the sky will not be green, gazelles will not hunt lions, rocks will not inhale, and fire will not be cold.

Yet man-made definitions of love and kindness change with the breeze—there is no universality. In the United States, cannibalism is bad, although it is an accepted rite in some African countries. In Cuba, private enterprise is illegal, yet for Cubans living ninety miles away in Miami, it is a noble pursuit. Alcohol was prohibited in 1920s America but accepted ten years later. Divorce is sinful in one Christian church but acceptable in another. Russia jailed religious practitioners for seventy-five years until the government changed and legalized all religions again in 1990. Indeed, goodness and love are in a state of constant flux as dictated by the social structure du jour. Thus, universal love can't be part of nature, because society's definitions of "good" and "bad" are inconsistent.

Universal love similarly fails during times of conflict and hardship. Witness a three-hour traffic jam in L.A., a supermarket running short of food before a snowstorm, or a three-day blackout in New York City. Is there universal love to be found there? If it is an integral part of a man's core, waiting to be reawakened by religion, then why does it go to sleep so easily? Surely such a powerful force as love would not disappear, especially after two thousand years of Christianity and twenty-five hundred years of Confucianism and Buddhism. Patriotic Japanese Americans must have wondered what happened to universal love when they were herded to the internment camps during World War II, as did millions of law-abiding Jews waiting in well-formed lines before Nazi gas chambers. Where was the kindness of man then? How could it disappear so easily? Or, instead, is it possible that universal love never existed in the first place?

Clearly, universal love can only exist in a confused mind; avoiding such confusion is one of the Tao Te Ching's most consistent warnings. As Chuang Tzu wrote,

> **It would seem that humanity and justice were not part of the nature of man!**
>
> —*The Wisdom of Laotse*, 60

Society uses labels to control the herd's thoughts and promulgate the belief in artificial kindness. It creates "tags" to influence the opinion of the masses, dictating what is "good" and what is "bad." The government calls foreign countries that act contrary to its interests the "enemy." Volunteering for the military is called "patriotic."

Helping unknown strangers is called "charitable." Even beauty is prescribed by social convention: once rotund women were considered beautiful; today they are labeled "fat." As Chuang Tzu wrote,

> To a person who is born beautiful people give a mirror. But if people did not tell him, he would not know that he was beautiful.
>
> —*The Wisdom of Laotse*, 67

Chuang Tzu continues the lesson by instructing us to distrust society's labels of kindness:

> To a Sage who loves his fellowmen, people give a name ("humanity"). But if people did not tell him, he would not know that he was kind.
>
> —*The Wisdom of Laotse*, 67

It is necessary to avoid the trap laid by society's labels, for only then can we elude the Siren song of universal kindness.

Impartiality

So can the individual take Lao Tzu's advice, ignore conventional labels, and like the Sage, "treat people like sacrificial straw-dogs"? Is there no room for any love in the world? Does the acceptance that nature is unkind mean that the man of Tao has to be a soulless predator? Fortunately, the picture is not so bleak. As Chuang Tzu explained in his dialogue with Prime Minister Tang of Shang,

> "Tigers and wolves are loving animals," said Chuangtse.

Principles of Tao

"What do you mean?" [asked Tang.]
"The tiger loves his cub. . . ."

—*The Wisdom of Laotse,* 67

Chuang Tzu explains that the most vicious and feared of nature's predators are loving animals when caring for their cubs. Nature allows for unconditional love, but only among a small handful of animals. Such love is most powerful and romantic. An individual would literally fight to the death to protect another within this small group, sometimes called a "cocoon." For a Taoist, it is natural to love and protect a few select people fiercely; all others are viewed as inconsequential sources of trouble—nothing more than straw-dogs. Importantly, this small cocoon of loved individuals transcends the traditional definition of family. As Chuang Tzu taught,

Perfect kindness has no regard for particular relations. . . . It is so much higher than filial piety.

—*The Wisdom of Laotse,* 67

Chuang Tzu clearly states that the family relationship is not a prerequisite for perfect kindness and love, blatantly dismissing the Confucian reverence toward family. He instead emphasizes kindness toward those who share true connections—tangible and intangible—to the individual. For the Taoist, kindness is extended only to those who share common values and interests. Further, in the case of man and woman, there should be a physical attraction that goes to the heart of animal desire.

Lao Tzu's description of natural love is harsh and brutal on one hand, as when he warns against extending any compassion toward the masses. On the other hand, it can be romantic and tender, as when he encourages passionate commitment toward a select few. This attitude of treating the masses with impartial indifference while showering a specific group with unfettered care is a central theme in Taoism and gives birth to the principle of "partiality."

The forces of the Tao—as manifested in nature—are impartial. Nature reserves no special treatment for any individuals. Hurricanes wipe out towns without distinguishing between victims, rain falls equally on all people under the clouds, the sun warms everything touched by its rays. Indeed, nature is brutally indifferent. Young animals are the easiest prey, and children are the most susceptible to disease. The forces of nature treat life's innocents as harshly as they do mass killers.

Nature gives no animal quarter. While the vulnerable antelopes live in constant fear, the lion—"king of all beasts"—must eat eleven pounds of meat a day and thwart the attack of other beasts; when age prevents him from hunting and fighting, hunger or other carnivores will kill him. The "circle of life" is simply one animal eating another. Nature doesn't favor one species over another, nor does it selectively punish one over another. And, just as nature is indifferent, it is also immune to the thoughts and feelings of its victims. Rather, it continues on in precisely the same way as it has through time immemorial.

The concepts of an unkind nature and impartiality combine to form the basis for rejecting Christian principles. Some scholars have tried to draw parallels between Taoism and Christianity by taking Lao Tzu quotations out of context to support apparently similar verses in the Bible. Such efforts disregard that these two religions are fundamentally opposed in their founding principles. With respect to impartiality, Lin Yutang noted,

> **One of the most important concepts about Tao is that it is entirely impersonal and impartial in its workings. This constitutes one of the most important differences between Tao and the Christian God. In this concept of impartiality, Tao resembles the scientist's concept of an impersonal law, which makes no exceptions for individuals.**
>
> —*The Wisdom of Laotse*, 66

Taoism's recognition of an unkind nature further illustrates differences with Christian beliefs built on the inherent goodness of man. It warns that any doctrine that tries to train man to be good is introducing artificial behavior and is doomed to fail. As Lin Yutang noted,

> **Both Chuangtse and Laotse emphasize that Tao benefits all without conscious kindness. In Chuangtse, the Confucian doctrine of *jen* ("humanity") is constantly under attack as being a doctrine leading to conscious affectation. In the world of unconscious goodness, the people were "kind," but they "did not know it was called humanity"; they "did right," but "did not know it was called justice."**
>
> —*The Wisdom of Laotse*, 66

Since nature is immutable, why waste time worrying over it or—worse still—trying to change it? In a realization that would horrify Christian missionaries, an individual finds that all he should care about is how the forces of nature affect him personally. In essence, since nature can't be changed, leave it alone. And this is the model after which a spiritual person patterns his behavior. Since man's unkind nature can't be changed, the Taoist leaves the common masses alone. He doesn't interfere with inconsequential persons unless they threaten him in tangible ways (as per the doctrine of noninterference).

But as oneness dictates, the Tao man's impartiality to the masses is offset by the partiality he exhibits to the small group of people about whom he truly cares. He treats these people as if they were indispensable parts of his own body. This cocoon is an extension of the individual, since it includes only those who share common values, likes, and dislikes.

True love, or "perfect kindness," entails action. Love without action is just a word. For the ever-skeptical Taoist, verbal expressions of caring are inconsequential, and only *acts* of love are recognized. This further reinforces the Taoist's impartiality toward the masses. When was the last time a stranger sacrificed something of significance for you? Universal love from the masses boils down to a bunch of sentimental blatherings supported by little tangible action. A Taoist, by contrast, voluntarily spends time, money, and effort on those within his cocoon.

This acknowledgment that action or energy is required in any truly loving relationship in turn leads to the recognition that such relationships must be limited. Perfect kindness takes effort—considerable effort. Universal love is therefore meaningless, for it entails spreading this effort over the multitude. It is akin to distributing wealth: one could give riches to a select few or pennies to the many. To care for the entire world (with corresponding effort) is to care for no one. Not wasting energy on the masses is therefore most consistent with the natural way, for it allows the individual to devote his limited resources to his cherished cocoon.

Camouflage

> . . . only the perfect man can go about in the modern world without attracting attention to himself.
>
> —*The Wisdom of Laotse,* 139

Using nature as a model provides an important technique that is crucial to surviving life's challenges: the use of camouflage. Nature's impartial harshness has taught animals how to avoid a predator by using their coats of fur to blend into their surroundings. Lao Tzu warns the Taoist to remain similarly inconspicuous to a fundamentally unkind society. Accordingly, Lao Tzu has been described as "the first philosopher of camouflage."

Modern society pushes the individual to seek the trappings of reputation and money as life's goals: a bigger house, a more luxurious car, and expensive clothes are all symbols of success and authority. Lao Tzu warns that this is a fool's path, for it makes you the target of the hundreds of jealous people who surround you. Despite their sweet smiles, they will resent and covet your success. In the business world, this puts your job at risk; in personal relations, your flashy lover will be courted by others; for the famous, vicious rumors will be a constant annoyance. As Chuang Tzu explains through analogy,

> **A tree with a straight trunk is the first to be chopped down. A well with sweet water is the first to be drawn dry.**
>
> —*The Wisdom of Laotse,* 143–44

As a Taoist, you embrace a philosophy that disdains many of the values of the society within which you live. It would be foolhardy to express those views to people outside your cocoon, for one of the most important ingredients in building a life of contentment is to blend in with society. Chuang Tzu urges,

> **To do what the others do and not be criticized by others, this is to be the sons of men.**
>
> —*The Wisdom of Laotse,* 86

In the past, various groups have set themselves up for the derision and wrath of their respective societies. All sorts of religious and ethnic groups—whether immigrants to a new country or simply the victims of changing times—have flaunted their unique heritage and consequently suffered persecution and expulsion. This is not the way of a Taoist, who instead disguises any differences to blend in with society. Chuang Tzu sagely states,

> **When you enter a country, follow its customs.**
>
> —*The Wisdom of Laotse,* 219

Just as it is futile to fight the inconvenience of rain, so should the Taoist accept the society around him and blend in. The Taoist learns to adapt to his surroundings rather than attempt to change them. Adaptation is the best form of camouflage; one learns to cover oneself with a cloak of pretend values.

The true Taoist would never involve himself in a revolution or mutiny. Revolutions simply replace one group of dysfunctional thieves with another. As such, they are of little concern to the man of Tao. Lao Tzu recommends heading to the mountains in times of conflict, returning only when things settle down. Taoism is not in the business of changing society. A practical Taoist recognizes that his society should be treated with fear and apprehension. He knows that one should never underestimate the fury of a society that discovers a group or an individual blatantly attempting to stand outside social convention. Thus, a classical Taoist warning is to live by the laws of God and respect the laws of man.

The Three Treasures

> **The Three Treasures are my possessions and I shall share them. They are sacred and possess magic power.**
>
> —*Lu Yang Tai (conversation with Master Anatole)*

The Tao Te Ching can be viewed as a collection of warnings organized within a structured set of philosophical principles. Its correct application in daily life helps the practicing

Taoist survive and find contentment in a world filled with "chaos, absurdity, and suffering." It is a testament to these principles that they remain as applicable to life in modern America as they did to life in ancient China. Lao Tzu's Three Treasures probably represent the most concise and explicit of these rules. Unfortunately—as is the case with so many of Lao's teachings—they have been distorted throughout the centuries and their current meanings are mere shadows of their author's original intent.

The First Treasure

The first is Love.

—*The Wisdom of Laotse*, 291

Lao Tzu's first treasure, "love," has been so misinterpreted by translators and philosophers that its common definition is now an absurd concept, totally inconsistent with Taoism's philosophical core. The Chinese character for love has many nuances. Unfortunately, this has resulted in a number of conflicting translations of the first treasure, from "love" by Lin Yutang to "simplicity" and "benevolence" by others.

In determining a correct explanation of any of Lao Tzu's writings, the practicing Taoist always turns to its application in reality. A correct interpretation or understanding is validated only by practical application, while an incorrect interpretation becomes obviously false upon intellectual or physical application. Using this method, it quickly becomes clear that translating the first treasure as "love" is blatantly

Principles of Tao

erroneous. When Lao Tzu says at the conclusion of the Three Treasures poem that "love is victorious in attack, / and invulnerable in defense," it is clear that the common interpretation of "love" is wrong. No survivor of any physical conflict would claim that love is the secret weapon to victory. Ask any combat veteran, police officer, or victim of a vicious crime if love is the key to survival; the absurdity of this notion is obvious. Using intellectual persuasion to turn "victory through love" into a valid life principle is a folly on a par with fantasy or the blind faith of religious dogma. Love *is* a powerful emotion, one that plays an important role in human existence, but it will never be taught at West Point.

So what did Lao Tzu mean when he wrote of love as the first treasure? The answer is a combination of three essential elements: acceptance, caring action, and simplicity. The three together yield a more correct definition of the first treasure.

The first requirement of Lao Tzu's meaning of love is *acceptance*. Genuine love requires accepting a loved one without reservation. In the same way, it is necessary to embrace the world around you. For example, if you don't embrace an idea, it is difficult to comprehend it at its deepest level. A mathematician must first accept math as an interesting field of study; otherwise, he will never be able to learn and comprehend its principles. An athlete must love his sport in order to train with the enthusiasm needed to excel. You cannot be partially committed to anything of value. Would you trust a doctor who was repulsed by the sight of blood but performed surgery anyway because it was a good source of income? Emotional acceptance is a prerequisite to functioning efficiently in any endeavor. It opens the senses and enables the mind and body to function correctly.

Implicit in this phenomenon is understanding that when you embrace anything completely, you accept it without change. Your acceptance of the first treasure must be unconditional, and you must not attempt to change people or phenomena to meet your desires or expectations. To divert anyone from his or her natural path will stretch everyone involved beyond their limitations to cope. This forced love is inconsistent with acceptance. How many couples are unhappy because one or both partners try to change the other to be what he or she can't? The unhealthy tendency of humans to change what they should not is a major source of discontent and sometimes conflict.

While acceptance is one of the elements of Lao Tzu's first treasure, Taoism requires that loving emotions be backed up with concrete actions. Verbal expressions of love are nice, but they are only words. True love must be manifested in *caring action* whereby practical care is freely provided to a loved one. A spouse is given physical and emotional support. A pet is given food, shelter, and medical attention when needed. Whether it is the mundane provision of a home or the romantic gift of flowers, caring action is a necessity in the Taoist definition of love.

Earlier in this chapter, love was described as the natural emotion that occurs when your attachment to a person or animal is so great that it virtually becomes a part of your being. Such genuine love is a simple and clear emotion; it is not complicated and does not have to be taught. In this way, it is much like its opposite—hate—which also requires no instruction. Religious institutions have tried to teach a complicated version of love for two millennia, succeeding in breeding only war and confusion.

Simple emotions, thoughts, and actions are the true manifestations of love. Without such sincere manifestations, love does not exist. *Simplicity* involves stripping away the complications with which countless social institutions have burdened you.

Simplification means returning to your natural core. This reconnection between the intellectual and natural (or animal) self is a vital step to achieving contentment and an important tool for navigating through life. The ability to analyze situations and reduce them to simple, uncomplicated observations is a powerful technique. It is one of the primary mechanisms for removing confusion, which is a major source of stress and a barrier to contentment. The value of this practical application cannot be understated, as the ability to simplify is the first step in becoming a "problem solver" in your professional and personal life. Lao Tzu noted,

> **The clever people become lost in their own devices, while the divine man can go straight to the truth.**
>
> —*The Wisdom of Laotse,* 308

Thus, the first treasure's meaning of *love* is better translated as acceptance, caring action, and simplicity. Applying this new definition to Lao Tzu's assertion that love is victorious in attack and invulnerable in defense, the passage becomes clear. Accepting a conflict for what it is and engaging in it with both simple, clear thinking and uncomplicated action results in victory. You "love" the enemy by understanding his motivations and tactics and then responding with unhesitating, decisive action.

With this definition of love, we see that Lao Tzu's first treasure cuts to the core of a spiritual existence. It teaches the student of Tao to embrace any phenomenon realistically and to rely on simplicity of thought and action.

The Second Treasure

The second is, Never too much.

—The Wisdom of Laotse, 291

Lao Tzu's second treasure, "Never too much," is Taoism's cautionary advice to avoid excesses. Physically, the harmful results of excess are obvious and well understood. If you eat too much, you get fat; if you smoke too much, your lungs become damaged; if you run too much, your knees deteriorate; if you work too much, you succumb to exhaustion. Excesses in the physical world are a prescription for disaster. Too much speed kills, too much oxygen poisons, and too much sun burns.

It is equally important to realize that Lao Tzu's second treasure is *not* a principle of denial or minimization. For example, the second treasure would not support a Buddhist monk's self-destructive abstinence from food, exercise, and sex. Using nature as its model, Taoism has no room for such bizarre, intellectual constructs that deny the body its needs. For just as too much oxygen poisons, too little results in suffocation; just as too much speed kills, too little stymies progress; just as too much food leads to obesity, too little leads to starvation.

If both excess and denial are to be avoided, how can a Taoist practically determine what is the correct level of any physical action? What measure or gauge identifies the proper level of such action? Chuang Tzu answers by observing,

The beaver slakes its thirst from the river, but drinks enough only to fill its belly.

—The Wisdom of Laotse, 226

Chuang Tzu uses nature to show that the gauge for the correct amount of physical action is necessity, or sufficiency. "Never too much" instructs the Taoist to ascertain and achieve these proper amounts in order to function correctly. By being sensitive to the effects of physical actions, the man of Tao naturally regulates his actions to the correct level. Therefore, if your eating habits cause weight gain, a diet slims you back down. If your car's tires squeal when you drive around a curve, then you apply the brakes to slow down. When your muscles are sore from excessive exercise, you take a break and recuperate. Understanding this trade-off between excess and denial, it becomes clear that "sufficiency" is the best translation of Lao Tzu's second treasure.

Sufficiency in the physical world has important implications for the American, particularly as it relates to material possessions. In the days before modern America's affluence, the acquisition of material wealth was needed to survive. When the typical family was no longer composed of self-sufficient farmers, the new industrial family unit consisted of wage earners making money for food and shelter. This shift in labor—from acquiring the means to survive to the more abstract notion of acquiring money—opened a Pandora's box. While the farmer's physical limitations enabled him to work only enough to support his family, the industrialist became a money-acquisition machine, limited only by his cleverness and desires. The farmer and frontiersman worked to the point of sufficiency, while the industrialist worked beyond the point of necessity to the limits of his aspirations. Material possessions became a validation of success and no longer a requirement for survival. This psychology grew at the urging of society and has become the primary prescription for discontent in modern America. In essence, individual contentment is sacrificed for the limitless quest for material possessions. Remarkably, Lao Tzu observed this even in ancient China and encouraged the man of Tao to embrace sufficiency of material possessions:

> **There is no greater curse than the lack of contentment.**
> **No greater sin than the desire for possession.**
> **Therefore he who is contented with contentment shall be always content.**
>
> —*The Wisdom of Laotse*, 225

A key feature of all Taoist principles is that, just as they work in the physical dimension, they also apply in the mental realm. This duality demands that the man of Tao apply the second treasure to his mental conduct. Thus, excessive thinking is as dangerous to one's well-being as any physical excess.

While physical excesses place the body at risk, excessive mental activity places peace of mind or contentment at risk. Too much thinking results in a disturbed mind that worries about life's every detail. A mind that constantly dwells on life's "what-ifs" cannot live in the moment. Constant calculations and planning fills the head with unnecessary doubts. This creates fear of the future, resulting in one of the most powerful barriers to contentment. As Lao Tzu wrote,

> **Who is calm and quiet becomes the guide for the universe.**
>
> —*The Wisdom of Laotse*, 223

The mind not only busies itself with constant planning and calculations, but also with the self-destructive need to dwell on unanswerable questions. The desire to know about life after death, the will of God, and other unknowns is a prescription for disaster. Such thoughts are not only a futile waste of energy, but they program a mental process that is divorced from reality. In time, the mind becomes a self-generating confusion machine. Chuang Tzu observed,

> **. . . our knowledge does not extend beyond the material universe. He who observes the working of Tao does not try to follow a thing to its very end, nor trace it to its very source. There all discussion ends.**
>
> —*The Wisdom of Laotse*, 148

Mental unbalance is not the confused mind's only danger. The Chinese knew three thousand years ago that stress was the primary cause of disease; modern science is only beginning to acknowledge its role in illness. Because of this well-documented relationship between mind and body, mental stress will lead to a host of psychosomatic diseases. Disorders ranging from back problems to heart disease and intestinal illnesses are often the direct result of a confused and stressed mind.

As the man of Tao builds a content lifestyle for himself, he remains constantly vigilant for threats. He trains himself to be sensitive to his surroundings and thus detect problems before they happen. The Taoist does not bury his head in the sand and wait for disaster to strike. Instead, his calm mind is constantly watchful for the small symptoms of threats to his well-being. Once impending trouble is detected, he immediately acts to avoid or destroy the threat. It is always easier to deal with situations in their early stages. As Lao Tzu said of threats, they "[m]ust be dealt with while they are yet easy" (p. 282).

Most people are so preoccupied with the trivialities of life, busying themselves with society's trappings, that they are oblivious to genuine warnings. Only the calm mind will be sensitive to these hints of trouble and thus be able to act before the threat is magnified. This philosophy carries practical implications in all aspects of life, including personal relationships, business affairs, and social interaction in general. Lao Tzu encouraged the Tao man to

Deal with a thing before it is there;
Check disorder before it is rife.

—*The Wisdom of Laotse,* 283

Principles of Tao

Lao Tzu's first treasure of simplicity and his second treasure of sufficiency are tightly coupled:

> **Reveal thy simple self,**
> **Embrace thy original nature,**
> **Check thy selfishness,**
> **Curtail thy desires.**
>
> —*The Wisdom of Laotse,* 120

The Third Treasure

> **The third is, Never be the first in the world.**
>
> —*The Wisdom of Laotse,* 291

Lao Tzu's third treasure is a warning to avoid one of society's greatest urgings—to be the best at everything. From birth, social institutions constantly push the individual to excel and best those around him. Schools push for higher grades, businesses push for the best production, sports programs push for stronger athletes, and advertisers push for gaudy displays of fancier clothes and cars. There is an implicit message that happiness can only be achieved through being the best and owning the most. Society wants the individual to be a racehorse in a contest with no finish line. Competition is king, and anything less than first place is for losers.

Lao Tzu recognized the dangers of this constant pursuit of first place. He saw that competition for rank and fortune is one of society's primary tools for manipulation, employed to the detriment of its citizens' happiness. Competition pushes the individual to exceed his limitations. It is a vicious directive that uses pride and vanity to enslave a population.

In a world of competition, achieving some small success makes one a target for others in their quest for first place. While a man of Tao will quietly enjoy material success only as a means to lead a content life, the common man will display his success and strive for more. This makes him a target for others who are driven by envy and jealousy. While Chuang Tzu reminded us that the tallest tree is the first to be cut down, Lao Tzu wrote,

> **When gold and jade fill your hall,**
> **You will not be able to keep them safe.**
> **To be proud with wealth and honor**
> **Is to sow the seeds of one's own downfall.**
> **Retire when your work is done,**
> **Such is Heaven's way.**
>
> —*The Wisdom of Laotse,* 79

Lao Tzu's three treasures represent three important warnings in navigating through life and finding contentment. They are practical and applicable to everyday challenges. They also have important implications that are profound and central to Taoism. Lao Tzu performed an amazing feat—combining daily pragmatism with a philosophy for the ages.

CHAPTER 5

Applying Taoist Principles

*Do not develop the nature which is of man,
but develop the nature which is of God.*

—*The Wisdom of Laotse,* 189

The Application Imperative

The purpose of any legitimate philosophy is to relieve the suffering of its followers. In a practical sense, it should help them live a happier and healthier life. Unless a philosophy is applied pragmatically, the entire belief system is relegated to nothing more than an intellectual exercise serving as entertainment. A philosophy or religion that works in the real world, however, bestows profound benefits. As Chuang Tzu said,

> Those who understand Tao . . . must necessarily apprehend the eternal principles and those who apprehend the eternal principles must understand their application.
>
> —*The Wisdom of Laotse,* 240

Think back to our earlier analogy: like driving a car, a practical philosophy cleans the car's windshield and affords the driver an unclouded view of the world. Seeing the road ahead—similar to one's path through life—becomes markedly easier. An impractical philosophy, by contrast, heaps dirt on the windshield, making navigation on the roads—or through life's journey—a dangerous process. Building on the analogy, an unclouded windshield is of little use on a car that never leaves the driveway. Only with the proper application of accelerating, steering, and braking is clear vision turned into safe driving that serves a purpose. For this reason, when the practitioner fully absorbs the teachings of a true philosophy and understands its application, the term *enlightenment* is used.

Several millennia ago, philosophy was labeled "the mother of all sciences" because it promised to clarify man's view of the world. Philosophy, in essence, is a science that deals with observed reality. And, as any scientist knows, theory must be validated through application. Thus, true philosophy—like science—must place great importance on the application of its respective principles to yield concrete results.

Unfortunately, most philosophies and religions have avoided subjecting themselves to rigorous testing through

Applying Taoist Principles

application. While the motives of the "social sages" who propagandized these beliefs varied, hypocrisy lay at the core of their intentions. Using blind faith as their tool, they fooled millions of unsuspecting victims into following principles built on fantastical constructs of the mind—often with catastrophic consequences.

As previously discussed, Lao Tzu divides mankind into two distinct groups. The first group—the "herd," or common man—dwells in complicated belief systems based on blind faith, uses superficial and obscure language, and finds comfort in the confusion of conventional thought. The common man avoids validating philosophical and religious concepts. Whether this is from a subconscious recognition of the impracticality of their doctrines or from a fear of challenging commonly held principles, no effort is made to apply them and determine their validity. Or perhaps the herd is merely lazy and apathetic and would prefer to be spoon-fed its beliefs by politicians, clergy, and television.

Lao Tzu's second group is composed of those rare individuals who sense that something is wrong with conventional beliefs. The disconnection between popularly held convictions and observed reality troubles them. Unhappy with this state of confusion, they desperately try to figure out what is going on and thus become "seekers" in search of life's answers. They are brave enough to think outside the constraints of conventional wisdom. And, as self-motivated skeptics, they are open to philosophical principles that abandon society's values, which have been ingrained since birth. They deeply *want* to eliminate their confusion and are motivated to fight their way to clarity.

It is important to note, however, that even certain so-called seekers can be fools. There are thousands of confused New Agers running from guru to guru, searching for some undefined version of enlightenment. Driven by the sincere goal of finding answers outside of traditional Western beliefs, they follow any teacher who dresses in exotic robes and speaks in wise tones. Their unquestioning devotion to fake gurus is ultimately little different than society's herd unquestioningly following its community's doctrines. The desire for New Age enlightenment may be noble, but—in reality—is nothing more than a fruitless search yielding only exotic, esoteric blathering.

The key characteristics of a true seeker of enlightenment are an inherent skepticism and a need to check things out constantly. His dispassionate testing of philosophical principles, akin to a scientist's impartial testing of his theories through experimentation, makes him a legitimate student of philosophy. It takes courage to ask *why* and *how*. Clarifying one's vision of the world is a serious pursuit, requiring acute observation and an unflinching demand for proof. For the true seeker, blind faith does not exist.

Curiously, some Western thinkers have segregated religion and philosophy from other disciplines, placing them in a category that doesn't require proof through analysis of reality. Rather, such beliefs rely on faith and the promise of a rosy future as the foundation of their belief systems. In the case of religions, the rosy future is only achieved in heaven after death. It is a development that would deeply sadden Aristotle, the father of Western analytic thought.

By contrast, Eastern philosophies and religions—with

Applying Taoist Principles

Taoism in the vanguard—have maintained their pragmatic core. Lao Tzu repeatedly emphasizes that clarifying reality is the goal of his philosophy. He advocates the use of nature (reality's unspoiled manifestation) as the model for philosophical principles. Taoism's founder instructs the man of Tao to "provide for the belly and not for the eye" (p. 90). In other words, Lao Tzu believed it was inconceivable to separate practical application from philosophy, for his belief system's primary purpose is to provide *tangible* benefits as quickly as possible.

This importance of applying Lao Tzu's principles is reinforced by the ancient division of his Tao Te Ching into two halves. The first half is called the Book of Tao and deals with his philosophical principles. The second half, the Book of Teh, elaborates on the practical application of his principles. This binary organization of Taoism's founding philosophical/religious text is decidedly unique.

The brilliance of Lao Tzu was his ability to develop an integrated system that dealt with both man's earthly existence and the unknown world of higher energy, that is, religion. His unified view of the seen and unseen did not, however, sacrifice the need for any theory—philosophical or religious— to be validated through practical application. He wrote that the realm of the gods is beyond mortal comprehension, but that their manifestations (teh) can be observed, understood, and applied.

The great Tao exerts its power over everything, including the gods. Taoism's principles, therefore, can be tested in tangible ways here on earth to provide some limited understanding of the ways of the universe:

The Truth of Tao

> These two (the Secret and its manifestations)
> Are (in their nature) the same;
> They are given different names
> When they become manifest.
>
> —*The Wisdom of Laotse*, 41

The Tao Te Ching is a book of warnings. One of its most persistent cautions is that man, being such a limited and fallible creature, should not attempt unverifiable speculation. The process of *not* testing theories ingrains undisciplined thinking, which in turn opens the door to confusion. Mankind's original, simple nature has been so corrupted that modern man must explicitly train to avoid mental flights of fantasy. Chuang Tzu further supports this warning:

> **Human life is limited, but knowledge is limitless. To drive the limited in pursuit of the limitless is fatal;** . . .
>
> —*The Wisdom of Laotse*, 174

The best way to ground a belief system in reality is to insist on its practical application. Application is the litmus test for correct thinking. True enlightenment, therefore, is not possible without constant testing and application. For this reason, classical Taoist temples always integrated physical disciplines with their mental programs. They thus ensured that their students' personal experiences were firmly cemented in reality, arresting any tendencies toward chimerical thoughts.

The idea that philosophical principles must be verified by action is a key Taoist principle in itself. For the man of Tao,

Applying Taoist Principles

words are cheap. A skilled talker can make almost any concept sound legitimate; only through application can its validity be ascertained. This attitude requires a discipline of thought that is rare. Further, because this nonpassive attitude is unconventional, it also demands unusual courage to challenge beliefs that have been cherished unquestioningly since childhood.

The lessons of Taoism also incorporated practical application because it allowed no room for individual interpretations. Even the most willing and sincere student can misinterpret the ideas communicated by a teacher. However, once such ideas are tested through action, the student witnesses the validity of his interpretation. If the student has misunderstood the meaning of an instructor's words, it will be obvious on application. Tangible results deem the interpretations correct or incorrect; no confusion or "maybes" are possible.

Further, teaching through application forces simplification. Overly complex explanations yield similarly complex, unworkable principles that cannot be applied by students. Thus, application fosters simplicity and clarity.

While application can help identify incorrect or misunderstood concepts, it can also help reinforce principles that have been understood correctly. Because they are physical creatures, students can more easily embrace newly learned concepts by experiencing them physically. For example, learning to drive a car by conceptual explanations and textbook study alone is virtually impossible. The principles of driving are abstract and difficult to grasp from verbal explanation. When those concepts are reinforced by practice behind the wheel, however, the student driver rapidly absorbs them. Eventually, he no longer needs to think about each action, and the principles become ingrained through daily application on the road. Executing principles without explicit thought represents a milestone in the quest for true enlightenment. For the Taoist, the ability to apply Lao Tzu's principles without explicit thought (ch'an) is the ultimate goal. Practical application is the best means to get there.

In the Taoist's quest for spirituality, it is essential to understand his limitations. The man of Tao best navigates through life by clearly observing reality and then acting within his limitations. Unfortunately, human nature's tendency is to overestimate one's personal abilities and thus overextend one's reach. While a philosophy's teachings can constantly emphasize the importance of understanding personal limitations, students don't typically appreciate this lesson until it is reinforced through personal experience. The concept of limitations becomes powerfully evident when the student encounters constant physical limitations through physical application. There is nothing like the pain and humiliation of martial arts, for example, to hammer home the idea of personal limitations.

Taoism's emphasis on practical application is consistent with its insistence that Taoists are responsible for their own actions. Inscribed above the entrance of classical Taoist temples is the adage "Every man is responsible for his own actions." While it is impossible to understand the ways of the gods, an individual's fate is his own responsibility. Man's willingness to blame everyone and everything but himself

Applying Taoist Principles

for his failings is directly linked to prevailing belief systems, ungrounded in disciplined action. To the man of Tao, excuses are the whine of weak-spirited individuals, the bleats of the herd. Because mastering Taoist principles requires constant reinforcement through application, the man of Tao builds the confidence to act—and disdains those who don't.

The personal confidence built by successfully applying Taoist principles also reinforces the commitment of a student to his master. By constantly witnessing and experiencing verification of his teacher's principles, the student's faith in the master grows. The student sees the master demonstrate, through application, his mastery of Taoism: the physical skills of martial arts and chi quong, as well as the mental abilities of meditation. Perhaps even more importantly, he observes his master embracing a lifestyle founded on the principles that he preaches. As a result, the master earns the faith of his students, in contrast to the blind faith demanded by most religions and philosophies. Respect, unlike most things in life, cannot be purchased. The master gains respect by demonstrating his knowledge through visible application.

Chi

**Draw upon it
And it serves you with ease.**

—*The Wisdom of Laotse,* 64

A unique characteristic of Taoism is that its tenets apply to worlds both seen and unseen. Its principles, for example, are central to the visible worlds of Chinese medicine and martial arts and to the realm of religion, communication with the unseen universe of the gods. Regardless of the application, Taoist theory achieves concrete results through its reliance on a proven, consistent set of principles.

In applying Taoism's doctrines, the use of energy is required. Without energy, concrete results are impossible—that is, no energy, no results. This energy abides by Taoism's laws of operation as defined within its principles, much like Newton's laws of physics. Yet in its practical application—be it acupuncture or martial arts—this energy cannot be measured using traditional scientific instruments. Instead, only the manifestation of this energy can be experienced in tangible ways. The energy itself, however, is unseen and immeasurable.

What is this strange energy that cannot be measured and yet has such power? Certainly it must be enormous, for it permeates all earthly existence and extends to the heavens, unifying all of creation in a single, elemental force. This energy functions as the cornerstone of Taoism's unification theory, similar to the one that eluded Einstein in the development of his extraordinary holistic view of the universe's physical laws.

Taoists label this far-reaching, fundamental energy *chi*. Though its origin is unknown, it operates under unambiguous principles that can be reliably applied to a number of disciplines. Lao Tzu wrote, describing its unknown nature,

> **The thing that is called Tao**
> **Is elusive, evasive.**
> **Evasive, elusive,**
> **Yet latent in it are forms.**
> **Elusive, evasive,**
> **Yet latent in it are objects.**
>
> —*The Wisdom of Laotse*, 132

Applying Taoist Principles

Chi is an elemental power possessed by all living things. It is this pervasiveness that makes it such a unifying force. Lao Tzu describes it as a life force:

> **Dark and dim,**
> **Yet latent in it is the life-force.**
>
> —*The Wisdom of Laotse,* 132

Lao Tzu also states that, since chi is so "elusive, evasive," it can only be grasped by witnessing its evidences, or manifestations:

> **The life-force being very true,**
> **Latent in it are evidences.**
>
> —*The Wisdom of Laotse,* 132

The Taoist works to understand the Tao by manipulating chi in practical, palpable ways. By dealing with the tangible world of the "seen" (yang), he better understands the "unseen" world (yin). Fundamentally, the application of Taoist principles is the application of chi.

Probably the most graphic example of manipulating this unseen chi to yield practical results is the Chinese science of acupuncture. Acupuncture was originally developed thousands of years ago to maintain the energy balance of the body and as an anesthetic to minimize death due to shock and pain during medical procedures. During his 1972 visit to China, President Richard Nixon was amazed to witness surgery performed without the benefit of conventional anesthesia. The Chinese doctors relied on acupuncture needles strategically placed in remote points of the patients' bodies.

By changing the flow of chi, the doctors controlled bleeding and pain.

When examined using Western science, there is no accepted explanation for the success of acupuncture. Yet billions of people for thousands of years have successfully relied on it to control pain and promote healing. Most serious Chinese doctors are educated in the principles of Taoism as the cornerstone of their practice because it describes the flow of chi.

Taoism's unified principles of chi can also be applied to a practical philosophy of life. For example, Lao Tzu teaches us that chi behaves like water, while also serving as a model for living better. He explains that, just as calm water is clearer than agitated water, chi flows better through a calm, unconfused mind. The calm mind is a happier mind, and consequently individual chi will be stronger, resulting in a sound mind and healthy body. While most philosophies and religions avoid making the bridge between their abstract principles and practical applications in life, Lao Tzu provides explicit direction. Chi acts as the glue that binds the abstract to the concrete.

> **Calm represents the nature of water at its best. In that it may serve as our model, for its power is preserved and is not dispersed through agitation.**
>
> —*The Wisdom of Laotse,* 77

Lao Tzu further explains that chi is everywhere, a unifying force woven throughout the fabric of the universe. It is a universal energy of cosmic origin that even the gods themselves use. For this reason, Taoist astrologers and shamans use the triangulation of the stars and planets to calculate the effects of cosmic chi on individuals. Chi's pervasiveness is described in the Tao Te Ching:

> **At its greatest, Tao is infinite; at its smallest, there is nothing so small but Tao is in it.**
>
> —*The Wisdom of Laotse*, 187

Man's limited ability to comprehend and explain the metaphysical makes explaining chi a formidable task. While practitioners use models or metaphors like yin and yang, reversion, and the behavior of water to describe its operation, Lao Tzu warns us that chi ultimately defies explanation by mere mortals. Given its cosmic origins, human speculation on its source and reasons for its behavior is an intellectual flight of fantasy—akin to speculating on the ways of the gods. To do so is to invite confusion.

> **Now Tao by its very nature can never be defined. Speech by its very nature cannot express the absolute.**
>
> —*The Wisdom of Laotse*, 53

With an emphasis on practical application and an attitude of enlightened skepticism, Taoism bred a culture of great experimenters for whom the manipulation of chi became a priority several millennia ago. The invention of gun powder in 1300 A.D., for example, was a by-product of Taoist experimentation, discovered when scientists tried to extend human life spans with a chemical designed to enhance individual chi explosively. Interestingly, this commitment to manipulate chi created a culture of inventors, very similar to the Yankees and their fabled ingenuity. The ancient Taoists who mixed thousands of ingredients to develop gunpowder have much in common with Thomas Edison, whose experimentation with thousands of filaments led to the invention of the light bulb.

The importance of chi cannot be underestimated in its pervasive application in our everyday lives. For example, the flow of chi in living spaces is the subject of feng shui. In this science, the flow of chi is optimized in the architectural design of homes and offices by using several basic principles. In Asian cultures, feng shui is checked stringently; in Hong Kong, a recently completed skyscraper remains vacant because the architect committed major, irreparable feng shui errors. As another example, Chinese wind chimes are used not only for their pleasant sound, but also to reduce the excessive flow of chi where required by feng shui theory.

It is important to emphasize that Taoism's primary concern is that its theories on the manipulation of chi ultimately yield results. Taoists are the ultimate pragmatists; even if certain explanations are vague or incomplete, if they work consistently, then they are usable and therefore embraced. This attitude of exalting practicality also means that a Taoist is always open to new and better ways to achieve results.

Such an approach breeds a flexibility of mind that is important to a Taoist, who constantly adjusts himself to observed phenomena. For example, enlightened Chinese doctors now incorporate Western medical procedures to augment their classic healing techniques. These Chinese healers don't stubbornly reject valuable Western healing methods because they rely on a different theory of medicine, but rather embrace them because they are the best in certain circumstances. Unfortunately, Western doctors are not so open-minded, often refusing to consider holistic medicine for illnesses for which they have proven remarkably effective.

Developing Individual Chi

The purpose of enlightenment is to live a better life. For the Taoist, this entails the cultivation of individual chi. Under the tutelage of a master, the student's body is incrementally improved through training techniques proven effective over many millennia. In classical Taoist temples, the physical exercises of chi quong and martial arts built strong bodies while providing an unambiguous demonstration of Taoist principles. Such initial focus on the physical is necessary because the novice student isn't ready to comprehend the subtleties of the mental and religious aspects of chi manipulation.

This initial emphasis on chi in the physical body is necessary, for we are all physical creatures; without a healthy body, a content life is impossible. Despite all of the so-called "spirituality" we may theoretically develop, intense migraine headaches, a bad back, or a severe case of dysentery makes "enlightenment" a secondary concern as we search for relief from physical discomfort. We must care for our physical vessels before we can tend to the loftier concerns of our minds. This obvious point seems lost on many practitioners of other religions, as their increased piety correlates to neglected, flabby bodies.

The fundamental purpose for developing the physical body is to build a suitable channel for the optimal flow of chi. Chi, like water, cannot flow properly in a poorly configured or substandard system of pipes. Further, if the pipes are weakened by corrosion, they can't handle the pressure of water rushing through them. Through physical development, the human body—with its many channels—is strengthened to handle increasing levels of chi. Two Taoist practices work synergistically toward this goal: chi quong is used to strengthen the channels, and kung fu accelerates chi through them.

An individual's chi is also affected by his mental condition. A confused mind weakens chi. With confusion comes mental stress, resulting in disease and illness. This psychosomatic connection between stress and reduced immunity—recognized by Chinese healers thousands of years ago—is only now being acknowledged by Western doctors. Despite its supposed sophistication, Western medicine cannot explain this link between mental contentment and physical health. The Taoist theory of chi, however, makes the connection obvious.

The student of Tao mentally develops chi by embracing a philosophy of life that brings contentment. By taking Lao Tzu's philosophy to heart, the Taoist gains a realistic view of the world—with all of its chaos, suffering, and absurdity—as well as a set of principles with which to navigate it optimally. This results in a content mind wherein chi flows unimpeded and thus flourishes.

In achieving a calm state of mind, Lao Tzu's principles are like a comforting beacon of light guiding practitioners out of a thick fog. While the confused man is lost and pan-

Applying Taoist Principles

icked, unable to find his path, Taoism offers explicit direction. The lost soul with no "ray of hope" is racked by fear, mentally agitated, and physically tired. The Taoist, by contrast, finds comfort in clear goals and consistent guidance—which breeds calmness. Calmness, in turn, allows chi to flow clearly and unimpeded. Thus, Lao Tzu's philosophical principles—via chi—manifest themselves mentally and physically.

In training the Taoist to have a quieter mind, meditation is used to augment the calmness achieved through a proper philosophical outlook. Unlike the recreational meditation taught in the West, which serves as little more than mental entertainment, Taoist meditation is a rigorous focusing exercise that is work. The payoff, however, is worth the effort: this meditation deeply relaxes the body, calms the mind, and "burns up" stress, improving both the flow of chi and the strength of the immune system.

The student's practical application of Taoist principles culminates in learning religious ceremonies and procedures whose primary purpose is to strengthen his individual chi's connection to that of the cosmos. While this connection's mechanism cannot be explained, specific religious procedures yield concrete, observable, and predictable results. Practical Taoists have no tolerance for nonperforming, purely ceremonial religious icons. In ancient China, for example, the statue of a spirit that failed to benefit its clan or village was destroyed; similarly, Taoist shamans who didn't perform were stoned to death. Religious procedures must be grounded in tangible results. Ultimately, as an individual's chi becomes more "in tune" with cosmic chi, the practitioner's life becomes easier by synchronizing its flow with that of the universe.

The development of individual chi through the tutelage of a master requires an integrated program of instruction. Classical training embraces a system with a core of practical application. The master carefully introduces each student to ever deeper concepts as the pupil progresses. This spiral toward increasingly profound teachings works in a carefully orchestrated manner; the master constantly evaluates his student's physical, mental, and spiritual development to determine when he is ready for the next level of instruction. With such a personalized approach to teaching the Tao, mass instruction of Taoism is obviously impossible.

The integrated nature of individual chi development—including philosophical instruction, physical exercise, mental development, and religious ceremonies—requires the student to commit himself wholeheartedly to Taoism. "Smugs," who accept only those parts of the system that they find appealing, need not apply. It is an all-or-nothing proposition.

Similarly, no legitimate master would waste his time on partially committed students. Classical training not only demands a highly personalized, decades-long relationship between master and student, but also involves an exchange of chi between the two. For this reason, the master can only share his chi with a few select students to minimize its dilution and ensure its maximum effect.

Physical Chi Quong

> To control one's breathing, expelling the foul air and inhaling the fresh, to stretch like a bear and crane like a bird for the purpose of achieving a long

Applying Taoist Principles

> life—these are the believers of mental hygiene. . . . Those who wish to strengthen their bodies and achieve longevity . . . love such teachings.
>
> —*The Wisdom of Laotse,* 272–73

By following the path to enlightenment, you make a personal commitment to develop your entire being, beginning with the physical self. Contentment—which is the goal of enlightenment—is nearly impossible to attain without a healthy body. Accordingly, the early masters of Taoism created an integrated program whose first priority was physical development. Modern man may believe that the mind is of paramount importance, but reality teaches us otherwise. When serious illness or advanced age exacts its toll, we quickly see that the body is a vessel for the mind. And if that vessel is faulty, the mind—despite all of its supposed intellectual power—is incredibly vulnerable and suffers.

The Taoist science of chi development gave birth to the practice of chi quong. Chi quong is a disciplined exercise program that not only builds the body's channels of chi but also regulates the flow of chi through them. Consistent with Taoism's recognition of the mind-body link, there are both physical and mental chi quong exercises. A Westerner would likely find that physical chi quong resembles the early morning tai chi exercises performed by Chinese people in parks throughout the world. Mental chi quong is known as "meditation" in the West and develops mental chi. Physical chi quong requires developing both mental and physical chi because the mind controls the body.

Discipline is the key to cultivating chi through chi quong. Benefits result from using rigorously structured exercises to direct chi in specific ways. Chaotic, undisciplined chi quong is not only ineffectual but also counterproductive. The fostering of discipline is why Taoist masters wean newcomers on physical chi quong. If a student can't discipline his body, he certainly can't discipline his mind. This is similar to Hindu instruction, which begins with *hatha* (physical) yoga before progressing to *raja* (mental) yoga.

Physical chi quong's required mastery of mind and body requires focus and concentration, thus teaching the practitioner how to control his thoughts and actions. In doing so, he also learns to manage his individual desires—the prerequisite for spirituality. An individual who is undisciplined in the physical realm can never be spiritual. Thus, physical chi quong is a practical means to achieve a spiritual state.

Discipline can be acquired by an external agent or self-motivation. For example, the military maintains discipline through the fear and punishment meted out by superior officers. The Taoist, by contrast, must be self-motivated. While a temple's supporting environment helps encourage an individual, his discipline must ultimately come from within. A student whose training is forced will develop chi quong that is overly mechanical and unsynchronized—limbs uncoordinated, breathing out of sync with the movements, and mind unfocused and thus out of touch with the flailing form.

Physical chi quong's primary goal is flexibility. The Taoist believes that flexibility is the best indicator of youthful, fresh chi. In short, flexibility equals longevity. Lao Tzu always encourages the man of Tao to return to a childlike state:

> When man is born, he is tender and weak;
> At death, he is hard and stiff.
> When the things and plants are alive, they
>   are soft and supple;
> When they are dead, they are brittle and dry.
> Therefore hardness and stiffness are the
>   companions of death,
> And softness and gentleness are the
>   companions of life.
>
> —*The Wisdom of Laotse*, 305

In the quest for longevity, Taoism's founder urges flexibility for health and a physical constitution best suited for survival; flexible trees bend freely and thus survive a hurricane, while old, hardened ones crack and splinter in the high winds.

The West's idealized male, by contrast, sports the physique of a bodybuilder—impressive, but hard and inflexible. Unlike the flexible Taoist ideal, his form is rigid and tight, sacrificing health and function in pursuit of an aesthetic ideal. And this ideal, though powerful in appearance, is vulnerable to the twists and impacts of everyday life and, worse still, the hardship of physical confrontation. His chi travels along rusted, rigid pipes that crack easily.

Further, inflexibility of body breeds inflexibility of mind and vice versa. If the mind is clear, it provides clear commands to the body and responds directly to the body's needs. In physical chi quong, the mind instructs the body to become more flexible, and this flexibility is mirrored in the practitioner's mental state. This elasticity of mind and body, much like a child's, is driven solely by simple wants and desires. In this way, the Taoist attempts to remain flexible and open-minded—removing society's artificial goals. As Lao Tzu wrote,

> **Who is rich in character**
> **Is like a child.**
>
> —*The Wisdom of Laotse,* 252

The second goal of physical chi quong, after flexibility, is to improve sensitivity. By feeling the body move through hundreds of prescribed motions, the practitioner becomes sensitive to the signals it emits. Consequently, he can detect a malfunction—whether illness or injury—in its early stages, allowing for early treatment. And early care is usually most successful, dealing with problems before they become irreversible.

Sensitivity is incredibly important to the Taoist. Sensitivity developed through chi quong is an early warning system, enhancing one's chances of survival. Whether in the abstract world of business or the more gripping environment of combat, the sensitive participant is the most likely to survive. In respect to such sensitivity, Lao Tzu encourages Taoists to "keep to the female":

> **He who is aware of the Male**
> **But keeps to the Female**
> **Becomes the ravine of the world.**
>
> —*The Wisdom of Laotse,* 160

In this passage, the Old Master warns the warrior breed of Taoists that their masculinity (yang) needs to be balanced with some femininity (yin). In the Taoist quest for a harmonious existence, a male with an overly hard,

Applying Taoist Principles

inflexible edge needs some softer, female characteristics such as flexibility and sensitivity. Of course, this balance should never be an even fifty-fifty split; this would result in an unnatural, confused creature. Rather, the balance should incorporate enough femininity to function optimally.

Importantly, the female sensitivity that Taoism embraces is not the weak-spirited version advocated by Western proponents of "liberal" thought. It is, instead, a vigilant attitude of caution developed by the most experienced of fighters. Lao Tzu describes this sensitivity, belonging to the "wise ones of old," as

> **Cautious, like crossing a wintry stream,
> Irresolute, like one fearing danger all around, . . .**
>
> —*The Wisdom of Laotse*, 106

Clearly, such sensitivity is not about politically correct thinking or concern for the feelings of others, but about the awareness of one's often perilous environment.

One practical implication of Taoism's yin/yang theory is its unabashed advocacy of a healthy sexual lifestyle. For example, the Taoist God of Longevity has an elongated upper head resembling the shape of the male organ, a reminder that a healthy male body necessarily possesses the ability to engage in sex. As Western medicine acknowledges, the loss of sexual desire is a symptom of health problems, including heart malfunctions, arterial blockages, and chemical imbalances. For Taoists, too, such dysfunction represents something more profound than a simple mechanical problem. The most obvious manifestation of the male animal—the ability to engage in sex—is a critical indicator of healthy yang energy. Conversely, the inability of a male to have sex is evidence that chi is blocked and disease will follow. Physical chi quong therefore includes exercises that ensure the flow of chi to specific body locations that help sustain this ability. Further, Taoism uses sexual (tantric) exercises to improve male and female sexual function even more directly.

In the male's sexual interaction with the female there is a powerful exchange of chi. The interchange of male and female energy is another aspect in Taoism's "embracing the female." The powerful male, bursting with yang, needs to interact physically with the yin-filled female. Men train in the fighting arts to breed hardness; they interact sexually with women to breed softness. On the other hand, women—who are trained to be more nurturing—receive strength and motivating energy from sexual interaction with men. This constant rotation of yin and yang energies helps the Taoist achieve a state of "oneness." As Lao Tzu wrote, yin and yang must coexist harmoniously and not be divided:

> **Being the ravine of the world,**
> **He has the original character which is not cut up,** . . .
>
> —*The Wisdom of Laotse,* 160

Overall, physical chi quong develops sensitivity for early detection of internal and external forces as well as flexibility for appropriate adaptation. Sensitivity and flexibility, coupled together, give the Taoist a survival mechanism. Lao Tzu's principles—a collection of warnings—are effectively applied in the real world through sensitivity and adjustment. Physical chi quong is the first step to attaining this capacity.

The Mechanics of Physical Chi Quong. Physical chi quong develops the human body's channels of chi, which are arranged in a configuration called the *meridian system*. Diagrammed, the human meridian system resembles the circulatory system, as it is composed of pathways that roughly follow the arteries and veins throughout the body. In essence, blood can be thought of as the life force of the visible world, while chi is the life force of the unseen world.

Along the meridian system's channels there are points used by Chinese acupuncturists to manipulate the flow of chi. These points can be "triggered" by acupuncture needles or the physical pressure of massage (acupressure), so changing the flow of chi can control pain, reduce bleeding and swelling, and balance the body's various energies to promote healing.

Physical chi quong exercises use various positions and movements to direct chi in precise ways. For example, one of the most basic chi quong positions is the "horse stance," a relatively wide-legged, low-hipped position resembling the posture of a person astride a horse, which directs chi in a spiral pattern into the reproductive organs. This area is susceptible to disease, particularly in older people, and remains untouched by Western exercises. Physical chi quong simply and elegantly prevents such illnesses.

Chi quong's positions must be exact, for even the slightest change in the angle of one's hands or feet, for example, can dramatically affect chi's flow along the various meridian channels. For this reason, effective chi quong requires the close supervision of an instructor. As the practitioner becomes more proficient, the master can add new subtleties to make the exercises more powerful and effective. And just as the various positions and movements of chi quong achieve various effects, there are also different levels of chi quong—ranging from "sitting" chi quong for infirm patients to combat chi quong for professional warriors.

Consistent with the Taoist's attempt to emulate the calmness of water, physical chi quong uses slow, fluid motions to move chi optimally. In contrast to Western exercises like modern aerobics, chi quong has no jerky accelerations that can damage joints, tendons, and muscles. Such rapid motions agitate chi, much like vigorously shaking a pitcher of water.

Physical chi quong synchronizes its movements with breathing. The deeper the breathing, the greater the volume of chi pushed through the meridian system. Simply stated, the body's position during chi quong controls the direction of chi flow while the depth of synchronized breathing controls the volume of chi flow. Such deep breathing yields powerful results but can be dangerous if misused. Shallow, natural breathing during chi quong accelerates low volumes of chi, so any misdirection is of little consequence. Uncoordinated deep breathing, however, is dangerous because it can damage organs, reinforcing the requirement for chi quong's close supervision.

The largest chi channel parallels the spinal column and is of paramount importance to an individual's health. In Chinese medicine, this largest line of life-energy is vital for radiating chi throughout the body. If it is not functioning properly, then like a clogged river, chi becomes stagnant and health will suffer. Thus, it is a priority of chi quong exercises to strengthen the mechanical construction of the back as well as its attendant chi meridian.

Applying Taoist Principles

A healthy back is the most obvious indicator of youth. An older person with a flexible back appears vigorous and youthful, while even a youthful person with a bad back appears aged and unhealthy. Western spinal surgeons now recognize that the flow of certain lubricating spinal fluids completely stop around the age of thirty. Physical chi quong offsets this effect by pumping large volumes of chi into the spinal column. Under the guidance of a chi quong master, remarkable improvements in back flexibility hail the first step in recapturing the health lost to age and disease.

As the practitioner's physical chi quong progresses, the master adds exercises to increase development of the vestibular apparatus, the mechanism responsible for equilibrium. Chi quong includes rotating exercises and one-legged stances to constantly improve one's sense of balance. There are less obvious benefits to this development: the Chinese discovered that the human immune system is directly related to equilibrium; that is, the better one's balance, the stronger one's immune system. Although the mechanism for this correlation remains unknown, the ever-practical Taoists incorporated this connection into their chi quong regimens thousands of years ago.

While the mechanical aspects of chi development are logical, predictable, and often in sync with Western medical theory, there is yet a deeper, more profound aspect to physical chi quong. As discussed earlier, chi has cosmic origins beyond human explanation, and one objective of the Taoist is to synchronize himself with this universal energy. In essence, the Taoist is a conductor of chi between the heavens (cosmic chi) and the earth (grounded, organic chi).

Resting between these two like butter between two slices of bread, the Taoist constantly strives to improve the flow of chi through his physical form as chi rotates from heaven to earth and back—with the Taoist in the middle. The better he becomes at conducting this life force, the more chi he has available for living. By opening the body's channels, physical chi quong makes the Taoist more receptive to cosmic chi. While all chi quong exercises are designed to improve this cosmic flow of chi, certain prayerlike positions are specifically intended to strengthen this connection.

Chi quong's metaphysical nature goes further when integrated with Taoism's religious aspects. From its origins in ancient shamanism, Taoism incorporates the belief that certain diseases stem from the body's invasion by malevolent "spirits." These nonphysical entities literally drain the chi from their victims' bodies like a virus invading a body with a weakened immune system. Since these spirits tend to attack a body with weakened chi, strong chi helps ward off these nonphysical leeches in a manner analogous to a strong immune system that repels viruses. Thus, by strengthening a Taoist's chi, physical chi quong has important implications for dealing with the spiritual realm.

Man's quest for eternal youth has been a legacy of every civilization in history, as evidenced through various manifestations from the ancient Egyptians and Greeks up to modern-day America. The icons of today's popular media are invariably the young and beautiful, displaying smooth skin, white teeth, and agile bodies. The few elderly people who are revered by Western cultures are those who have aged gracefully, for it isn't fashionable to be old. By contrast,

Applying Taoist Principles

Eastern cultures venerate their elders: they respect the wisdom and counsel gained from those who have survived and prospered. The open-minded Taoist is similarly anxious to learn from those who have successfully navigated life's path.

Taoists recognize that the healthful characteristics of youth—not its outward appearance—are critical to a content existence. Since our minds and souls are saddled with a physical form during their short stay on earth, a healthy body is a prerequisite for our contentment. The various characteristics of youth—a flexible back, sound joints, and strong muscles—are therefore treasured "possessions."

Modern America (and other Western countries) has limited its pursuit of youth to superficial appearances. The result is a legion of constantly dieting, health club–addicted, surgically enhanced proponents. Ironically, many "youth-preserving" activities actually yield the opposite result: steroids not only enlarge muscles but also destroy kidneys; aerobics burn calories and also wear down knee joints; and bizarre diets foster bad nutrition.

The Taoist, by contrast, focuses on the important *characteristics* of youth and uses physical chi quong to develop and maintain them. For the Taoist, physical appearance is secondary to the real benefits of youth. In Taoist temples, statues of the gods depict mature men with thick, powerful builds—in contrast to today's skinny, teenage-looking popular icons.

Physical chi quong is truly the Taoist "fountain of youth," performing remarkable feats in transforming the body into a stronger, more flexible, and healthier vessel. Some speculate that its amazing efficacy since ancient times is a testament to its mystical origins. Regardless of its source, however, physical chi quong is an important, practical application of Lao Tzu's principles.

Mental Chi Quong (Meditation)

> When the mind is overworked without stop, it becomes worried, and worry causes exhaustion.
>
> —*The Wisdom of Laotse,* 108

In understanding the link between mind and body, one must recognize that the mind controls the body—not vice versa. While the two are interdependent (the mind without the body is a chunk of immobile neural matter; the body without the mind is little more than an oversized vegetable), the mind controls the combined organism, creating a functional human machine. This means that mental control is of the utmost importance, as reflected in Chuang Tzu's warning that the minds of men should not "let their bodily desires run away with them" (p. 155).

Developing the mental facet of human existence is necessary for the Taoist to achieve enlightenment. The mind is responsible for correctly perceiving reality and then issuing the proper commands to the body; this is the mechanism by which a spiritual man translates his understanding into action. For this reason, the mind can be one's friend or one's enemy. By issuing correct commands to the body, the spiritual man can optimally navigate through life's hardships; for the confused, incorrect commands cause the human vessel to batter itself senseless while traveling through life's dangerous waters.

Applying Taoist Principles

In essence, a clear mind enables the Taoist to synchronize himself with reality. The opposite of clarity—confusion—is the biggest sin in Taoism. Lao Tzu teaches us that common values (labeled by society as good or bad) are merely constructs of a dysfunctional society. In contrast, the only true sin for the Taoist is individual confusion. Confusion prevents the mind from accurately perceiving reality and issuing commands for action while remaining mindful of the body's limitations. Therefore, spirituality can never be achieved unless confusion is eliminated.

Recognizing that confusion is caused by the perverted values of society is required to eliminate its deleterious effects. By identifying the harmful influence of social values on your ability to comprehend reality, you take the first step in repairing their damage. In other words, "damage control" can only begin once damage is detected and its source identified. Lao Tzu is clear on this point:

> **And who recognizes sick-mindedness as sick-mindedness is not sick-minded.**
> **The Sage is not sick-minded.**
> **Because he recognizes sick-mindedness as sick-mindedness,**
> **Therefore he is not sick-minded.**
>
> —*The Wisdom of Laotse*, 297

So in following Lao Tzu's advice, once the Taoist understands his "sick-mindedness," how should he repair its consequential damage? What is the practical method of dealing with a lifetime's worth of society-implanted values that distort his perception of reality?

One answer is to use philosophy to gain an understanding of reality. Correct philosophical principles teach the mind to perceive reality accurately and thus counter the effects of sick-mindedness. In this regard, Lao Tzu's philosophy uses nature as its model for reality, unpolluted by man's complicated distortions. In this manner, it teaches principles that reflect the true dynamics of reality. By contrast, hundreds of philosophical and religious systems created over the millennia are merely based on fantastical constructs of the mind, failing to ground their tenets in reality. Built on principles designed to manipulate individuals and elicit behaviors that sacrifice individual well-being for society's "greater good," these systems invariably blind their victims to the reality of the current moment.

Belief systems that use the promise of a bright future are immediately suspect to the trained Taoist. He hears warning sirens when hearing of principles that sacrifice the current moment for future rewards. Replacing *current* with *future* is a common and overwhelmingly successful method for distorting one's perception of reality, making people vulnerable to "promise-makers."

Forgetting the principle of the "current moment" doesn't simply expose one to becoming a victim of professional manipulators. Its true harm is that it destroys an otherwise able mind's ability to correctly perceive what is directly in front of it. In essence, the mind has the amazing ability to distort direct observations to fit its sick-minded view of the world. This can be the result of ridiculous belief systems promulgated by society's constructs (usually the church and state) or the individual distortion machines of pride and arrogance. Regardless of the source, however, the result is the same: mental confusion runs rampant. Only a philosophy of reality, such as Taoism, can repair the damage.

While a philosophical system's principles can help the rational individual find his way out of confusion's fog, it needs a practical means of fighting competing thoughts that have been instilled since birth and reinforced each day through all types of communication, including television. Taoist principles make *logical* sense but must battle emotions born of years spent following countervailing beliefs. Such ingrained patterns dog the mind; thoughts, ideas, and beliefs disturb one's mental state, causing it to run amok. For this reason, Chuang Tzu encourages the Taoist to

> **not . . . allow the mind to lead one astray from Tao, and . . . not supplement the natural by human means.**
>
> —*The Wisdom of Laotse*, 107

So how is one to deal with a runaway mind? Emotions are activated by a life of planning and calculating, a state seemingly necessary to pay bills, keep one's job, deal with relatives, coexist with supposedly benign neighbors, and do all of the other things expected of a member of today's society. Millions of possibilities and fears plague the mind. Retirement planning, health insurance, nuclear holocaust, global warming, and a spreading midriff wrinkle one's brow with stress. Yet they all seem to comprise the "reality" of modern life. What can Taoism possibly offer as an answer to one who must interact with this dysfunctional society and is unwilling to hide behind the walls of a monastery? It's fine for Chuang Tzu to write that one should "make not your mind a clearinghouse of plans and strategy" (p. 110), but what technique can one employ to follow that advice? One needs a practical method.

Lao Tzu asks the same question, then provides the answer by returning to his metaphor of water:

> **Who can find repose in a muddy world?**
> **By lying still, it becomes clear.**
>
> —*The Wisdom of Laotse*, 106

Lao Tzu encourages stillness as a way to clear the quagmire of runaway thoughts that blocks one's view of his path. Chuang Tzu corroborates this thought:

> **The Sage uses his mind like a mirror.**
> **It remains in its place passively, . . .**
>
> —*The Wisdom of Laotse*, 110

Both passages provide a context for Taoism's concept of "mental hygiene," the use of a prescribed process to rid oneself of the confused thoughts born of social values. It is the mental equivalent of bathing. As Chuang Tzu clearly describes it,

> **You have given yourself a bath . . . and the dirt seems to have come off with the hot steam, but something still circulates inside. When you are disturbed by the external senses and worried and confused, you should rest your mind and seek tranquility inside. When your**

Applying Taoist Principles

> mind is blocked and gets beyond your control, then you should shut out your external senses.
>
> —*The Wisdom of Laotse*, 85

When Chuang Tzu explains that mental hygiene is the act of shutting out your external senses, he advocates a concrete, practical solution. The individual must learn how to turn off his senses and shut down his brain for a rest. In essence, Chuang Tzu suggests teaching the brain how to *not* think.

This concept of explicitly learning how to not think is alien to Westerners. All of American society, with its vigorous engines of commerce, is geared toward planning and calculating. Consider a strange colloquial expression that demonstrates this particular cultural trait: people will isolate themselves—shutting the door, turning off the phones—because they say they need time to think. However, you'll never hear a person declare that he needs time to not think.

This advocation of not thinking led to the science of mental chi quong, or meditation, the practical application of Lao Tzu's mental hygiene. Therefore, the Taoist's holistic approach to health and well-being is twofold. It prescribes physically training the body in a manner consistent with Taoist principles using physical chi quong and mentally training the mind with Taoist principles using mental chi quong.

Just as physical chi quong develops the body to function better physically, mental chi quong extraordinarily improves the functions of the mind. By teaching the mind how to not think on command, it conversely allows one to focus better when intense concentration is needed (a good example of applying Taoism's principles of inaction and noninterference to the mental realm). A mind that knows how to dwell in repose can spring into focus better and with greater intensity than a constantly frenetic and fatigued brain. Mental inaction allows for improved mental action. Therefore, the conscious act of disciplining the mind is equivalent to disciplining the body.

Train the body, train the mind; the goal for the holistic Taoist is to maximally develop both the soma and the psyche.

The Mechanics of Mental Chi Quong. Mental chi quong is called meditation in the West. Its definition here has been vague and unclear. Most Americans would describe meditation as the act of sitting in a relaxed position, thinking pleasant thoughts, and perhaps chanting. In short, they see meditation as really nothing more than mental entertainment.

The pleasant thoughts of a wandering mind may indeed be relaxing, but so is watching a movie, reading a book, or listening to music. So what is to be gained from such idle recreation? Clearly an exercise dedicated to mental *entertainment* isn't going to discipline the mind and repair its sick-mindedness. Entertainment doesn't equate to training and thus shouldn't be expected to produce similar benefits.

Meditation, or mental chi quong, is more precisely described as a focusing exercise that employs visualization techniques to accomplish specific objectives. It uses a disciplined process of mental imagery to yield practical results. Discipline is key. It isn't entertaining to sit in place for hours, forcing the mind to focus on specific images while

Applying Taoist Principles

preventing it from wandering to other, competing thoughts. Indeed, meditation is focused visualization—and it is most definitely work.

Although there are many forms of mental chi quong, the two most important are (1) "emptiness," or *ch'an*, meditation and (2) "burning" meditation. Emptiness meditation teaches the mind to not think and thus to rid itself of thoughts, while burning meditation "burns up" the stress of daily life. Both techniques use mental acuity to open the individual's channels of chi and remove the blockages caused by nervous stress or physical dysfunction. Opening the meridian system through such mental cleansing enables chi to flow unimpeded.

Mental cleansing is doubly important because its benefits extend beyond the cerebral to the core of psychosomatic illness. Unlike its Western counterpart, Eastern medicine emphatically contends that most diseases can be traced to physical imbalances triggered by mental dysfunction. Empirically, most laymen have found this to be true, noting that their susceptibility to the common cold increases during times of stress. Quite simply, stress reduces the body's immune system. Therefore, it becomes clear how a discipline like mental chi quong that helps eliminate mental stress would also yield physical benefits.

Both ch'an and burning meditations begin with the practitioner sitting on a straight-backed chair, both feet planted flat on the ground. Meditating in a chair is deemed appropriate for Americans because, unlike their Asian counterparts, they're accustomed to sitting on furniture. And for reasons related to nothing more than cultural heritage, Asians meditate seated on the floor in a position in which they're most comfortable.

It is important to note that, unlike Buddhists who sit in the lotus position, meditating classical Taoists do not cross their legs. This seemingly minor nuance has important implications for the flow of chi. Taoism views the human body, sandwiched between the earth and the heavens, as a conductor of chi. It is therefore vital that the practitioner properly align his body to allow chi to flow optimally. The "uncrossed legs" position facilitates this requirement: cosmic chi originates from the heavens and flows through the Taoist's head, down his channels, and through his feet in a "straight shot" into the earth. The Buddhist view, by contrast, is that chi should be preserved and recirculated within the individual; therefore, Buddhists cross their legs to configure their channels circularly.

It is interesting to note that the system's core philosophical beliefs are so profoundly reflected in the sitting position that it prescribes for meditation. Lao Tzu's principles, dedicated to interacting with the surrounding world rather than inwardly withdrawing from it, lead the Taoist to cultivate the exchange of his individual chi with that of the surrounding environment. Consequently, the Taoist meditative position is one that opens the practitioner's channels to the outside environment.

Once the Taoist is seated comfortably, he begins "shutting down" his mind. Classically, he starts by staring at a lit candle for a short time, allowing the mind and body to settle into the meditative process. When ready, the practitioner closes his eyes and imagines himself (along with his chair and candle) on a peaceful beach, with the ocean's waves crashing in front of him.

At this point, the practitioner begins to relax his body fully. This is more difficult than it sounds, for the human body is rarely relaxed; even during sleep, it tenses and twitches, constantly fidgeting and rolling about. It takes only several hours each week of deep relaxation—achievable only through meditation—to combat persistent tension and significantly improve chi flow. Chuang Tzu encourages such effort by warning,

> **When the body is kept hustling about without stop, it becomes fatigued.**
>
> —*The Wisdom of Laotse,* 108

The practitioner totally relaxes the body by systematically progressing through it, one muscle at a time. He begins with the left big toe, commands it to relax, and then continues up the left side of the body. Continuing in a similar fashion down the right side of the body, he ends with the right big toe. Each muscle in the body—even those in the face and scalp—must be fully relaxed before moving on to the next. If the practitioner is unsure whether a muscle is truly relaxed, he can tense it and immediately relax it. By experiencing the contrasting feel of contraction, the practitioner can understand and achieve relaxation. If, after completing one cycle of relaxation, the practitioner doesn't feel sufficiently relaxed, the process should be repeated.

Once the body is fully relaxed, it is time to remove the streams of intruding thoughts that have been dogging him. His confused, calculating mind constantly disturbs his tranquility with millions of thoughts. And these mental trespassers are maddeningly difficult to stop. It is a key part of mental hygiene to accomplish this through emptiness, or ch'an, meditation. Unfortunately, the art of not thinking is much more difficult than it sounds, often requiring years of cultivation. Ironically, the more one worries about not thinking, the worse it gets.

The trick in removing unwanted thoughts is not to try to stop them altogether, but rather to simply let them go when they inevitably appear. As thoughts enter his mind, the practitioner doesn't allow himself to dwell on any particular one. Instead, he lets them flow past. He meets each one with the greeting "later" and pushes it away. Akin to a cup with no bottom, his mind should allow thoughts, like water, to enter and pass through unimpeded. Thoughts come but immediately depart. For the period of meditation, thoughts have no home and are thereby rendered inconsequential.

As the practitioner's mind settles, thoughts appear less frequently or halt altogether, and visualization of the candle and beach becomes clearer. The relaxed body may feel either unusually heavy or light and invariably like a relaxed, single mass rather than a collection of limbs and organs. All perception of time is lost. Hours pass like minutes.

Once this meditative state is achieved, it is time to deal with the accumulated stress of daily existence through burning meditation. There are many such forms of mental chi quong, but all share a common protocol. The practitioner visualizes stress as black dirt or tar trapped throughout the body. He then envisions drawing golden light into his body from any of several different sources—the candle's flame, for example.

Applying Taoist Principles

This golden light represents good, healing energy that fills the body and pushes out the black dirt of stress. The meditator then visualizes this expelled dirt combusting on contact with outside air and burning with a vigorous, deep red flame.

Over a period of one to two hours, the meditator continuously draws in golden light, pushes out the dirt of stress, and burns it. By repeating this cycle, the mind deals with stress's harmful effects until the visualized dirt is completely expelled and "burning" is no longer necessary. Much like a bather leaving the bathtub once he's been scrubbed clean, the meditator can now end the session with a mind rejuvenated through mental cleansing. He feels refreshed, having taken concrete action that can be felt immediately, just as Chuang Tzu explicitly prescribed when recommending "calm as a counter-agent against nervousness" (p. 110). Thousands of years ago, in a manner as relevant in today's America as it was in ancient China, he urged Taoists to use such mental cleansing:

> Rest is conducive to a patient's recuperation. . . . Tranquility can cure a man of nervousness.
>
> —*The Wisdom of Laotse,* 110–11

Amazingly, this continuous process of using golden light to push out and burn stress is a powerful tool in dealing with the psychosomatic harm of stress. Meridian system blockages—formed by stress—are destroyed by burning meditation. This practical method improves chi flow and enables the immune system to function more effectively.

Practical Immortality

Ultimately, by quieting the mind and eliminating the detrimental effects of society-dictated thoughts, the calm mind can begin to find itself. Since spirituality is the process of clearly seeing one's own path, the contribution of mental chi quong toward achieving an enlightened state can't be overestimated. Chuang Tzu writes,

> A man cannot see his own image in flowing water but sees it in water which is at rest.
>
> —*The Wisdom of Laotse*, 108

Further, combining mental chi quong with a proper philosophical outlook helps the individual recover his unspoiled original nature. By "washing away" the mental effects of social contamination, the individual recaptures his lost core. He returns to a childlike love of life:

> Can you let unimportant things go? Can you learn not to depend on others but to seek it in yourself? Can you come and go unfettered in spirit and can you purge your mind of knowledge? Can you be (innocent) like a newborn child?
>
> —*The Wisdom of Laotse*, 85

Remarkably, the practical application of Lao Tzu's principles yielded physical chi quong to recapture and maintain a youthful body while simultaneously prescribing mental chi quong to recapture and maintain a youthful mind. A flexible and strong body, a flexible and strong mind—a compelling recipe for *practical* immortality.

The metaphysical implications of meditation become even more profound as one contemplates time, life, and immortality. This intellectual unearthing begins by recognizing that time is a phenomenon that needs explicit recognition. During meditation, the practitioner experiences hours literally melting away and seeming like seconds. The disconcerting implication of this discovery is readily apparent; just as a meditative state of unawareness can make precious time fly by at the speed of light, so too can the blur of mindless daily activity squander an entire lifetime. Irretrievable time evaporates in the seeming blink of an eye. Harboring a faulty mental state is akin to sleepwalking through life's journey.

Perhaps the most common of our sick-minded mental tendencies is our predilection for placing "markers" in time. Our constantly planning mind has a propensity for identifying and anticipating a point in the future when things will be better or dwelling in the lost "good old days" of the past. We sacrifice the current moment in order to focus on these "time poles," taking our consciousness out of the present to a point in time that offers solace from our discontent. The tragic result is that we are robbed of the present, literally destroying time. We must remember that the past is but a memory and the future only a dream. All that is real is the present. If we squander it, we squander our lives.

For example, the typical American labors fifty weeks each year while eagerly anticipating his two weeks of vacation. He makes no effort to enjoy the nonvacation period, "saving" any real fun until the next summer or winter vacation. He doesn't spend his time in the present, focusing instead on the time poles of vacations past or those yet to come. Time flies by, and with it any passion for life.

Viewed on an even grander scale, much of an American's life from age twenty to sixty-five is spent working, for which the payoff is retirement. But when one's focus is constantly drawn to this marker of an anticipated future, the present is sacrificed. Forty-five years of youthful life disappear in a puff of evaporated experiences. Time poles destroy the current moment, devouring chunks of one's life. As Chuang Tzu writes,

> **These students of human affairs watch with happiness the changes of circumstances and the arrival of opportunity, and whenever they *can do something*, have a chance to do something, they cannot keep still. And so all these people follow their routine year in, year out, submerged in their own affairs, and cannot get out. They let their bodily desires run away with them and get tangled up in the thousand and one affairs until they die. Alas!**
>
> —*The Wisdom of Laotse,* 154–55

In a meditative state, the body becomes inconsequential and time disappears. Mental chi quong teaches the mind how to operate in this state of noncorporal existence. Focus and discipline are used to train the mind how to function without the body. This state of being—the mind functioning in the body's absence—is analogous to a form of death. Indeed, for the short period of deep meditation, one experiences a kind of "micro-death." The implication for the practitioner, therefore, is that meditation is a practical means of training for that period when the soul is released from its bodily shell. As Chuang Tzu describes it,

> **Human life in this world is but as the form of a white pony flashing across a rock crevice. In a moment it is gone. Suddenly waking up, all life is born; suddenly slipping off, all silently creep away. With one change, one is born; with another, one dies. Living creatures moan, and mankind weeps. Remove its bondage, slip off its skin-carcass, and curling up, where shall the soul of man go and the body with it? Is it perhaps on the great journey home?**
>
> —*The Wisdom of Laotse*, 236–37

For the practitioner of Taoist meditation, such training is a simulation of that certain period when corporal life "slips off." Thus, meditation not only allows us to recapture and maintain a youthful mind here on earth, but also prepares us for our "great journey home."

Martial Arts

> . . . he can sit still like a corpse or spring into action, like a dragon, . . .
>
> —*The Wisdom of Laotse,* 61

The practicing Taoist, who looks to nature for an unspoiled representation of life, observes a constant struggle for survival in the animal kingdom. Whether referring to fish, insects, or mammals, nature's most obvious characteristic is the instinct to kill in regular, brutal fashion. *National Geographic* television programs graphically depict the harsh but inescapable reality of strong animals feeding on their weaker victims. To our Disney-bred horror, we watch cute baby antelopes viciously attacked and eaten by strong, powerful lions. We recoil when these so-called noble beasts turn innocent deer into lunch. As Lao Tzu wrote, there is no ambiguity in the natural world:

> **Nature is unkind:**
> **It treats the creation like sacrificial straw-dogs.**
>
> —*The Wisdom of Laotse,* 63

While our minds *intellectually* comprehend what is meant by "survival of the fittest," *emotionally* we cry out, insisting that surely mankind is somehow different, somehow better! Our instinctive repulsion at the sight of slaughtered creatures causes us to hope that man can elevate himself above the animal world's brutality. Certainly the builder of great societies, architect of structures that reach to the sky, creator of sophisticated philosophies and heartfelt poetry is a superior creature! Can't man embrace the warm, natural love displayed by animals while shedding the ugly, predatory side of his nature?

When Chuang Tzu answers by observing that "tigers and wolves are loving animals" and that "the tiger loves his cub" (p. 67), he states that even the most vicious predators are loving animals that, by necessity, resort to violence in order to survive. There is no "evil" associated with their natural desire to fight. Rather, it is necessary for existence. Just as animals' love is natural, so too is their killer instinct.

In the oneness of nature, the ability to love and the ability to destroy are inextricably bound, because in nature the ability to destroy means the ability to survive. A tiger that can *only* love will soon starve as its unthreatened food strolls by. Thus, it's impossible to find an animal whose sole modality is compassion. Similarly, the ability to care deeply for oneself and one's family (the Taoist cocoon) is not exclusive of the ability to do harm when necessary. Like it or not, the human animal is mostly animalistic; therefore, Lao Tzu wrote that man's natural core is unkind:

> **The Sage is unkind:**
> **He treats the people like sacrificial straw-dogs.**
>
> —*The Wisdom of Laotse*, 63

Various pillars of society have tried to purge mankind of its "ugly" nature. For two millennia, religious institutions have preached universal love in a futile effort to eliminate an element of human nature that is impossible to purge. Yet, despite the tenets of countless religions, man's violent tendencies continue unabated. Ironically, those institutions impossibly committed to eradicating this predisposition have been the worst offenders: religious wars have killed millions on a grand scale, and the perfection of torture during Christianity's Inquisition brought personalized cruelty to a new level.

Meanwhile, apparently undeterred by centuries of failure, religious institutions continue their efforts to eliminate man's violence. Implicit in this quest is the hope that man can learn from past transgressions and elevate himself out of a quagmire of viciousness. In essence, religious leaders are arguing that man is no longer part of nature but rather some new form of being. Theirs is a futile dream, however; only gods are above nature, for our mortal bodies hopelessly ground us. And these physical bodies, with all of their needs and weaknesses, bind us to nature's root.

It is good to remember that—in accordance with the Taoist concept of duality—social institutions' inability to eliminate man's violent nature carries strangely comforting implications. If institutions could eliminate natural violence, they could also eliminate natural love. They could thus destroy passion altogether, and in doing so, create a loveless world. Fortunately for us, government and religious structures can only suppress our natural instincts; they can't exterminate them entirely. Passion cuts both ways—love and violence are kissing cousins. Chuang Tzu knew this and in a parable of rulers warned,

> **Man's heart may be forced down or stirred up. In each case the issue is fatal. . . . Like an unruly horse, it cannot be held in check. Such is the human heart.**
>
> —*The Wisdom of Laotse*, 125–26

Applying Taoist Principles

Regardless of the reasons for man's combative nature, it must be understood that the Tao is a reflection of life—and that life is not always peaceful. Thus, a Taoist seeking to see things as they truly exist must recognize the darker side of human nature. Filling a society with people who can only love is not an option, for such a fantastical world only exists in dreams and fiction, or perhaps in the seclusion of a remote monastery.

The plea that "people should treat others as they themselves wish to be treated" is an ignorant bleat. In an ideal world, goodness would be rewarded with goodness and the weak wouldn't be victimized. Unfortunately, our world is not an ideal one, and nature prescribes that goodness is *not* rewarded and the weak are the *first* to fall. Further, because man is inextricably bound to nature, human interactions also follow this pattern. This reality is lost on oblivious Americans who, when attacked in parks at night or robbed in crime-infested neighborhoods, are surprised. One can only achieve contentment through correct expectations, and thus one must adjust one's daily behavior in recognition of man's fundamentally unkind nature.

The Tao Te Ching's flowery, poetic words, like the gentle tones of a lullaby, often leave the untrained reader with an almost indefinably soft and gentle feeling. Yet the poetry's content tells a different story. In concert with life's constant dangers and imminent confrontations, Lao Tzu regularly employed military themes to explain Taoism's precepts. He wrote, for example, of using deceptive military tactics to survive:

> There is the maxim of military strategists;
> I dare not be the first to invade, . . .
> That is, to march without formations, . . .
> To charge not in frontal attacks, . . .
> There is no greater catastrophe than to underestimate the enemy.
>
> —*The Wisdom of Laotse*, 293–94

Lao Tzu even displayed an in-depth knowledge of military hierarchy in his writings:

> The things of good omen favor the left.
> The things of ill omen favor the right.
> The lieutenant-general stands on the left,
> The general stands on the right.
>
> —*The Wisdom of Laotse*, 167

He also exhibited his profound knowledge of the martial arts by describing the effect of sharpening a sword's blade excessively:

> Temper a (sword-edge) to its very sharpest,
> And the edge will not last long.
>
> —*The Wisdom of Laotse*, 79

But perhaps the best illustration of the Old Master's comfort with life's martial aspects is his repeated urgings to embrace the principle of camouflage to mask the Taoist's noncompliance with social norms. This theme was so prevalent in Lao Tzu's philosophy that he has been called the "first philosopher of camouflage," a title befitting a military tactician.

Applying Taoist Principles

Remarkably, despite the Tao Te Ching's explicit description of our world's warlike state and his abundant use of military analogies, pacifist interpretations of Taoism abound. For example, some philosophers have misinterpreted Lao Tzu's poem, "Weapons of Evil," as a demonstration of a Taoist's desire to avoid fighting at all costs:

> **Of all things, soldiers are instruments of evil,**
> **Hated by men.**
> **Therefore the religious man (possessed of Tao) avoids them.**
>
> —*The Wisdom of Laotse,* 167

Contrary to the pacifists' claim, Lao Tzu is warning the man of Tao to avoid the violent soldiers of *society*. Soldiers aren't "evil" due to their fighting profession, but rather because of their role as forceful implementers of the plans laid by society's dysfunctional leaders. Politicians use their gift of persuasion to push their ideas onto the herd of mankind, while soldiers use the force of arms. Either approach is distasteful to the Taoist.

A warrior, by contrast, fights for those things that matter deeply to his personal well-being while remaining indifferent to society's goals. A soldier is a *blind* enforcer of society's plans, while a warrior is a *thinking* fighter dedicated to his personal self-interest. While the two may share professional fighting skills, soldiers and warriors are as different as night and day, motivated by entirely contrary desires.

Anyone harboring doubts regarding Lao Tzu's characterization of life as war needs only to walk into a classical Taoist temple. At its entrance one is greeted with a stand of swords and battle flags. Venture deeper within and the pantheon of Taoist gods includes statues of powerful figures, clad in armor, wielding a variety of weapons: swords, axes, halberds, and maces. And these deities' facial expressions are not those of gentle pacifists but of focused combatants prepared for action. Indeed, the holiest of Taoist places is literally a hall of warriors.

The Warrior Way

Once the Taoist understands that life is a continuous battle, he is left with little choice but to deal with this reality. Given the inevitability of confrontation, there are only two options to consider: run away or fight. With these alternatives, a spiritual person—understanding that one can't spend a lifetime fleeing from the inevitable—opts for the latter, preparing himself mentally and physically for combat.

This enlightened attitude is the spirit of a warrior: danger is near, conflict is expected, and personal responsibility requires action. The alternate approach of running away from confrontation leads to continuous victimization. While it may be fashionable to embrace gentler philosophies that passively accept the harm dealt by others, it is not the Tao way. The Christian tenet that "the meek shall inherit the earth" isn't validated by reality, for in our world, the meek inherit only consistent beatings. Actually, the coward's path of avoiding conflict at all costs invites trouble. Those who wish to do harm, whether on the street or in business, can sense fear and are drawn to it. Ironically, the attitude of running from confrontation actually summons it.

Applying Taoist Principles

Embracing the coward's path is a significant betrayal of the soul. When you walk away from the responsibility of fighting for that which is important, you no longer *navigate* through life but rather let it batter you about in no discernible direction. The spiritual person, focused on achieving a content life, must fight. Without a mind and body willing to claw a way to contentment, a soul is lost. The confused individual's passivity results in a soul disconnected from reality and out of sync with its natural core. Wholeness of mind, body, and spirit are lost.

> . . . one who embraces the Tao has wholeness of character, from wholeness of character comes wholeness of the body, and from wholeness of the body comes wholeness of the soul.
>
> —*The Wisdom of Laotse,* 268–69

In assuming responsibility for your contentment, you understand that you must fight for *everything*—your job, your health, and your mental clarity. Coworkers and competitors will try to steal your livelihood, disease will attempt to rob you of your health, and society's channels of communication will work hard to confuse you. It takes focus and energy to counter these threats to your spirituality. For this reason, the warrior's way must permeate your entire life.

The ultimate threat to your well-being is physical violence. In America's wonderfully affluent and safe environment, most experience violence solely through television and movies. In these Hollywood depictions of life, good guys overcome violence in dramatic ways, leading to happy endings. The ugly reality of an unexpected, brutal attack—far different from that depicted on the silver screen—is rarely witnessed firsthand on the street. Because we don't see and viscerally understand the horrible consequences of physical violence, such encounters remain abstract notions which are given little thought by our complacent society. Responsibility for personal security is abdicated by most Americans who hope that they can call the police in time to save them. As Chuang Tzu warned,

> **Guard carefully your body, and material things will prosper by themselves.**
>
> —*The Wisdom of Laotse,* 240

If the physical being doesn't accept the responsibility for its safety and survival, then the mental being is lost. Being a tough businessman in the office and a wimp on the street is a contradiction of attitudes that breeds only confusion. By contrast, adopting the attitude of countering all threats—be they physical, mental, or financial—with passionate, aggressive responses favorably affects the entire being. A person who does this benefits from applying a consistent philosophy across all aspects of life.

The typical American's response to conflict is strangely remote and impersonal. And society must be blamed, for it controls its citizens' unpredictable behavior by programming them to avoid personal responsibility during confrontation. In essence, it has built a social structure peopled by perfectly behaved robots. Consequently, it is rare in this "civilized" society to find anyone willing to "duke it out." In business, it's "my lawyer will call your lawyer." In health, it's "call the doctor and get me a pill." Under threat of physical violence, it's "dial 911." Sadly, unlike this nation's great founders, who were men of action, we have become men of words. With this attitude, the American Revolution would never have happened; it would have been a tax dispute settled in litigation.

Though a true warrior is willing to deal with confrontation, he doesn't look for trouble. Anyone trained to fight— and thus schooled in the reality of confrontation—understands that violence is a last resort. Conflict is unplanned and uncertain by nature, often resulting in unexpected and dire consequences. Therefore, Lao Tzu referred to the use of force as a "regrettable necessity" (p. 166), and of its reluctant use, Chuang Tzu wrote,

> **He responds only when moved, acts only when he is urged, and rises to action only when he is compelled to do so.**
>
> —*The Wisdom of Laotse*, 273

Lao Tzu clearly mandated that a warrior should fight for *personal* gain rather than social goals. To a Taoist, the notion of fighting for others' gains is thus inconceivable, because he would never risk life and limb for those for whom he has no concern. Society proudly marches its easily manipulated adolescents into battle, cheered on by the applause of a confused herd. Those who survive return, often maimed, to an uncaring nation with a short memory.

A Taoist avoids all forms of social conflict. Revolutions do not concern him, for he is indifferent to one set of leaders over another. A Taoist pays his taxes and keeps his mouth shut. Should conflict erupt, Chuang Tzu observed,

> In consequence, virtuous men sought refuge in mountain caves, while rulers of great states sat trembling in their ancestral halls.
>
> —*The Wisdom of Laotse,* 127

As the Taoist navigates through life, his warrior attitude teaches him to be aware of all that is going on around him. Because a surprise attack immediately puts one at a disadvantage, Lao Tzu encourages the Taoist to be exceedingly vigilant:

> Cautious, like crossing a wintry stream,
> Irresolute, like one fearing danger all around, . . .
>
> —*The Wisdom of Laotse,* 106

Anticipating unexpected attacks causes the warrior to be constantly prepared. By dealing with conflict's *inevitability* rather than hiding from its *possibility*, fear is replaced by vigilance. This transformation, triggered by years of training and mental preparation, leads to a psychological state of calmness. Potential aggressors can sense a well-prepared fighter, and this has a deterrent effect. As the ancient Romans said, "To live in peace, prepare for war."

Anything of value requires taking risks and exposing oneself to financial, mental, or physical harm. Without the will of a warrior, the frightened lack the courage to try to improve their situation. Cowards won't undertake significant action, for they lack the willpower to bear the consequences of a tough fight. And, as a result, they are doomed to suffer the fate dealt by those around them. The fighter, by contrast, clearly identifies his goals and then aggressively pursues them. He tries to take control of the situation and, if necessary, suffers the necessary cuts and bruises. The warrior may ultimately succeed—or fail—but he is willing to try to do his best.

The warrior way invokes a deep appreciation for life. Keenly attuned to the possibility of brutal attack, the warrior develops a love of each day. Constant training causes the physical body to endure pain while the mind deals with constant humiliation—all for the purpose of handling potential conflicts. Hundreds of hours of such training every year pounds the truth of man's frailty into the student's head. Whether from an attacker's knife or a sudden heart attack, life's precious days can be stolen in an instant. Carrying death as a constant companion causes the Taoist warrior to live every day as if it were his last, thus freeing him from society's meddling plans and calculations. He recaptures the fresh air of life as long-term burdens are eased from his shoulders. Head down, eyes focused, the fighter shrugs off the artificial constraints of a confused world and struggles toward the freedom that his soul craves.

True Martial Arts

The practical applications of Taoist principles to counter physical threat are martial arts. There are hundreds of styles of such disciplines originating from every corner of the globe, including karate, judo, aikido, and tae kwon do. Western cultures label the most classical of the Chinese martial arts *kung fu*. The term is a misnomer, for it actually refers to the achievement of a profound ability in any skill. A computer programmer, for example, is said to have good "kung fu" for his extraordinary ability to write computer code. Classical Taoist martial arts would more accurately be called "Chinese boxing," with the most powerful of its styles referred to as *zho bo*. Regardless of technical inaccuracy, however, this book will use the familiar Western term *kung fu* when referring to Taoist martial arts.

Let's examine the phrase *martial art*. *Martial* refers to war or combat, while *art* is a skill acquired through practice or study. Quite simply, a martial art is a system of personalized combat skills. There should be no confusion about its purpose: to counter unexpected attacks with powerful responses that destroy the aggressor. Martial arts may have health benefits, but they're not only a fitness program; they may have mental benefits, but they're not only a psychological exercise. Martial arts are simple and pure: they enable practitioners to fight and survive while suffering minimal damage. And, because personalized combat is so unambiguous, martial arts are among the most practical skills an individual can acquire.

Remarkably, despite such clear purpose, martial arts are hugely misunderstood. In Western cultures, television and movies portray them as an exotic collection of punches and kicks accompanied by much shouting and screaming. Cinematic images of lean combatants who fight their way to victory with nary a scratch are imprinted on the public's mind. Thousands of martial arts schools support this view with their own unique brands of flailing arms and legs, huffing and puffing, and carefully orchestrated routines.

Applying Taoist Principles

In the Taoist's quest for enlightenment, he quickly learns that any theory or technique must be verified by genuine application before acceptance, and martial arts is no exception. This is required because our confused society and its disingenuous teachers manipulate the mind easily, twisting legitimate concepts into dysfunctional systems. Reality is masked by these illogical practices until confusion reigns.

Fortunately, kung fu is the easiest of Taoist applications to check out. The ability to handle physical confrontation can be tested readily; simply have a partner—preferably one who's bigger and stronger than you—strap on some pads, and with no exotic technique, try to pound you into oblivion. It approaches slapstick comedy to watch confident "black belt" martial artists turn into panicked victims as their sophisticated fighting systems rapidly evaporate under the barrage launched by an untrained two-hundred-pound construction worker. As humiliating as this test may be, it's better to fail with a friend wearing pads than in an unforgiving street fight.

Sadly, modern America is riddled with thousands of "karate" schools that have turned martial arts into little more than the practice of choreographed dancing with the illusion of a fighting style. Visit any of these schools and you'll witness students performing structured routines (*kata*) and executing punches, kicks, and blocks in the air while making fierce sounds. Fancy uniforms are worn with colored belts of rank, and much bowing is practiced. Yet there is strangely little physical contact between the students, nor do they use impact equipment like a heavy bag.

The student of such limited-contact martial arts uses his imaginary punches in the air to defeat imaginary opponents.

Image becomes reality and reality becomes image. Worse still, the naive student begins to believe his fanciful battles are an indication of an emerging fighting ability. Instructors support this natural, though faulty, psychological development by bestowing praise and awards of rank. False confidence is built and unrealistic expectations are set. Eventually, the hundred-pound black belt, without a second of actual fight training, believes he can handle a two-hundred-pound aggressor in a street brawl.

False martial arts thrive in America because our safe society makes it unlikely that the overconfident black belt will ever encounter genuine physical confrontation. So these systems prosper, creating students sure of their own indestructibility. And why not? Each has survived thousands of hours of pretend fighting without a scratch, bolstered by instructors assuring him that his training is preparation enough for the real thing. There is no conflict to slap him back to reality. With no understanding of his limitations and a lack of humility, such a student becomes a superman in his own mind. It's a comforting illusion—until an enraged street fighter teaches him a painful lesson.

Given that it is so easy to test the validity of any martial arts system, how can so many false ones develop and thrive? What has perverted fighting—the most basic of human survival skills—into a nonsensical practice?

As we have seen when examining other practical applications or philosophical concepts, the most likely sources of this confusion are social institutions. Throughout modern history, governments—either explicitly or through indirect influence—have encouraged their populaces to practice

Applying Taoist Principles

weakened forms of self-defense. Even China, the birthplace of ancient martial arts, has pursued such a program throughout its history. Historian Nigel Sutton describes why the Chinese government actively worked to destroy legitimate fighting styles:

> In China the martial arts have been changed to emphasize the sporting aspects so that the art presents less danger in the form of a core group of highly-trained potential rebels both to the participants and more importantly to the State. In order to justify the new emphasis and to deprive potential rebels of their traditional identity as members of resistance movements, the historical development of the art has been recast so as to emphasize aspects that fit with the new society's version of history. Those elements of the art that the State regards as dangerous have been criticized, discredited, and as far as possible, removed. That private groups still exist practicing and teaching some, if not all, of the traditional aspects of the art, shows that the State has not been entirely successful. Things, however, are made as difficult as possible for these groups and they are swimming against the tide of the public perception of the art carefully created by the State. One question I was frequently

asked while I was in China was why I didn't want to learn Western boxing where people actually hit each other, as opposed to wushu where it was all choreographed and "not useful."*

In addition to demonizing legitimate martial arts, the Chinese government also used less subtle means of suppression, employing the military and police to destroy clans of powerful martial artists. The ruling elite of China viewed these groups as potential adversaries—all of whom could fight better than any of the royal guard—and as a genuine threat to their security.

This scenario has no parallel in modern America, since martial artists are by and large ineffectual and thus of little threat to the government. Indeed, the American citizen-robot has no bite. The U.S. government attempts neither to discourage effective martial arts nor to nurture impractical ones. What then has caused the proliferation of such ineffectual fighting systems? The answer lies in society itself, where confused members of the herd follow equally confused instructors driven by greed.

American society doesn't really *want* effective martial arts. The parents who send their children to neighborhood dojos just want their kids to sample a taste of self-defense and would be horrified if their offspring actually learned to kill. The American martial arts student doesn't want to endure the broken knuckles and constant humiliation of full-contact-

---

* Nigel Sutton, "Gongfu, Gushu & Wushu," *Journal of Asian Martial Arts* 2(3): 113 (1993).

training. Completing the farcical circle, martial arts instructors are more than happy to give their customers what they want.

And so it goes. Pretend warriors perform their fighting dances, fooling themselves that their black belts translate to practical knowledge until a real physical confrontation destroys both their false confidence and their facial structure. With the probability of a genuine fight being so small, American martial artists get what they deserve—the hollow shell of a fighting system.

Key Principles Reinforced by Martial Arts

> Action is man's nature in motion.
>
> —*The Wisdom of Laotse,* 120

Kung fu is not only the most practical application of Taoist training, but it also reinforces each of Lao Tzu's principles. It is so fundamental that Taoism's priests had to be skilled in the martial arts. Indeed, all classical Taoist principles can be demonstrated and validated through martial arts training. Or, put another way, a practitioner of true martial arts can better absorb Taoist teachings and thus become a spiritual person.

Lao Tzu's principles and true martial arts are inextricably bound. For instance, his philosophical principles for surviving the battlefield of life have been applied to the conduct of war by history's greatest military strategists. Sun Tzu's *The Art of War*, considered the definitive text on the principles of warfare, draws extensively from the Tao Te Ching.

For example, Sun Tzu—in a passage that reads much like Lao Tzu's poetry ("Nothing Weaker Than Water")—uses the Old Master's analogy of flowing water to encourage battlefield flexibility.

Sun Tzu's principles are also the basis for many books on *business* strategy. Similarly, Taoist principles form the basis for a number of texts ranging from physics to health. The common link among these writings is the examination of collisions between competing energies, a topic on which Taoist principles provide deep insight. Be it fierce competition in business, colliding particle beams in nuclear physics, viral infections within the body, or swinging fists on the street, the martial aspect of existence is ever-present. Therefore, training in true martial arts is nothing less than a curriculum for life itself. What follows is the syllabus of that curriculum.

Clarity

The Taoist yin/yang symbol consists of black and white elements in its circular pattern. The two are distinctly opposite; there is no middle ground, no gray. The pure black and pure white elegantly represent the concept of clarity. One of the first lessons for a martial arts student is that there is no gray territory when it comes to fighting. Seasoned fighters understand that the most important factor in any confrontation is attitude. The opponent who has the most aggressive attitude will likely prevail; one cannot be a casual combatant. Polite warfare doesn't exist. The committed fighter passionately desires to destroy his opponent. There is no middle ground. Such is life.

Applying Taoist Principles

In dealing with people, the same warrior philosophy holds true. Just as the warrior ignores noncombatants, so does the Taoist eschew the herd of mankind. They are inconsequential and thus left alone. If, however, a particular individual becomes a threat in the Taoist's path—an obstacle that can't be avoided—then he removes (destroys) the problem through passionate, aggressive action. Conversely, should the Taoist identify a true friend or loved one—part of his cocoon—he takes an equally aggressive, *caring* attitude. In the oneness of passion, the Taoist is a true fighter, caring friend, and attentive lover. Chuang Tzu encourages such clarity, whether toward friend or foe:

> . . . he discriminates between safety and danger, is happy under prosperous and adverse circumstances alike, and cautious in his choice of action, so that none can harm him.
>
> —*The Wisdom of Laotse*, 241

Martial arts training teaches clarity throughout the daily learning process. A student will often incorrectly believe that he understands his master's instruction until he attempts to apply the technique in question and receives immediate feedback in the form of pain. This lesson, reinforced through decades of training, is that there is no room for confusion in anything of value. Further, the training process demonstrates that everything learned must be verified by application, because the mind often believes that it fully comprehends subjects of which it is actually ignorant. As his instruction is constantly reinforced by verification, the practicing Taoist develops genuine confidence in his technique, not the false version created by popular karate training.

Limitations

Nothing hammers home the concept of limitations like kung fu. For the typical American, smugly certain of the incredible power of his mind and body, the pain and humiliation of true martial arts are strong, corrective medicine. It is similar to an unprepared powerlifter who fools himself into believing that he can bench-press five hundred pounds; once the bar leaves the rack, reality sets in. In martial arts, the pain of contact with hard objects and the inability to defend himself against an aggressive opponent (who may be smaller), work to reinforce the student's conceptual grasp of limitations. Even seemingly simple exercises in balance, coordination, and flexibility mock the student's pride. This constant humiliation profoundly humbles the student.

The lesson of limitations has important implications in life outside the training hall. The kung fu student, humbled while learning simple kung fu techniques, develops a more realistic approach to his desires and aspirations. By experiencing physical limitations, he's less likely to overextend his reach in career goals, financial obligations, promises to loved ones, and so on. And—consistent with almost all religions, including Taoism—limiting desires is one of the most important steps to achieving contentment, because *unconstrained* desires are the prerequisite for suffering.

Applying Taoist Principles

> **Stretch (a bow) to the very full,**
> **And you will wish you had stopped in time.**
>
> —*The Wisdom of Laotse,* 79

True martial arts teach another concept of limitation: vulnerability. In learning the art of destroying another human being, the Taoist quickly understands how vulnerable the human form really is. Our bodies are held together by a thin epidermal layer that is easily cut open. Life can end quickly, for we are mortal. This vulnerability teaches the martial artist to live every day as if it were his last. By carrying death on his shoulder, an appreciation for life causes the warrior to savor each day.

> **He who knows where to stop**
> **May be exempt from danger.**
>
> —*The Wisdom of Laotse,* 172

Camouflage

The martial artist who learns his limitations and is sensitive to his vulnerability quickly realizes that it pays to assume a low profile. Like an animal whose coat resembles the surrounding brush or a soldier whose painted face blends into the jungle foliage, the Taoist learns it is often advantageous to alter his appearance. Such deception is a prime technique for a weaker fighter, enabling him to defeat a larger opponent: feigning a limp or faking a punch, for example, serves to gain the element of surprise and capture a small advantage. In the serious business of physical confrontation, one can't afford to overlook a single trick.

This principle of deception is central to Lao Tzu's persistent recommendation that the man of Tao use camouflage to hide from his biggest adversary—society. He urges the Taoist to lay low and not make himself a target. By displaying all of the values of society—while not taking them to heart—he blends in with the surrounding mass of mankind. He is never trying to be the first in anything, not bragging or boasting, paying his taxes, and observing the customs of his neighbors. Lao Tzu instructs,

> **Conservatism, compliance and caution, feeling oneself not the equal of others—these three are the signs of success.**
>
> —*The Wisdom of Laotse*, 193

While using camouflage to avoid detection, the Taoist is also on the lookout for surprise attacks. Such caution is a survival mechanism that most Americans, coddled by their protected environment, have lost. Nevertheless, just as a fighter always sits with his back to the wall, the Taoist adopts a similar attitude of wariness in his dealings with others. He constantly looks for clues as to the true intentions of his "friends," coworkers—even his spouse. The sensitivity developed through martial arts teaches the warrior to detect deteriorating situations before they become irreversible. And, by avoiding surprises, the Taoist can better navigate through the battlefield of life.

The importance of detecting problems and acting quickly to avoid or fix them is a principle of martial arts experienced in each training session. The martial artist who reacts first

Applying Taoist Principles

and counters an attack as it's launched has an advantage. For example, blocking a punch just as it is thrown is far easier than when it is at its peak of power and speed. So it is in life, where dealing with any situation is easier in its early stages than when it matures. Examples include the early stages of disease, the inception of a business competitor's attack, or the first signs of a frayed friendship.

Principle of Inaction

Warriors learn that all fights must be resolved in seconds. Unlike the movie versions of fights which last many minutes, genuine physical confrontations are handled in mere seconds. The timing is as follows: a fraction of a second to deflect the attack (block or parry), a second to counterattack and gain the advantage, and then a final second to put the opponent down. These two to three seconds require an unbelievable concentration of mental and physical power. Indeed, the trained fighter works decades to be able to perform three seconds of unleashed, explosive action.

> **To take rest is to be passive; passivity means having reserve power, and having reserve power implies order. Passivity means calm and when calm reverts to action, every action is right.**
>
> —*The Wisdom of Laotse,* 195

Training for such sharp bursts of intense power reinforces Lao Tzu's principle of inaction. The martial artist learns a central life principle: reserving power is crucial for those situations when it's most needed. Too many Americans fritter away their energy on inconsequential activities, leaving nothing for those things that really matter. They spend time worrying about global issues when life at home is a disaster; they fret about aged relatives when their own health is marginal; they spend twelve hours a day at the office while their children become strangers. By contrast, prioritizing and conserving energy is an indication of observing life through spiritual eyes.

The principle of inaction is closely tied to the principle of noninterference. While the former encourages the Taoist to conserve energy until it is needed, the latter instructs the Taoist when to draw on the reserved power. The principle of noninterference states that action should be taken only when something threatens to remove the Taoist from his life's path. This is the previously discussed concept of wu wei, which warns the Taoist not to look for battles to wage. Fights are only a last resort. The Taoist prefers to let the world wallow in its confused state, getting involved only when it affects him personally. It is, in essence, a laissez-faire approach to life.

> **It is because he does not contend**
> **That no one in the world can contend**
>   **against him.**
>
> —*The Wisdom of Laotse,* 134

Ch'an

As the fighter gains experience, he learns that the only way to function successfully during the heat of combat is to react without thought. There is a blur of action, a furious three-second span allowing no time for mental calculation, only ingrained action and reaction. Similarly, there is no time to anticipate or plan, only to act with 100 percent ferocity. Technique must manifest itself automatically, as if part of one's natural instinct. It must be spontaneous, a state developed through years of intensive contact training. Even then, such spontaneity only occurs if the fighter's training has correctly embraced natural movements while avoiding false, artificial constructs like kata.

This "no-thoughts" approach to combat is not only tactically sound, since a fight's brevity allows no time for mental computation, but is also necessary to block out a fighter's enemy: fear. By shutting off thoughts and viewing the opponent merely as an inanimate target to be annihilated, there is no opportunity for doubt or fright to surface. This enables the ch'an fighter to capture the high ground of aggression, suppressing fear while summoning his ferocious animal nature.

> **Let your ears and eyes communicate within but shut out all knowledge from the mind.**
>
> —*The Wisdom of Laotse*, 228

This lesson gleaned from the Taoist theory of fear is represented by the following formula:

Fear = Thoughts + Time

Originated by ancient Taoist warriors, it expresses their realization that fear can only exist if combatants *think* in the heat of battle, combining such thoughts with excessive worry about future possibilities or consequences of the past. Dwelling on such ruminations allows fear and doubt to enter one's mind. Ch'an instructs us to do the reverse, to avoid thinking about the past or future and instead live for the moment.

The past is but a distant memory, the future but a dream. So the Taoist dwells on the present and inoculates himself against fear. Indeed, ch'an shatters the equation of fear and releases the Taoist from the constraints of conventional apprehensions.

Ch'an's thought-free, machinelike state is one in which only the current moment exists. All of one's mental and physical abilities are focused on the immediate situation—there is no tomorrow, no next hour, no next minute, no next second. Rather, everything is committed to the present. This mental state is but an extreme version of the overall attitude that the Taoist adopts to embrace life.

"Live for the day" is the motto of a warrior, an approach that erases many of life's complications. There is no longer a need to worry about careers, retirement planning, global warming, or prestigious cars and the other trappings of luxurious lifestyles. Living for the moment lifts the burden of modern complexities from the Taoist's shoulders.

Another reason that a ch'an-like attitude is needed during combat is because planning is inevitably futile. Every fight is, by its nature, unpredictable. Any good fighter not only employs a number of fakes in his arsenal, but will also admit

Applying Taoist Principles

that in the passion of a fight, the combatants themselves don't know their own next moves. Combat is chaos, wherein unpredictability reigns. There is no role for planning.

Life is similarly unpredictable. Intricate, long-term plans look good on paper, but reality has an annoying habit of destroying the best of those blueprints. Retirement planning, which sacrifices the current moment (monthly investment contributions) for the distant future (retirement account returns), is an example of such apparently "common-sense" planning. Unfortunately, unforeseen developments—like disease or death—have a way of cropping up, shattering such carefully laid schemes and making a mockery of a lifetime of sacrifices. In essence, the planner often prepares for a future that never arrives.

Since plans have a way of failing due to unanticipated developments, the fighter must learn that any strategy for a confrontation can only include a few basic principles. From these he draws tactics in an ad hoc linear progression, one step at a time. He learns that the best approach is to focus on step A before proceeding to step B.

If, for example, a combatant thinks about his counterattack before he deflects the opponent's strike, then he will neither block the attack nor execute a well-delivered countermove. By not concentrating first and fully on step A, all subsequent actions are useless, and the well-constructed, complex plan of multiple steps is meaningless. This also explains yet another reason why kata training is folly for true fighters.

The principle of taking things one step at a time applies across the breadth of one's life. The spiritual Taoist has the ability to focus on the single task at hand rather than fret over the millions of future possibilities. And he doesn't get frustrated when his efforts don't work; instead, he tries another approach. Just like an experienced fighter who doesn't give up when his first strike misses the target, a Taoist keeps his wits about him throughout life's surprises. He doesn't adhere to a rigid plan and thus remains flexible. He adapts.

Discipline of Mind and Body

Martial arts training strengthens the link between mind and body. As the Taoist progresses in his training, he learns to focus his mind and issue the correct commands to his body; the body responds by following those mental instructions. Correct training develops a discipline of mind and body that improves over time. Ultimately, the two work in concert to recapture the natural harmony they've lost in the artificial lifestyle of modern life.

Mind-body discipline is most severely tested under an attacker's furious assault. It takes years of training to teach the mind to focus and exclude extraneous thoughts so as to achieve victory with as little damage to oneself as possible. This is no easy task; unlike the movie representations of hand-to-hand combat, even the best of fighters expect to get hurt in real conflicts. Not even the most adept fighter, for example, walks away from a knife attack without suffering cuts (hopefully not mortal). Not a pretty picture. Having a correct expectation enables the fighter to embrace confrontation with grim determination, knowing—after years of full-contact training—that only disciplined technique will save him.

Applying Taoist Principles

Such reliance on time-tested strategies and the avoidance of panicked motions is an important lesson to carry throughout life. The warrior Taoist understands that *fighting* principles and *life* principles are one and the same; both require a full commitment that doesn't evaporate under stress. Life, like physical confrontation, deals out harsh attacks requiring composed responses. By maintaining discipline, the Taoist protects himself from lethal damage and maintains his path.

Lao Tzu was adamant that nothing of value comes easy. He prescribed that the spiritual man identifies a path in concert with his natural core and in sync with the universe. By going with the flow of his *natural* desires and his surrounding environment, the Taoist can live a more content existence. Unfortunately, external forces interfere with the spiritual man's contentment. These impediments can be attacks on his psychological or physical well-being, attempts to steal his job, harm to his loved ones, or loss of freedom. While the cowardly herd of mankind runs from these confrontations and blindly accept its "fate," the warrior, by contrast, aggressively responds by fighting for his spiritual health. With this determination, the warrior doesn't allow unfortunate circumstances to destroy his contentment. By disciplined adherence to timeless principles, the man of Tao *earns* enlightened peace:

> **Concentrate your will. Hear not with your ears, but with your mind; not with your mind, but with your spirit.**
>
> —*The Wisdom of Laotse*, 228

Metaphysical Aspects of Martial Arts

As martial arts build a stronger connection between the mind and body, the mind becomes more at ease with its host's warrior spirit. By developing the ability to marshal every ounce of energy to survive mortal conflict, the trinity of mind, body, and spirit is forged into a holistic union. Dealing with physical confrontation by disciplining the entire being to work toward a common, urgent goal becomes an exercise in tuning the self to its core.

The crucible of conflict also serves as a test of character that gets at the heart of an individual. And while countless literary works have romanticized this aspect of combat, life is far harsher than fiction. Violence isn't romantic at all. Rather, the terror and pain suffered during physical confrontation scrapes you raw. Still, perhaps because of this harshness, you'll learn more about yourself during martial arts training—and the infrequent occurrences of actual physical confrontation—than through any other endeavor. It unmasks your character and exposes your soul, providing a lesson in understanding your true core that no amount of New Age psychobabble could unearth.

> **Man's mind . . . is more treacherous than mountains and rivers, and more difficult to know than the sky. . . . man hides his character behind an inscrutable appearance.**
>
> —*The Wisdom of Laotse,* 250

This character-exposing aspect of kung fu carries an important lesson: the only way to assess a friend, spouse,

Applying Taoist Principles

or coworker is to see how they behave during conflict. It doesn't have to be the extreme case of physical confrontation, but one of the thousand instances when things go wrong in daily life—a flat tire, business setback, sickness, lack of money, or jail time. When stressful situations hit, the reactions of those important to you become indicators of their character.

Chuang Tzu recognized this as an essential means to identify the character of those individuals with whom you share a common bond. He described nine tests (explained in this book's final chapter) that serve as excellent trials for one's character. He advised looking for those positive and negative symptoms a person displayed under the fire of confrontation in order to see the true man. For example, the seventh test is:

> **He . . . announces to him the coming of a crisis to test his integrity.**
>
> —*The Wisdom of Laotse*, 251

Lao Tzu's system for dealing with the reality of conflict between physical beings is equally powerful in handling the mystical arena of conflict in the nonphysical world. A Taoist temple resembles a martial hall, filled with images of spirits dressed in armor and poised ready for combat. At its crudest level, this depiction is a simple warning that one must prepare for a tough life among earthly mortals; at its most spiritual, it is a reflection of the conflict among nonphysical beings. Within the Taoist pantheon, the Jade Emperor is one of the highest rulers who sends spirits to fight in heaven's conflicts. Unlike the Christian depiction of heaven, the Taoist celestial world requires armor and weapons of destruction. No wonder the Taoist views true martial arts as both relevant and urgent.

Reflecting Taoism's shamanistic origins, Taoists believe that spirits can dramatically affect the achievement of a content life on earth. Spiritual forces can work in one's favor, or they can bring catastrophe. It is the universality of chi that enables the spiritual dimension to affect mortal fate. For this reason, a classical Taoist priest serves as a spirit fighter, using timeless procedures to ward off uninvited spirits. Disease, for example, is the result of a victim's weak chi, which allows "evil" spirits to inhabit his body and literally drain the life out of him. Taoist priests, drawing from their shamanistic ancestors, use religious procedures to make the victim's body inhospitable for these "chi vampires" and force their expulsion, much as the body's immune system rejects infection.

The struggle between individuals is even more directly related to the interactions of chi. The outcome of any physical confrontation is determined by the adversary who can most effectively accelerate his chi and direct it to his opponent's vulnerable areas. Thus, any true martial arts training teaches the student to accelerate chi through the application of Lao Tzu's principles. Armed with this knowledge, a trained Taoist fighter can overcome a much larger opponent.

While physical confrontation is infrequent, the course of daily life includes numerous nonphysical confrontations. At work, for example, people are consumed with competitiveness and jealousy despite management's constant plea for

Applying Taoist Principles

teamwork. The natural conflict of personal interests in the workplace yields bad thoughts, resulting in "negative energy" being directed toward the source of their ire. Even if you stay away from petty jealousies and have not purposely set out to harm anyone, the weak character of those in your workplace may send damaging chi toward you. Make no mistake; this form of attack is as dangerous as exposure to an infectious disease. In older cultures, where people haven't lost their natural sensitivity to this phenomenon, some members will literally kill those who give them the "evil eye."

The Taoist who trains in martial arts easily grasps this state of mental warfare, for it is but a logical extension of the physical combat with which he is familiar. Under the tutelage of a master, the student learns to use his cultivated chi to build a suit of protective mental armor against such attacks. This technique is instrumental in surviving a modern lifestyle in which it is often necessary to interact with hundreds of strangers each day. Unfortunately, even the most casual meeting on the street can result in a harmful exchange of chi that the Taoist must counter.

As the martial artist becomes more skilled, he develops increased sensitivity. The *third eye*, represented as a point on the forehead in depictions of Taoist and Buddhist gods, is the mechanism by which the mind detects and receives information for processing. Through constant feedback gained by deflecting and delivering energy (chi) in full-contact training, the student fine-tunes his third eye. This sensitivity to external forces becomes increasingly refined, reaching its apex when the seasoned practitioner can detect otherwise invisible energies emanating from anyone with whom he has contact. Cultivation of this mystical ability is another bridge to the religious aspects of the fighting arts.

All Taoist principles have concrete applications on earth. Even Tao's most mystical teachings are applicable to living life contentedly in a world filled with potential adversaries. Yet Taoism does not shy away from detailing the connection between the spiritual man's earthly development and the possibility of an afterlife. Under Taoist theory, by becoming a spiritual person able to function optimally in the absurity of mortal life, one is better prepared for a celestial existence without a bodily shell. Because the principles for both existences are consistent—a logical consequence of both realities being subservient to the Tao—one's efforts at acquiring spirituality pays dividends in both *life* and *afterlife*. There is no "downside" to preparing for life after death.

The path for this development involves the ability to handle life's challenges. The confrontations and hardships encountered on this planet are tests of character that serve as a prerequisite for a better nonbody existence. Under Lao Tzu's theory, nature is a manifestation of heavenly Tao. And, in nature, the ability to handle confrontation is the first sign of a creature with substance. For this reason, the ancient religions revered animals that possessed extraordinary fighting ability because they served as proxies for spiritual development.

> **. . . the Sage follows nature in his life and goes back to nature at his death.**
>
> —*The Wisdom of Laotse,* 273

In all religions, entrance to the heavens is not free. Taoism, however, stands alone in asserting that good deeds aren't what opens heaven's gates, but rather proper preparation of a fighting soul. When Lao Tzu identified nature as the model for the universe, he made it clear that being able to handle confrontation is the ultimate test of character. One must fight for everything—food, money, health, free time, mental peace. Life on earth is an endless cycle of peace and war waged on a personal level.

Thus, for the Taoist, developing mind, body, and spirit to fight through the absurdity of mortal existence is nothing less than preparation for the final journey—a journey home to the welcoming embrace of the Tao.

> . . . all living things spring from the dust and to the dust return. But I will lead you through the portals of Eternity to wander in the great wilds of Infinity.
>
> —*The Wisdom of Laotse,* 240

Religion

> He who does not understand God will not be pure in character.
>
> —*The Wisdom of Laotse,* 78

In the quest for enlightenment, the man of Tao learns to adjust himself to his environment. With a clarified view of the world, he becomes sensitive to the forces that affect him and learns how to navigate among life's hazards. Fending off confusing social values, he finds contentment in simple daily pleasures. In the process of becoming more spiritual, the Taoist limits his desires to only those things that truly matter—and sufficiency becomes his goal.

To operate within this narrowed scope of existence, however, the Taoist needs to understand the principles governing the world at large. Even with his desires reduced to manageable levels, he must develop a comprehensive global view. This attitude of "comprehend globally, while acting locally" allows the spiritual man to function better within his immediate environment. By avoiding a myopic outlook and broadening his vision, the spiritual man improves his ability to anticipate, detect, and handle emerging situations.

Just as an experienced sea captain uses his understanding of meteorology, ocean currents, lunar tides, and astronomy to guide his ship safely, the Taoist's comprehension of the broad forces that influence the world improves his chances to navigate through life's perils successfully. Further, both the seafaring captain and the Taoist know that they can't control global forces—nor can they even hope to understand their origins—but they can still use them in practical ways. And both the man of the sea and the man of Tao clearly recognize that ignorance of consequential forces spells catastrophe.

For this reason, Taoism's broad holistic view of the universe unflinchingly includes religion within its system of practical concepts. For the Taoist, a workable knowledge of the forces that guide the world would be incomplete without incorporating religious practices. A comprehensive picture of a spiritual person's mortal existence is crippled without an appreciation of heaven's way. Indeed, in the hierarchy of universal forces, man and his natural

Applying Taoist Principles

environment are subservient to the gods, just as they are to the principles of the Tao. As Chuang Tzu clearly explained,

> ... Tao existed by itself from all time. It gave the spirits and rulers their spiritual powers, and gave Heaven and Earth their birth.
>
> —*The Wisdom of Laotse*, 133

Taoist philosophy's inclusion of religion is profound. While philosophies and religions are generally perceived as mutually exclusive, Taoism integrates the two. Since the forces of the Tao act on the heavens as well as the earth, the two are indivisibly coupled. Separating Taoist *religion* from Taoist *philosophy* would be akin to having different theories of physics for round objects versus square ones—an absurd idea, since both operate under identical, measurable equations of behavior. Indeed, both religious and philosophical principles represent interlocking facets of the brilliantly clear "diamond of the Tao":

> These two (the Secret and its manifestations) Are (in their nature) the same; ...
>
> —*The Wisdom of Laotse*, 41

Philosophy is labeled "the mother of all sciences" because it provides a clear picture of the world in the same way science elucidates physical phenomena. Through experimentation and observation of physical reality, both science and philosophy embrace logic and deduction to define workable principles. Their respective views of the world allow for a broad appreciation of the forces that govern physical existence and provide techniques for practical application of their theories.

So while man has relied on philosophy and science to deal with the immediate practicalities of daily life, he has always possessed an instinctive urge to extend his vision beyond the observable and reach toward the invisible heavens. And this intense, innate desire is the source of history's great religions. Regardless of their specific beliefs, all religions promised to provide not only a view of heaven's ways, but also the implications for mortal existence. Professing to relieve their followers' sufferings, prophets acted as "middle men" between the untouchable gods and earthly mortals. It was the prophets' responsibility to explain those heavenly forces that influenced earthly contentment and to demonstrate how to apply them.

And this is precisely where Taoism dramatically differs from other religions. All other faiths preach religious doctrines supposedly prescribed by the word of God and then convince their followers to embrace such dogma. Based on these fabricated "good" values and using artificial notions like humanity and justice, they indoctrinate their believers to conform to group-approved behaviors. Claiming the authority of "God's word," each congregation proudly envisions itself as "the chosen people." Inspired by the passion of their convictions, religious leaders spread their ideology to the initiated—sometimes using the power of the sword to persuade nonbelievers.

In Taoism, by contrast, logic prevails and emotional fanaticism is left to others. Chuang Tzu writes of the need for intellectually sound religious theory:

Applying Taoist Principles

> Oftentimes, one strips oneself of passion
> In order to see the Secret of Life; . . .
>
> —*The Wisdom of Laotse,* 41

In this regard, Taoism warns against embracing the emotionally seductive values of humanity and justice, which are used to fabricate the labels *good* and *bad.* Instead, Lao Tzu instructs us to look to unblemished nature as an observable manifestation of heaven's way. In this paradigm there is no manufactured value system, no good and bad. Rather, there is only the way of nature, the sole model for the Taoist's behavior and values, viewed as an unspoiled reflection of the heavens. Accordingly, Lao Tzu urges us to ignore the Siren call of society's cluttered values and open our minds to the simplicity of the Tao:

> **What I call good is not what is meant by humanity and justice, but taking good care of one's character.**
>
> —*The Wisdom of Laotse,* 142

Taoism's view of religion can be traced to its shamanistic origins. Lao Tzu combined an elegant philosophy with a well-structured system of shamanistic practices (dating from the birth of mankind). Because Taoism's religious practices originated in peoples who were living in an unspoiled natural environment, artificial notions like humanity and justice were irrelevant. "Goodness" was a luxury for the civilized man of the distant future. For many millennia, the stress of mere survival kept shamanism, Taoism's predecessor, grounded to an essential, practical goal; it applied its rudimentary understanding of the heavens to help mankind endure the challenges of mortal existence.

It is important to understand that Taoism's continual warnings against humanity and justice are not the teachings of a mean-spirited faith. As a logical consequence of its principle of noninterference, Taoism is arguably the most "humane" of the world's religions. Taoism's core tenet to avoid interfering with others' paths is much more humane than those of other faiths that push their beliefs onto the herd of mankind. Competing religions vigorously impose their dogmas on all members of society—sometimes augmenting the power of verbal persuasion with the threat of the blade.

Taoism, by contrast, embraces a practice of "live and let live." Lao Tzu believed few could receive the message of the Tao; consequently, most of society should be left alone to wallow in confusion. His teachings warned Taoist priests to be low-key in disseminating the lessons of the Tao and advised all Taoists to avoid intruding into the lives of others. Ironically, this implication that Taoism—the religion that proclaims "nature is unkind"—is the most humane of all religions, for its practice of noninterference allows others to live their lives and follow their beliefs as they see fit.

Because religion deals with the unseen world of the gods, Lao Tzu instructs the Taoist to be careful in what he endeavors to learn and to believe only what can be experienced. He warns that beliefs without practical application have no tangible value and are irrelevant. All principles—philosophical or religious—must pass the litmus test of functionality. There is no room in Taoist belief for unverifiable beliefs or blind faith. Shamans and their

Applying Taoist Principles

descendants, Taoist priests, had to prove their value or suffer expulsion or death at the hands of their tribesmen. For example, the shaman of a starving tribe in what is now Russia, after communicating with the spirit world, was expected to advise where to find food to survive the harsh Siberian winter. If his advice didn't deliver the promised sustenance after days of hard travel, the shaman could expect harsh punishment for his incompetence.

Despite its flowery poetry, the Tao Te Ching is an earthy, reality-grounded philosophy. Its principles are concrete, only hinting at its religious aspects. Accordingly, Lao Tzu and Chuang Tzu warn against speculating about the ways of the gods. For the Taoist, who accepts his mortal limitations, discussions about the workings of the heavens are a fool's pursuit that can only breed confusion—akin to ants discussing the principles of aerodynamics. Therefore, Lao Tzu warned that Taoists must first understand that their comprehension of the way of heaven is extremely limited before beginning religious instruction:

> **What man knows is very little. Although that knowledge is little, man must rather depend on what he does not know before he can know the meaning of God.**
>
> —*The Wisdom of Laotse*, 174–75

While the Taoist avoids speculating about the invisible forces of the gods, he is open to well-structured theological concepts that can be verified. Further, it is important that these beliefs are consistent with the natural world. In this way, a logical system is reinforced as the principles of religion and mortal reality are coupled in the same way the heavens and earth operate within the same universal structure—both subservient to the Tao and thus governed by the same laws.

Given the limitations of words to describe the intangible world of the gods, the Tao Te Ching uses allegorical passages in its religious references. Since effective instruction—particularly in a discipline as difficult as religion—requires a master, Lao Tzu knew that any attempt to define his religious teachings through the written word would be counterproductive and instead breed confusion. The Old Master knew that literal explanations of the Tao would be distorted by ignorant, arrogant readers who would turn his holy teachings into an awful perversion of the Way.

> **There are some things that you can talk about, and some things that you appreciate with your heart. The more you talk, the further away you get from the meaning.**
>
> —*The Wisdom of Laotse*, 313

The passages were written with the expectation that they would be received by a student under the tutelage of a master continuing Taoism's history of oral tradition.

Perhaps written instructions are limited because of the central role chi plays in Taoism's physical and metaphysical practices: chi can be experienced but is difficult to describe. As discussed earlier, chi is the unifying mechanism that enables the forces of the Tao to manifest themselves. And so

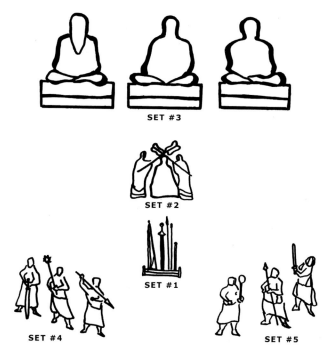

TEMPLE MAP

This map depicts the layout of the Suzhou Mysterious Essence Temple, one of China's oldest places of Taoist worship. Upon entering this sacred place, you are greeted by a stand of swords and battle flags signifying the "life is a struggle" theme (#1). Above the stand is the Jade Emperor, the great deity (#2) whose orders bring harmony to Earth and restore unpolluted manifestations of the Great Ultimate, which is represented by the Three Pure Ones. Unlike the Christian version of God, the Jade Emperor's mission is not to carry goodness to man, but is instead to reestablish the natural state of harmony that mankind has lost. In charge of this world, the Jade Emperor issues orders to his celestial Generals (#4 and #5).

Towering above the Jade Emperor are the images of the Three Pure Ones (#3). To the left sits "Heavenly Worthy of The Virtue of Tao" (Lao Tzu). Next, representing the elemental forces of Yin and Yang respectively, are "Primordial Heavenly Tao" and "Heavenly Worthy of the Sacred Jewel." These images of the Three Pure Ones characterize manifestations of the Tao, the Great Ultimate. They serve to remind us that the forces of Tao surpass all. They also exemplify a very powerful message: everybody and everything, including humans and Gods, are subject to the power of the Tao. There are no exceptions. The enormous size of the Three Pure Ones further serves to remind us that we all must accept the force of the Tao and obey its power.

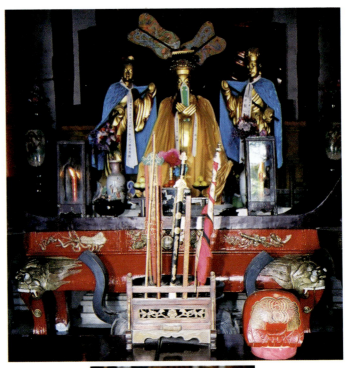

Above: Jade Emperor - The Great Deity of Supreme Power
Below: Sword and Battle flags at entrance of traditional temple
(Suzhou Mysterious Essence Temple; Suzhou China)

Three Pure Ones
(Suzhou Mysterious Essence Temple; Suzhou China)

Celestial Generals and Reincarnated Marshals line eastern walls of temple
(Suzhou Mysterious Essence Temple; Suzhou China)

Celestial Generals and Reincarnated Marshals line eastern walls of temple
(Suzhou Mysterious Essence Temple; Suzhou China)

Celestial Generals and Reincarnated Marshals line western walls of temple
(Suzhou Mysterious Essence Temple; Suzhou China)

Celestial Marshal of Mysterious Path
(Suzhou Mysterious Essence Temple; Suzhou China)

Incense offered in respect to spirits
(Suzhou Mysterious Essence Temple; Suzhou China)

Zodiac Gods in White Cloud Temple
(White Cloud Temple; Shanghai, China)

Above: Grand Master Anatole with Abbot Leiu in White Cloud Temple
Below: Grand Master Anatole in front of the image of
the Governor of Internal Essence and Sovereign of Underworld
(White Cloud Temple; Shanghai, China)

Governor of Internal Essence and Sovereign of Underworld
(Temple of Original Simplicity; Boston, Massachusetts)

Lao Tzu
(Temple of Original Simplicity; Boston, Massachusetts)

Above: Spirit of Perfect Warrior, Master of Change
Below: Celestial Lord of the Waters
(Temple of Original Simplicity; Boston, Massachusetts)

Star Gods: God of Longevity(left), God of Good Counsel(middle),
God of Good Fortune(right)
(Temple of Original Simplicity; Boston, Massachusetts)

Celestial Spirit of Ghost Hunting
(Temple of Original Simplicity; Boston, Massachusetts)

God of War
(Temple of Original Simplicity; Boston, Massachusetts)

God of Literature with Attendants
(Temple of Original Simplicity; Boston, Massachusetts)

God of Wealth
(Temple of Original Simplicity; Boston, Massachusetts)

Celestial Warrior of Water Virtues
(Temple of Original Simplicity; Boston, Massachusetts)

Supreme Protector of Mysterious Virtues
(Temple of Original Simplicity; Boston, Massachusetts)

Goddess of Mercy
(Temple of Original Simplicity; Boston, Massachusetts)

God of Primordial Energy
(Temple of Original Simplicity; Boston, Massachusetts)

Supreme Marshal of Warlords and Celestial Dragons
(Temple of Original Simplicity; Boston, Massachusetts)

Above: Supreme Lord of Heavenly Virtues
Below: Warlord of Celestial Heavens
(Temple of Original Simplicity; Boston, Massachusetts)

Abowe: Lord of Magical Powers of North Star
Below: Lord of Heavens, Protector of Taoist Virtues
(Temple of Original Simplicity; Boston, Massachusetts)

Celestial Fox Spirit
(Inari Temple, Kyoto, Japan)

Altars of Celestial Foxes
(Inari Temple, Kyoto, Japan)

Above: Grand Master Anatole in front of Inari Temple gates
Below: Grand Master Anatole in front of Inari altar
(Inari Temple, Kyoto, Japan)

Altars of Celestial Foxes
(Temple of Original Simplicity; Boston, Massachusetts)

I-30

Celestial General of Heavenly Troops

On page I-30:
1. Liaison Officers of the Governors of this World and Waters
2. Celestial General's Five Banners of Knights
3. The Thunder God
4. General of the Divine Empyrean

(Temple of Original Simplicity; Boston, Massachusetts)

Grand Master Anatole performing purification ceremony
(Temple of Original Simplicity; Boston, Massachusetts)

Applying Taoist Principles

it is with the religious aspects of Taoism, since chi's unseen energy governs both the ethereal and physical worlds. Consequently, Taoism's religious practices rely on manipulations of individual chi similar to those in such grounded endeavors as martial arts and holistic healing.

Taoism's religious practices build a bridge between one's earthly body and the heavens. In the quest for oneness with the universe, the man of Tao works to understand his path—which ultimately leads to the Great Ultimate. The allegorical representations of the Tao Te Ching instruct the Taoist how to find his absolute path. Unfortunately, despite the assistance of Taoist teachings, the limitations of bodily existence prohibit him from fully comprehending heaven's way and his ultimate path. Such knowledge is only possible when one sheds one's mortal shell:

> **I have freed myself from my body, . . .**
> **I have discarded my reasoning powers.**
> **And by thus getting rid of my body and mind, I have become One with the Infinite.**
>
> —*The Wisdom of Laotse*, 276

So how does one build a bridge to the Great Ultimate, given the limitations of the physical form? How can one's pathetic human manifestation have any hope of finding its spiritual path? Aren't we lost on a hopeless search for spiritual oneness, hindered by our inability to "rid ourselves of body and mind"?

The solution is to combine a Taoist master's instruction with assistance from the gods (in the form of prayer). By praying, one opens a two-way communication channel to the heavens. The Taoist sends an appropriate message to the Great Ultimate and receives a concrete answer in return. In this way, guidance from the gods augments spiritual training to clarify one's path.

There is a prerequisite, however, before prayer can yield tangible results. A confused mortal, a physical and mental wreck, would be wasting his time trying to communicate with the heavens. Confusion clouds an individual's chi, destroying the sensitivity needed to receive communications from those immortals who govern mortal existence. A confused individual can't even possess the ability to formulate a correct question, let alone detect the heavenly answer. Conversely, if the student of Taoism has clarified his world vision, he is ready for this most practical and personal of religious practices.

As prayer strengthens his connection to the Great Ultimate, the Taoist also taps into an unlimited source of celestial chi. By cultivating sensitivity to both earthly and heavenly chi, he improves his mortal contentment and makes the leap to the Great Ultimate easier when his soul is liberated from his body. The metaphysical bridge built while on earth serves as a transit mechanism for the soul's final journey.

While our body grounds us to earth and its physical existence, the things we experience have both physical and supernatural effects. The Taoist's actions turn the guidance received through prayer into tangible benefits, both physical and spiritual. Only by combining prayer with action does the spiritual man take responsibility for his entire being. As the Taoist works to tune himself to his surrounding forces, he engages in a concrete training process that's as grounded in reality as are martial arts. By tuning himself to the "frequency" of our cosmic origins, the Taoist increases his harmony with the universe. Deliberate action transforms prayer into reality, while prayer without action is merely wishful thinking.

> Spiritual, yet not to be devoid of action, that is God.
>
> —*The Wisdom of Laotse*, 78

Taoism's Shamanistic Roots

> He who holds fast to the Tao of old
> In order to manage the affairs of Now
> Is able to know the Primeval Beginnings
> Which are the continuity of Tao.
>
> —*The Wisdom of Laotse*, 102

What theory—validated by application—explains the remarkable abilities of shamans, the precursors to Taoist priests? The word *shaman* is the English translation of the Tungus' *Saman*, which means one who knows or communicates with spirits while in a trance. Indigenous to the Altai Mountains in Siberia, the shaman works with fire and heat. In practice, he is a conductor and manipulator of the energy, or chi, that resides in all manifestations of nature. In the shamanistic arts, flame is not only viewed as a source of heat, but as an agent of change. This change can be physical or of even greater consequence, influencing fate or changing the future.

The shamanistic process is consistent with the Taoist formula that *energy* causes *movement* that results in *change*. Following this energy-movement-change paradigm, shamans use the energy of fire to redirect or move the mystical connection of an individual to the cosmos, an action that changes the development of future events (fate). For the shaman, time is an artificial construction, a marker created for convenience. Using ancient ceremonies, shamans enter trances wherein the past and future mean nothing, "time walking" effortlessly through the ages.

Shamans and Taoist priests use their power to improve the fate of individuals. According to classical theory, each person is born under certain astrological signs representing specific configurations of stars. Accordingly, each individual possesses his own "frequency," associated with his inherent chi energy as determined by the star configuration at the time of birth. These celestial alignments serve as channels of the cosmic energy beamed to each person; changing this "beam pattern" affects one's fate. The shaman's objective is to realign an individual's personal chi with that of the cosmos, as dictated by astronomical configurations. This technique corrects ill fate that results from "misalignment" caused by internal mental confusion or external metaphysical forces.

Corrective "realignment" is accomplished using prayers, rituals, ceremonies, and talismans bestowed by the ancient masters and shamans from millennia ago. For convenience in their calculations, the shamans developed a system of classifying these frequencies into groups of animals, trees, and stones. Augmenting this manipulation is the sphere of chi that a powerful shaman or Taoist master radiates around

Applying Taoist Principles

himself, favorably affecting the fate of those within the holy man's temple or clan by realigning beams of cosmic energy.

There are also rhythms and cycles to the universe that affect all of nature, including man. If an individual's frequency is out of sync with the cycle of the universe, then that individual will suffer poor fate. It is as if the doomed individual is swimming against a powerful current. The shaman uses special amulets and procedures to synchronize the individual's frequency with that of the cosmos. Such action, if successful, helps the individual work in concert with the flow of events instead of against them. The individual's path is corrected.

Invisible to most humans is a world of universal chi that includes nonphysical creatures existing within their own dimension: "spirits." While Taoists refrain from labels such as *good* and *evil*, some of these spirits are harmful, with the ability to invade the body and suck the chi, or life, out of the victim. The weak, confused individual is more likely to be attacked by these malevolent spirits, and those infected suffer illness, disease, financial hardships, and interpersonal problems.

These spirits are "vampires" of chi. Some have existed forever; others originate from the focused thoughts of ill-intentioned persons—in other words, they are born from a curse. Many societies, unlike modern America, are attuned to this phenomenon and take the threat so seriously that they won't hesitate to kill someone who has cursed them.

Among their many duties, shamans and Taoist priests deal with these evil spirits. By understanding an individual's cycle of chi as it relates to universal rhythms, they can identify weak periods and warn those who are vulnerable. The shaman or Taoist priest can then use his own internal chi to help the vulnerable person, as well as use rituals and talismans to focus the power of the cosmos to ward off the invading spirits.

Classical Taoist theory identifies three levels that influence universal forces acting on mankind: the heavens above, man in the middle, and the earth below. Man is a conductor of chi between heaven and earth. All Taoist sciences, from chi quong to meditation, are built on this principle, which also forms the basis for shamanistic and Taoist religious practices. Operating within this paradigm, Taoist astrology is a systemization of the heavenly forces above man, and minerals and animals represent the earthly forces below. These fundamental ideas codify the two realms that bracket man and affect his fate.

Ancient Taoist scientists and alchemists identified twenty-eight major and thirty-two minor stars in the sky. These astronomical bodies are correlated to the sixty-year Chinese calendar with its sixty guardians, each of whom control a cycle of chi in the universe. An individual's birth date corresponds to a particular star, which in turn identifies which cycle will govern his fate. The sixty stars are mapped to five constellations, including Virgo, Leo, and the Great Bear.

While Taoist astrology describes how the forces of the heavens manifest their action on mankind, the earthly dimension of universal energy exerts equally powerful effects. And the combination of these forces either increases or decreases an individual's animal power. Animal power reflects the corporal aspect of one's existence which, if weakened, makes one vulnerable to physical hardship and disease. Taoist shamans perform astrological calculations and then adjust them to factor in the effects of earth's natural cycles through the use of specific minerals (like quartz and malachite), herbs, and other techniques. The shaman uses these activities to invite the appropriate missing animal power back into the weakened individual, thus restoring balance. The master also uses the power of certain animals to serve as liaisons between the guardian spirits and the affected individual.

In summary, shamanistic practices use chi to benefit those individuals who are sensitive enough to receive their manipulations. While Taoist sciences can be incredibly complex, their roots can be traced to shamanism; they are, therefore, grounded in the simple, natural ways of a people uncontaminated by civilization's intellectual confusions.

Taoism's religious tenets—grounded in and consistent with its philosophy—get at the core of metaphysical reality. They avoid the blathering so common to other creeds that seem determined to force their values on others, based only in blind faith. For the man of Tao, legends of the past can be taken at face value or simply viewed as allegorical representations of a functional construct. In either case, they are instructive to the spiritual seeker.

Celestial Evolution

> **Your nature is not possessed by you; it is a natural evolution lent to you by the universe.**
>
> —*The Wisdom of Laotse*, 95

Both ancient shamans and their more scientific successors, the Taoists, relied on chi as the mechanism connecting earthly existence to the heavens. The universality of chi makes its role in religion as relevant as that of its more physical applications, such as holistic healing and martial arts. Because of the connecting power of chi, as a Taoist develops his body and mind, he engages in a religious exercise. This means that physical and mental development are necessary for religious development.

An individual with a slovenly, inflexible body and a confused mental state has no hope for the Taoist version of "salvation." Unlike Christian dogma, which preaches salvation through good deeds, Taoism mandates *effort*; it has no tolerance for lazy "do-gooders." For a classical Taoist, this effort involves the constant attuning of oneself to physical and metaphysical reality—the sole means by which to gain access to the heavens. Goodness plays no role. This implies individual responsibility for taking correct action, with success measured by results rather than a theoretical scale of piety.

As the Taoist strives to become more in tune with the universe, he is not sacrificing his daily contentment. The goal of Taoism—even as it relates to religion—is to increase one's enjoyment by experiencing life's pleasures. Ancient Taoists poked fun at doctrines preaching abstinence and voluntary hardship as the path to a higher plain of development. Indeed, Chuang Tzu thought it absurd to sacrifice physical comfort and mental peace for some abstract notion of spiritual development:

Applying Taoist Principles

> It causes a man to live strenuously and die cheaply, and must be considered too severe. It also makes men sad and austere and is a doctrine difficult to practice. I am afraid this is not the teaching of the sages. For it goes against human nature, and few people can stand it.
>
> —*The Wisdom of Laotse,* 27–28

Chuang Tzu instead taught that sacrificing the current moment for an unknown afterlife is not only incorrect, but actually counterproductive. Success in tuning oneself to universal energies is measured by improving one's contentment while on earth. In developing himself spiritually, the Taoist must learn to enjoy life and recapture those simple pleasures that have been suppressed by social values. Only when physical existence, mental contentment, and religious convictions converge has one truly achieved a "state of grace."

So how do the metaphysical and physical interact within the man of Tao? What is the mechanism by which daily actions on earth affect the nonphysical soul of an individual? And how does Taoism's religious instruction on heaven's way manifest itself within the mortal being?

To answer these questions, one must first explore the Taoist's theory of *karns* (not to be confused with the Indian theory of karma). Karns are nonphysical particles contained within everyone and formed at birth. Like chi, traditional scientific instruments cannot measure them, for they aren't composed of electromagnetic energy as defined by Maxwell's equations. Nevertheless, the importance of karns is not to be underestimated, for these nonphysical particles comprise the very "soul" of man.

Karns form a configuration unique to each individual, comprising the energy matrix of the soul. This energy pattern interacts with universal energies. For example, if an individual's karn pattern aligns with the universe's cosmic pattern, then his life improves, as he is synchronized with heaven's way. Accordingly, the goal of a Taoist is to tune his karns to this universal pattern.

So how does a Taoist go about tuning his "frequency" to that of the cosmos? What are the practical means by which one aligns karns and thereby achieves universal synchronization?

The answer, quite simply, is that the Taoist consciously tries to execute correct actions throughout his life. Challenges and tests constantly present themselves, and how the Taoist deals with these tests determines whether his karns will move toward a more correct alignment or become more scrambled. In other words, improper action is the result of a confused mind—and a confused mind yields confused karns. Conversely, a clear vision of reality, as demonstrated by correct action, is the mechanism by which physical existence favorably impacts nonphysical karns. In essence, the "chaos, absurdity, and suffering" that life presents are the tests by which mortals can "prove" their spirituality through correct action. For this reason, the mythology of the great quests appropriately included challenges as a prerequisite for enlightenment. But they had it wrong in

Applying Taoist Principles

that no artificial trek was required; life's daily hassles are challenge enough.

> **To adjust oneself to events and surroundings casually is the way of Tao.**
>
> —*The Wisdom of Laotse*, 78

The concept of how to handle life's challenges has profound implications. Taoist theory holds that all individuals are given several big tests during the course of their lives. And if the individual makes incorrect decisions, his karn pattern changes unfavorably and hardship follows. Indeed, the Taoist understands that mistakes cannot be taken lightly, for they carry serious consequences—sometimes physically, sometimes spiritually.

The Taoist belief that one's ultimate fate is determined by prior action is somewhat consistent with the popular notion that one's fate is based on the accumulation of good deeds. The difference is that Taoism believes it is correct action, as opposed to good deeds, that is important. For the Taoist, it is inconceivable that universal correctness could be based on man's definitions of *good* and *bad*, which change at the whim of society. Accordingly, it is illogical to believe that one's ultimate fate could be determined by collecting deeds whose worth seems to shift with society's values du jour. The universe is indifferent to mankind's values; therefore, action based on popular values will only serve to confuse an individual's karn pattern.

One way to understand the impact of the choices one makes throughout life is through the analogy of a tree. The tree's main trunk represents life's correct path, beginning from the roots within the earth and progressing skyward toward the heavens. As one moves up the tree, forks divide the trunk. These forks represent life's big tests, for one must decide which direction to follow. One leads away from the tree's trunk and onto dangerously narrowing branches. The other allows one to progress safely up the trunk, ever closer to the heavens, until one meets another fork—yet another test.

While a mistake may lead the Taoist off the trunk and along an incorrect branch, it is generally possible to progress to another fork along that branch that allows him to rectify his course and proceed back to the mother trunk. Such opportunities are finite, and after a number of mistakes, he finds himself scrambling along precarious, distant branches from which there is no hope of returning to the trunk safely; mortal life is problematic, the soul burdened.

This analogy illustrates why Taoists are so sensitive to the correctness of their decisions. It has nothing to do with adding to one's list of hypothetically "good" deeds; rather, it is the singular means by which one proceeds through mortal existence, drawing closer to the Tao. Lao Tzu emphasizes the importance of making correct decisions at each fork in life's progression:

> **Walking on the Main Path (Tao),**
> **I would avoid the by-paths.**
> **The Main Path is easy to walk on,**
> **Yet people love the small by-paths.**
>
> —*The Wisdom of Laotse*, 246

Taoism advises its followers that mortals have no control over their soul's entry into this world or any control over its exit. Just as point A (birth) was beyond our control, so too will be point B (death). However, it is up to the individual to journey from point A to point B with as much contentment as possible. Ultimate fate cannot be changed, but the Taoist has the freedom of will to select the best path possible. Returning to our previous analogy: the tree of life (one's path) is set and cannot be altered; it is, however, up to the individual to travel up its comforting trunk or scramble in confusion along its outer branches. This freedom to choose our path means that we have the responsibility to fight for our fate. While the certainty of death is constant, a content life is an achievable goal requiring effort and perseverance.

> **Each one's destiny cannot be altered. Time cannot be stopped, and Tao must not be blocked up. With possession of the Tao, one can go wherever one likes. Without the Tao, one is lost wherever one goes.**
>
> —*The Wisdom of Laotse,* 319

The similarity between classical Taoism's view of fate and the more popularly held version is evident in the concept of reincarnation. Conventional New Age thinking—borrowed from Hindus—asserts that by living a life of "goodness," one will be reincarnated at increasingly higher levels of existence. This ascendance continues until one is eventually accepted by the Great Ultimate, and the hassles of mortal existence are no longer required.

The Taoist version, by contrast, asserts that it is not "goodness" that determines whether a soul will be accepted by the Great Ultimate, but the process of tuning one's karns to universal energies. An improperly configured karn pattern won't be absorbed by the Great Ultimate and thus will be rebounded or "reincarnated."

This rebounded soul represents the Taoist version of Christianity's original sin. A confused karn pattern that is rejected by the Great Ultimate reappears as the soul of a newborn child. Therefore, the soul brings with it the confusion and scrambled karns of prior lives—its "original sin." This reinforces why confusion is Taoism's greatest sin, for it dooms the soul to a discontented mortal existence with no hope for joining the Great Ultimate.

To the classical Taoist, life is an ongoing effort to unscramble the confusions of the soul. Always striving to live a more content life, he uses mortal existence to train himself to behave in ways consistent with the Tao. In his efforts, he uses Taoist philosophy for principles to live by and guidance from the gods to see reality more clearly. (Prayers are for clarity, not material desires.) The two—philosophy and religion—work in concert to help him achieve spirituality.

The task of becoming a true man of Tao is difficult. Taoists recognize that their limitations are severe and confusions are many. Indeed, society works against clear vision. The Taoist can repair the damage of his confused soul, however, by using his time on earth as a training ground. The process is arduous and requires many years of mortal existence to straighten out his misconfigured karn pattern. For this reason, longevity is important to Taoists. Time, the most precious of commodities, is needed to rectify individual confusion to prepare for the Great Ultimate. Taoism's preoccupation with longevity doesn't derive from a fear of death, but from an understanding of the appropriate preparation it demands. For a Taoist, death is the next stage of a journey for which he wants to be ready. Only then can he truly welcome its embrace.

> . . . he knows his form is subject to change, but his mind remains the same. He believes not in real death, but regards it as moving into a new house.
> —*The Wisdom of Laotse,* 237–38

The Taoist Temple

> Use the light,
> And return to clear-sightedness— . . .
> —*The Wisdom of Laotse,* 243

As the ever-practical Taoist searches for help in achieving an enlightened state, the temple is his most accessible source of guidance. For all religions—Taoism among them—temples are where religious institutions formally apply their creeds under the supervision of a priest or master. From ancient times, it was the role of each community's church, temple, or monastery to bring some measure of contentment to its congregation. In its unspoiled state, a place of religion—a church or temple— was where images of deities worked in conjunction with the power of their priests to facilitate communication with the heavens. These "houses of God" were designed and consecrated as places of prayer; there, mortals could receive celestial guidance on how to be more content with their lives.

As with most large institutions, religions' noble goals have become secondary to their self-interest. Whether driven by greed or power, large religious organizations have a record of distorting their core tenets to achieve their ignominious objectives. Sadly, these institutions—whose purpose should be to facilitate unspoiled communication with the gods—have been turned into merchants of distortion, propagating manipulative values in search of cash and status. Indeed, the "word of God" has taken a backseat to the "word of nonprofit corporations."

For this reason, anyone searching for a religious institution—including a Taoist temple—should avoid the largest, most popular organizations. Private temples, by contrast, are meant for a select few and reflect the personal needs of each member. Instruction between the priest and his congregation is direct, and there is no conflict between the goals of the institution and its members' spiritual development. Religious practice in private temples is pure, uncontaminated by self-aggrandizing organizational desires. This reflects Chuang Tzu's observation that

> . . . the highest teachings are not accepted by the minds of the common men, and the words of wisdom are not popular, because they are overshadowed by conventional teachings.
>
> —*The Wisdom of Laotse,* 130

Applying Taoist Principles

Despite the limitations of large institutions, however, *popular* Taoist temples still provide some benefit to their congregations. The messages contained within the images spread throughout these temples are simple and consistent with Lao Tzu's teachings. Above each main entrance, for example, is inscribed, "Every man is responsible for his actions." Similarly, the images inside the temple encourage health, caution, and clarity and warn against the excesses of material desires. And consistent with most religions, Taoist temples reinforce man's minuscule position within the universal scheme while instilling a healthy "fear of God."

Due to their much smaller size, private temples can dedicate themselves to the correct instruction of each member. For this reason, their integrated curricula include mental, physical, and spiritual development. A classical Taoist temple teaches chi quong, meditation, martial arts, and religious practices. And because of its private status, membership is not open to the public; new members are carefully screened and chosen. In most cases, the private temple's master—also its priest—approves all new initiates. The more desirable temples are virtually impossible to join, since each master accepts no more than a handful of students in his lifetime.

The most important criterion for selecting students is their intense desire to learn Taoism. With religion at the apex of its curriculum, pupils begin instruction by developing their bodies, then their minds, and finally their spiritual core. A student must possess the necessary desire in order to warrant a master's investment of several decades in his development. Because Taoism is fundamentally a philosophy of limitations, each student needs the willpower to survive the many pains and humiliations associated with the training process. When one's goal is as profound as becoming more in tune with the Great Ultimate, a casual attitude yields only failure. Indeed, the burning desire required of all serious students must be innate and inextricable—part of their nature. As Chuang Tzu observed,

> **Because if you haven't got it in you, you could not receive Tao.**
>
> —*The Wisdom of Laotse,* 317

The role of a master, or priest, within a private temple cannot be overstated—quite simply, the master *is* the temple. Beginning with the temple's foundation, the master makes his mark using various devices (for example, a chi compass) and astrological signs to locate and position the temple. Subsequently, his energy—chi—gives the temple its power. This chi also activates students' internal desire to learn, providing the catalyst that reanimates their souls.

The temple's master also uses his chi to protect the congregation. Just as a monastery's walls protect its inhabitants' physical bodies, the master's power protects their nonphysical forms. And just as food nourishes the body, the master's teachings nourish the soul. As Chuang Tzu observed,

> **And he who is thus fed by God has little need to be fed by man.**
>
> —*The Wisdom of Laotse,* 137

As in any church or temple, the temple's priest is essential to establishing communication with the heavens. In this

Applying Taoist Principles

capacity, Taoist priests use ancient procedures to "open the eyes" of the figures of deities placed throughout the temple, thereby asking Taoist spirits to be receptive to the congregation's prayers. This procedure is necessary to activate the spiritual power of the temple and build dynamic communication channels to the heavens.

In his role as a spiritual instructor, the master's relationship with each student is profound, not casual. In classical Taoist temples, there is earned devotion between the two; indeed, actual chi is exchanged. While the student's quest to find a good master is difficult, the master is equally challenged to find a few good students. The master earns the devotion of these students by continually providing tangible proof of his teachings. And by leading them along rewarding paths of self-discovery, the master never asks his students for blind faith—only earned conviction. He lives as he preaches, and his teachings are pragmatic with immediate benefits. Indeed, as in any profession, respect can only be earned, never purchased.

As the student progresses, the master carefully exposes him to increasingly deeper knowledge, eventually progressing to religious practices, the most "hidden" art. Given the limitations of learning from a book, especially one as deceptively complex as the Tao Te Ching, personal lessons from a master are the only means by which a student can truly comprehend the Tao. As in any viable exchange, both parties benefit. In this case, the master earns the respect of his students, while the students earn the attention of their master by sacrificing their time and money. The master, never abusing his students' generosity, always provides tangible benefits for the money and respect given by his students. Unlike typical religious organizations, where benefits are rarely witnessed firsthand, the master-student exchange is tangible and concrete. Obscure benefits belong to the realm of charlatans.

Pantheon of Gods

> Therefore all things of the universe worship Tao and exalt Teh.
> —*The Wisdom of Laotse,* 242

While private Taoist temples also teach the grounded applications of physical chi quong, meditation, and martial arts, the temple is first and foremost a holy place. If a student wishes to learn only martial arts, he should go to a dojo; if he wishes to improve only his physique, he should go to a health club; if he wishes to learn only philosophy, he should go to college. The core of a Taoist temple is the *religion* of the Tao. Accordingly, religion permeates all that is taught—it can't be separated out.

Spread throughout the temple are icons that serve as reminders of the various Taoist principles. For example, the yin/yang circle reminds students of this central principle that binds all natural phenomena—light with dark, action with inaction, and life with death. Similarly, swords and battle flags at the temple's entrance remind all visitors that life is a war.

Most prominent, however, are images of Taoist gods, each representing a specific principle or an important life lesson. The God of Longevity, for example, reminds the congregation of the importance of maintaining the physical body, the house of the soul.

Applying Taoist Principles

The images of Taoist deities are crafted according to specific conventions. Again using the God of Longevity as an example, he is always depicted with a domed head, holding a dragon staff in one hand and a peach in the other. Although statues are usually made from wood or clay, these images are sometimes painted on scrolls; this was the case for mobile Taoist clans who needed their temples to be portable. The master invites the appropriate spirit to inhabit these images using ancient "eye-opening" ceremonies—the Taoist equivalent of consecration. Once activated, they serve as the communication portals by which the congregation can pray to the heavens.

The spirits who inhabit the temple's images are celestial creatures who have achieved their position in one of three ways. Consistent with Taoism's martial theme, the first category of spirits is that of mortal heroes who suffered and died a violent death. Similar to Christian saints, these spirits protect those Taoists who sincerely communicate with the heavens and try to live spiritual lives. In this sense, Taoists *earn* the right to be "chosen people" favored by the heavens, unlike other faiths in which one is either born into such status or simply self-selected.

The second category of Taoist spirits—which includes the God of War—is composed of those celestial creatures who were careless or cocky in their prior mortal state but learned from their mistakes. The exalted position of these beings reinforces the important Taoist lesson that one should always endeavor to take correct action and not make careless errors; this is important because the Taoist's willingness to take action must be tempered by careful, deliberate consideration. Despite such warnings, imperfect Taoists still have the courage to try to do what is necessary—and bear the consequences of their mistakes. In short, while mistakes are inevitable, the true sin for the man of Tao is not the actual mistake itself, but rather not learning from that error. Indeed, the ability to learn from mistakes is indicative of a Taoist's skill in adjusting himself to reality. Chuang Tzu repeatedly emphasized this principle:

> . . . he discriminates between safety and danger, is happy under prosperous and adverse circumstances alike, and cautious in his choice of action, so that none can harm him.
>
> —*The Wisdom of Laotse*, 241

The final category of Taoist spirits comprises those celestial creatures born directly into the celestial world, including, for example, the Goddess of Mercy. Since these occupants of the nonphysical world were never burdened with a physical body, they are ideal prayer media, linking earthly mortals and the heavens.

There are literally hundreds of Taoist spirits. Like a military force, they are organized according to a strict hierarchical system, with their consecrated images arranged throughout the temple in accordance with this structure. While each master has limited freedom to accentuate certain deities, there remains a specific layout that is consistent across all classical temples.

As mentioned earlier, when you first enter a Taoist temple (usually through a southern entrance), you are greeted by a

Applying Taoist Principles

stand of swords and battle flags signifying the "life is a war" theme. Above the stand is the Jade Emperor, who issues orders to his generals—those spirits charged with bringing harmony to the earth.

Above the Jade Emperor are images of the Three Pure Ones which represent manifestations of the Tao: On the left is a statue of Lao Tzu, to his right is a statue representing the primordial forces of life (yang) and to the far right is a statue representing the primordial forces of death (yin). This is important symbolism, indicating that the Tao is above all—even the Jade Emperor, the most powerful of all gods. Orders from the Jade Emperor bring balance and harmony to earth and help restore the original, unpolluted manifestations of the Great Ultimate, represented by the Three Pure Ones. Unlike the Christian version of God, the Jade Emperor's mission is not to bring "goodness" to man; instead, he shows the ways of the Great Ultimate—values not defined by earth's inconsequential humans. In essence, his noble goal is to try to reestablish the harmony of nature that thousands of years of mankind's confusion has disturbed.

The most familiar Taoist images are the famous "Star Gods." Commonly seen in the West, this trio is composed of the God of Longevity, the God of Good Counsel, and the God of Good Fortune. The God of Longevity urges Taoists to care for their bodies and is depicted smiling to remind followers of the important role of mental contentment in good health (Western medicine's recognition of the psychosomatic nature of illness).

> **When a man's body is at ease, and his spirit is recovered, he becomes One with heaven.**
>
> —*The Wisdom of Laotse*, 221

The God of Good Fortune is also the God of Luck, reminding Taoists that acquiring wealth requires both ability *and* good fortune. Accordingly, the Taoist lucky enough to make a great deal of money should never get cocky. Taoism is not antiwealth, in contrast to the hypocrisy of other creeds that preach poverty while coveting millionaire members and supporting priests who live in palaces and wear gilded robes. Lao Tzu warned against the dangers of sacrificing the enjoyment of life for the pursuit of money, but he also advised that money could help mortals enjoy physical existence. Paired together, the gods of longevity and good fortune speak to the adage, "It's better to live rich and healthy than poor and sick."

The third Star God is the God of Good Counsel, whose message is the importance of understanding one's indigenous social structure and navigating its hazards. Many Taoist principles, like the principle of camouflage, help Taoists survive society's traps. Mortal contentment, therefore, is virtually impossible without sensitivity to society's power. Accordingly, Taoists are urged to live by the laws of God but respect the laws of man.

In surveying a Taoist temple, one is invariably struck by the warlike images of most Taoist gods, whose statues possess powerful physiques clad in armor and wielding a variety of weapons like swords, halberds, and maces. This appearance, coupled with their intense, threatening

Applying Taoist Principles

expressions, sends a clear message: life is the process of dealing with conflict. Reflecting unspoiled nature, these gods make it painfully obvious that one's survival is dependent on the ability to persevere when threatened.

The God of War is illustrative of this viewpoint. Clad in thick armor and carrying a drawn weapon, he reflects Taoism's realistic outlook that anything of value in life requires a fight. You fight for your money; you fight for your health; and you fight for your loved ones. Indeed, metaphysically, you fight for your fate.

The most feared of Taoist gods is the Governor of Internal Essence and Sovereign of the Underworld. Clad in armor, he holds a drawn sword in one hand and a diagram in the other. This diagram depicts a gold ingot surrounded by rotating chevrons, symbolizing that, while wealth (gold) is one means of enjoying mortal life, the Taoist must rotate (use) and not hoard it. This important Taoist principle teaches us that anything that doesn't circulate goes bad: stagnant blood leads to gangrene, stagnant water invites disease, and hoarded wealth brings misfortune.

> **. . . he who loves most spends most,
> He who hoards much loses much.**
>
> —*The Wisdom of Laotse*, 218

The Celestial Marshal of the Mysterious Path is seen in two versions. Both wear armor, but one version shows the god standing in a watchful posture while the other depicts him as combat-ready with a drawn weapon. This pairing reflects the inaction/action dynamic (wu wei) employed by the Taoist as he pursues his path through life. The watchful guardian warns the Taoist to be constantly aware of his path in a manner consistent with heaven's way, that is, reposed but on guard. The combat-ready guardian, on the other hand, reminds the Taoist that action is required once there is a threat to one's path. Combined, these two versions advocate both vigilance and action in order to maintain one's spiritual core.

The Lord of Magical Powers from the North Star reflects the Taoist respect for that which is tangible yet unexplained, such as the Taoist temple's mystical, religious practices which yield concrete results. Lao Tzu warned that many phenomena cannot be understood by limited mortals and that to speculate about their source is folly; yet, if there are tangible results to be gained, this power may be used when necessary.

In addition to deities represented in human form, many Taoist temples display representations of animals to establish spiritual connections with the desirable qualities of these creatures. Harkening back to Taoism's shamanistic heritage, such animals represent unspoiled nature; they possess many pure qualities that mankind has lost. For example, a tiger commonly represents power, grace, and ferocity—qualities man has lost to the effects of civilization.

Significantly, the temple's master often pairs various gods in specific ways to represent the duality (yin/yang) of Taoist principles. For example, the God of Literature is often paired with the God of War. Otherwise identical to his more combat-ready counterpart, the God of Literature carries a scroll or book instead of a sword. This emphasizes that one's fighting spirit must be balanced with the discerning intelligence of a scholar. The ideal model for a Taoist's spirit is not an aggressive brute, but rather a warrior-scholar. Another pairing commonly seen in classical Taoist temples is that of tigers with dragons. This animal manifestation of a revered earthly spirit (the tiger) combined with its celestial counterpart (the dragon) reinforces the duality of existence—grounded earthly existence with the way of the heavens.

Religious Ceremonies

> For a thing which retains its substance but has lost the magic touch of life is but a ghost (of reality). Only one who can imagine the formless in the formed can arrive at the truth.
>
> —*The Wisdom of Laotse*, 245

The purpose of Taoist religious ceremonies is to bring contentment to their participants. Historically, private Taoist temples had fewer members, so they relied less on rituals and more on simpler ceremonies. The larger public temples, by contrast, were influenced by the need to exert social influence and generate the revenue needed to maintain their larger infrastructures; in some cases, these enormous facilities covered several blocks within major Chinese cities.

The most important ceremony today, by far, is the personal act of praying in private, direct communication with Taoist spirits. During this communication process the Taoist asks for guidance; prayers tend to be general in nature, used to elicit the help of the gods in removing mortal confusion. Reflecting the acknowledged limitations of human comprehension, lay Taoists are reluctant to ask for anything specific—for who can understand the plans of the gods? A misguided individual could ask for money, for example, and end up with poor health; or ask for fertility, only to have his infant born with a crippled leg. Mortals have little ability to intuit what is important to achieving their future path. Most of the lotteries' instant millionaires end up with miserable lives, broke and friendless. For this reason, the Taoist is always cautious to ask only for clarity and guidance from the pantheon.

In sorting through the significant options that life presents, prayer should yield concrete benefits. For millennia, Taoists have insisted that the deities contained within their temples provide sound advice in the conduct of life. Since the congregants house the deities in comfortable quarters and sacrifice money, they expect positive benefits from these revered spirits. If a statue provides unreliable celestial answers to prayers, it is dragged from the temple and exposed to the elements or destroyed. For this reason, any statue that has survived for centuries in Taoist temples is a proven, reliable connection to the Great Ultimate.

As the Taoist prays for guidance, he generally starts by reciting that he is weak and confused. This recitation reinforces his humility before the gods and ensures that pride and arrogance do not impede his sensitivity to any celestial messages. Incense is often burned at the commencement of prayer to signify personal sacrifice; since the incense was purchased with money, its burning represents the offering of personal time and effort in exchange for spiritual guidance. This is required because Taoism teaches us that nothing of value is free; all worthwhile gains involve an exchange of energy. In this case, money from mortals is exchanged for guidance from the heavens.

While prayers by laypersons are personal, the temple's priest performs religious ceremonies before the congregation at large. These rituals generally fall into one of three categories: the initiation of new priests, communication with the celestial world, and the reparation of an individual's diseased soul (as manifested by physical or mental illness).

In these public ceremonies, the priest (or shaman) first burns diagrams or paper images designed specifically for a particular purpose. Next, he places himself in a trancelike state and then acts as a "medium" through which the celestial world responds to the congregation's questions. For ever-practical Taoists, these answers must be validated in the real world, lest the congregation lose faith in its priest. This is in stark contrast to the ceremonies of Judeo-Christian faiths, whose preachings are not borne out in tangible reality; prayers that don't work are conveniently explained away by citing the mysteries of "God's way." Clearly mortal comprehension of the gods is limited. But if a priest cannot achieve dependable results from his ceremonies, what is the value of those rituals?

The Theological Mission Redux

> To be in harmony with men is the music of man, and to be in harmony with God is the music of God.
>
> —*The Wisdom of Laotse*, 196

From Taoism's perspective, a properly functioning religious organization—whether church, mosque, synagogue, or temple—must achieve a symbiotic relationship with its respective congregation. The fates of any religious institution and its congregation should be inextricably bound—an impossibility for the large, corporate organizations familiar in the United States. A true religious institution activates a person's soul and helps him achieve mortal contentment. Indeed, that is its holy duty. In the case of Taoism, this obligation covers the entirety of what it is to be human—one's physical health, mental outlook, and spiritual core.

In order to remove man's confusion, the religion of the Tao establishes links between grounded mortals and the Great Ultimate. Counteracting the distorting effects of society, Taoism brings the purity of the Way to mankind. While most of society's herd lacks the courage to step outside convention, a few are able to commit themselves to a different paradigm—one based on observed reality and living for the present.

As these more content mortals grow increasingly in sync with reality and recapture life's passions, they engage in a metaphysical process that attunes their "spiritual DNA" (karns) to cosmic energies. In this manner, Taoism's theology and philosophy are indivisibly bound. Navigating around society's traps, the classical Taoist has the courage to fight for his soul. And in this battle, his temple and its master are indispensable allies, for they are pathfinders to spirituality.

> **He who clearly apprehends the scheme of existence does not rejoice over life, nor repine at death; for he knows that external limits are not final.**
>
> —*The Wisdom of Laotse,* 52

CHAPTER 6

The Conduct of Life

He who follows Tao is strong of body, clear of mind and sharp of sight and hearing. He does not clutter up his mind with worries, and is flexible in his adjustment to external conditions.

—*The Wisdom of Laotse,* 65

Grasp the Tao

This book's principles, comprising one of the most powerful philosophical systems ever created, draw their strength from Taoism's simple elegance and relevancy to life's mortal challenges. While Lao Tzu and Chuang Tzu constantly reiterated the futility of book-based learning—particularly of profound subjects—it's nevertheless possible to acquire a general appreciation for broad concepts and simple applications through written material. A good example is the reading of an instruction manual for a new piece of machinery. In this context, *The Truth of Tao* is a "training manual" for Taoist philosophy and religion, bridging the gaps of time and culture from ancient China to modern America.

If you've found the preceding chapters compelling and its logic irrefutable, you are doubtless anxious to apply its Taoist teachings to your daily life. This is a natural consequence of Taoism's emphasis on the use of practical applications to validate its principles while providing tangible benefits. As Chuang Tzu explained, readers who grasp Lao Tzu's beliefs are inextricably drawn toward the *application imperative*:

> **Those who understand their application do not suffer material things to injure them.**
>
> —*The Wisdom of Laotse*, 240–41

Some students, on examining Lao Tzu's teachings, express concern that many of the Tao Te Ching's eighty-one poems seem written for rulers—which the student is not. Or they hesitate to embrace its lessons because some scholars argue that the Tao's principles were for China's nobility and ruling class. Nothing could be further from the truth—the Tao is universal, meant for men of all social statuses. Lao Tzu wrote his elegant poetry in the sophisticated Mandarin familiar to his "target market," the social elite. This isn't because the Tao pertains only to them, but because, in agrarian China, only government officials, nobility, and scholars were literate. Given his undisputed disdain for social convention and artificial constructs, Lao Tzu's teachings apply to men of all walks of life—rulers and plebeians. Chuang Tzu makes this clear:

> **The sons of Heaven know that both themselves and the emperor are equally sons of Heaven... .**
>
> —*The Wisdom of Laotse*, 86

Some scholars speculate that Lao Tzu, while harboring no desire to delve into the affairs of government, tried to nudge rulers toward forms of leadership that were more consistent with nature's principles. With his urgings for a more laissez-faire approach, Lao Tzu taught that the people would flourish by governing themselves and realizing their individual paths, rather than those dictated by ruling structures. In reading his passages on the role of government, it is apparent that his homeland's twentieth-century experiment in communism was the height of irony:

> "In the government by the best ruler," said Laotse, "its effect is over the entire nation, yet it appears not to stem from him. He changes and influences all things, and the people are not dependent on him. His influence is there, but you cannot put your finger on it, and everybody is pleased with himself... ."
>
> —*The Wisdom of Laotse*, 118

Lao Tzu's writings for rulers contained another vital message. Just as leaders oversee the affairs of their kingdoms, so does the man of Tao strive for mastery of his domain. In this regard, the Taoist constantly fights to carve out a content life within his limitations. Unwilling to fall victim to society—or even his own confusions—the Taoist is a sort of warrior king, recognizing that ruling oneself is all that matters in the contest of life. The Old Master wrote,

> He who conquers others has power of muscles;
> He who conquers himself is strong.
>
> —*The Wisdom of Laotse,* 176

While Taoists don't discriminate based on social status, Lao Tzu defines a strong line of demarcation between "men of Tao" and the "herd." If not based on social position, race, gender, or other physical attributes, what then are the differentiating factors between the two? Indeed, for students wishing to apply the Tao, what is needed to achieve the spirituality and contentment that eludes the herd of mankind?

The answers to these questions go to the core of what it means to be "spiritual." The first criterion is that the student must be motivated to discard conventional thinking and embrace a new paradigm. It takes a rare individual to observe the absurdities of life, grasp a clarified view of reality, and withstand society's countervailing tide of confusion. To win this battle, one must be motivated by a yearning for clarity that cuts to the soul. No amount of intellectualization can instill the courage needed to swim against society's current. Rather, there must be passion and commitment, both deeply emotional and born of the heart—a desire to discard the conventions of a "civilized" world gone terribly wrong. Chuang Tzu notes this with the following:

> **. . . if you haven't got it in you, you could not receive Tao.**
>
> —*The Wisdom of Laotse,* 317

In addition to such intense motivation, the individual must possess the intelligence to understand Taoist teachings and then apply them. The Taoist model of the "perfect man" is the warrior-scholar; the warrior has physical power and ferocious intent and is balanced by the scholar who uses intellect to navigate through life and choose battles wisely. In essence, "fire in the belly" is combined with "reason of the mind":

> **To be stupid is to be taken advantage of.**
>
> —*The Wisdom of Laotse,* 193

The "intelligence" prerequisite described here is not of the type generally revered by society, measured by IQ and professional skill. Rather, from the Taoist perspective, many Ph.D.s and surgeons are mentally limited with no sense of reality, blinded by social convention. Gather a bunch of university professors in a room and witness an ocean of collective confusion! The Taoist version of intelligence relies instead on the ability to comprehend its simple principles and—more importantly—the aptitude to discern reality, reason deductively, and act appropriately. Overall, the "perfect man's" intelligence can be thought of as scholarly reasoning combined with "street smarts."

Assuming the student possesses these prerequisites, his next step is to define the goal of contentment. Only by understanding what contentment entails can the emerging Taoist measure his progress toward that goal. Contentment won't appear magically in a burst of enlightenment; rather, it's achieved incrementally throughout life. Along the way, forces outside one's control will invariably cause setbacks, but overall there should be measurable progress toward one's goal. If at any point progress halts and stagnation sets in, one must recognize the need for drastic change.

For the typical American, contentment is tied to the messages put forth by society's media, particularly by the powerful venue of television. Superficial images prevail: health is represented by big biceps and white teeth, friendship is represented by the presence of many golfing or drinking buddies, success is represented by luxury cars and a big house, caring is represented by charitable giving, and filial success is represented by a large family. Image is everything in American society.

Even love, the most powerful driver of the human soul, has been reduced to empty images. In an increasingly emotionless society, love is false and lacks sincerity. Despite declarations of filial loyalty, elderly parents die alone in nursing homes; despite oaths of fealty, friends disappear in times of need; and despite the professed love of God, prayer is reduced to a superficial observance grudgingly performed for an hour on Sundays.

Among all the aspects of life driven by the superficial values of society's images, money is paramount. The size of an American's wallet determines his level of contentment.

The Conduct of Life

Most believe a large bank account is the elixir that will heal life's ills, and mental peace is only a fat checkbook away. During the forty years of adulthood preceding retirement, one's hard-earned money pays for a big house to win the admiration of neighbors, luxury cars to win the admiration of strangers, and children's college tuitions to win the admiration of reproducing peers. If any money is left over, it goes to build a retirement nest egg, so at the ripe old age of sixty-five the good citizen can finally sample daily pleasures.

This bizarre program is labeled the "American dream." Work like a dog until retirement, and only then enjoy life. The problem is that there's no guarantee you'll make it to retirement. And even if you're lucky enough to get there, you'll have little vigor left to enjoy it. Even more damning, your natural instinct to spend money and enjoy the current moment is stifled over decades to the point where it cannot be reactivated. Thus, ironically, sacrificing daily pleasure for a promised rosy future likely prevents that future's realization. This recipe for disaster is not peculiar to modern America; it was found in ancient China, too, as Chuang Tzu observed:

> **And so all these people follow their routine year in, year out, submerged in their own affairs, and cannot get out. They let their bodily desires run away with them and get tangled up in the thousand and one affairs until they die.**
>
> —*The Wisdom of Laotse,* 154–55

Given that the American prescription for contentment is riddled with such obvious flaws, how does the Taoist version differ? What did Lao Tzu prescribe to enable an individual to achieve a content life?

It is here that the motto "live for the day" becomes the light at the end of the tunnel. As previously discussed, the tenets of "ch'an" comprise a mental state focused on the current moment. All practical applications of Taoist theory— meditation, healing, and kung fu—use this concept of living for the moment. And it is equally applicable to the conduct of life, deeply profound as it runs contrary to conventional thought and permeates most decisions related to everyday life.

Unfortunately, working to counteract this "live for the day" philosophy are proponents of the American dream who extol materialism at the expense of daily contentment. They are augmented by a most powerful ally: America's Judeo-Christian religious structure, which advocates suppressing natural desires for the sake of greater humanity. These two foes of daily contentment are the Taoist's formidable combatants, aggressively challenging his healthy perspective on life.

America is not alone in championing a false dream of sacrificing daily contentment for the promise of a bright future. For example, several generations of Russians were subjected to the enslavement of Communism, lured by the promise of a perfect society. They suffered for decades under totalitarian regimes, falsely believing a better life was just around the corner. While America's conscription of its citizens using societal pressure is subtler than Communism's iron fist, they both trade today's reality for tomorrow's hollow promises.

Taoism's battle on two fronts—philosophical and religious—directly results from its combined goals of relieving mortal suffering while saving souls. Traditionally, the role of philosophy is to deal with mortal existence, while that of religion is to deal with nonphysical existence. Taoism takes a different approach, viewing physical contentment and spiritual development as two indivisible sides of the same coin. For the Taoist, the "live for the day" motto isn't only a philosophy for mortal existence, but also a religious doctrine for saving the soul. That is, by not separating the two, as in classical Western theory, a unified strategy for life's conduct is feasible while here on earth.

A desirable consequence of Taoism's unified approach for achieving mortal contentment while simultaneously recapturing one's spiritual core is its establishment of a method for "tuning" one's nonphysical form. Under the previously discussed theory of karns, this process of adjusting to physical reality not only yields worldly contentment, but also trains the nonphysical being to be sensitive and flexible to ultimate reality (as manifested by universal energy, or chi). Consequently, living for each day also facilitates one's progress toward spirituality.

The Perfect Day

Perfect happiness is described as success.

—*The Wisdom of Laotse*, 94

Goals need to be clear. The clearer one's objective, the more likely one is to achieve it; the more obscure one's destination, the more difficult it is to reach it. Such clarity is generally tied to simplicity, so goals must be easy to understand and verbalize. To achieve contentment, one must define a tangible goal in a manner that eliminates confusion. A Taoist recognizes that his personal goals for contentment are contrary to those promulgated by society and represent the foundation on which the man of Tao builds his lifestyle.

In this context, the Taoist's daily goal is the "perfect day," defined as the one you'd wish to experience every day for the rest of your life without the requirement to work. While the typical American can talk endlessly about the perfect two-week vacation, he has no idea what to do with himself if granted twenty-four hours of free time every day without work to fill the hours. Explicitly defining how you'd spend all of your waking hours to relish the joy of life is an exercise that cuts to the core of your soul. It challenges you to verbalize those things that give you pleasure. And it will probably cause you to revisit childhood loves trampled by society's maturation hammer. But once you've defined and arranged the simple joys of life into your theoretical perfect day, you've created an uncomplicated, tangible goal consistent with Chuang Tzu's urgings:

> The man of character lives at home without exercising his mind and performs actions without worry.
>
> —*The Wisdom of Laotse,* 129

To mentally craft the perfect day, begin with waking up. You'd probably eat breakfast and then shower. What next? A walk with your dog or some time spent reading the newspaper? Midday might include a light lunch, then a

The Conduct of Life

workout a bit later to energize the body. Follow that with a favorite hobby, or some time reading or swimming. Sunset approaches. Time for a small snack? A walk on the beach? End your day by sharing cocktails and dinner with friends. Time for bed after a full day without the stresses of work. This is just an example of what such a day could entail, depending on your preferences. But no matter how you arrange it, the perfect day is a routine that provides comfort and contentment.

Interestingly, while constructing your perfect day, you'll discover that many of the things that you enjoy don't cost much money. If you enjoy reading, you can borrow library books for free. If you enjoy walking, it costs nothing to visit a park. If you love fishing, bait is inexpensive. If you love to paint, materials are affordable. Evenings with friends can be had for the price of a good bottle of wine. Enjoy the fresh air, visit art galleries, tinker in your garden—it all costs little.

The true cost of the perfect day is free time, and your challenge is to "buy" it. Time is money, and money is time. Thus, the conventional path of modern life—dedicated to acquiring a bigger house, a more expensive car, and additional children—results in a commitment of both time and money. Coveted professional promotions may mean more money but also entail more responsibility, more stress, and less freedom. Lao Tzu witnessed this trade-off in ancient China:

> **Fame or one's own self, which does one love more?**
> **One's own self or material goods, which has more worth?**
>
> —*The Wisdom of Laotse,* 218

Having clearly defined the perfect day as your goal, you can now make decisions in order to achieve it. Begin with your monthly budget. What does it really cost to live your perfect day? Many people reminisce of happier days when they had little money, a cheap apartment, and few responsibilities. Why can't they be recaptured? Would you trade a life of stressful days in expensive surroundings for perfect days in a small beachside cottage? Big house, big car, big career, and miserable days—or a rental property, small car, no career, and countless perfect days? This apparently easy decision is quite difficult, because for choosing the perfect day, society will label you a "loser"— but you'll be the ultimate victor by Taoist standards.

Achieving the perfect day won't happen overnight. Instead, by making correct decisions throughout life, you progress toward that goal. On a practical level, it takes time to achieve the perfect day because most of us don't have adequate financial resources. By carefully making life's big choices, however, you can better position yourself over time. For example, does having another child move you closer to, or further from, your perfect day? Society will applaud you for having a large family, but is it really what you want? Similarly, a promotion that moves you away from lifelong friends may promise more money, but does it bring you closer to your perfect day?

An important guideline in weighing your options is that society's recommendations always move you away from the perfect day. With depressing regularity, decisions that move you closer to your goal fly in the face of social convention. Society's gain is your loss.

Society's propaganda manipulates us, saying we should put off the perfect day until retirement. The American dream sacrifices our youthful years—when life can be enjoyed to the fullest—by making a hypothetical goal decades away. The Taoist, on the other hand, works to achieve the perfect day as soon as possible. He tries to make every day as close as possible to the perfect day. And, regardless of financial resources and social status, he seeks contentment by acting to increase the pleasurable side of life's "balance sheet." With the intelligence and willpower to first define and then fight for this goal, he can achieve contentment.

Achieving the Perfect Day

> My teachings are very easy to understand
> and very easy to practice,
> But no one can understand them and no one
> can practice them.
>
> —*The Wisdom of Laotse,* 297

Once you've defined the perfect day, the next step is more difficult—translating this goal into reality. Indeed, it's nothing less than life's primary mission. All philosophical and religious concepts are a waste of time unless translated into action. Thoughts and words are nothing without tangible manifestations. And the perfect day is the most concrete means to demonstrate your mastery of Taoist principles.

The bad news is that society will use its power to prevent you from realizing this content state. The good news is that in today's America, you have the freedom to pursue almost any lifestyle *quietly*, and society's interference is limited to social pressure rather than the physical coercion of most of history's civilizations. In this unique country—and this prosperous time—the opportunity to realize the perfect day has never been better.

One who pursues the perfect day moves incrementally toward a lifetime goal. Each day presents challenges to keep one from reaching this destination. Some challenges are subtle, like the barrage of confusing messages from society's various media. Television ads, for example, instill dysfunctional material values by linking images of success with material gain—luxury cars, expensive clothing, and so on. Other times, however, the challenges are more urgent, like a serious illness or the loss of one's livelihood. By dealing with these problems, you demonstrate your ability to function as a spiritual person.

Navigating through life to achieve the perfect day is pursuing one's path. Stated another way, in deliberating about his path through life, a man clarifies the means of achieving the perfect day. In evaluating whether you are "on your path," you need only consider whether your daily life is progressing closer or further from the perfect day.

The Tao Te Ching is often described as a book of Tao or "the Path." This is an accurate characterization because Lao Tzu's poems comprise a manual for navigating one's path through life, or put simply, for achieving the perfect day.

If one were to evaluate the success of the world's various philosophies and religions, the primary criterion should be the contentment of each community's followers.

The Conduct of Life

That is, how well do members of each group understand and move toward their individual perfect days? Thus, despite all the esoteric theories and debates about mankind's path, the issue boils down to how one achieves the perfect day. Of the myriad systems, only Taoism maps a specific path toward achieving the perfect day—making the Tao Te Ching a most pragmatic "bible."

In embracing the path toward contentment, you commit to a journey with many challenges and hazards. While the Tao Te Ching is a comprehensive manual, you still need a teacher to navigate effectively. The most important step to achieving the perfect day is finding your teacher or master. Without such guidance, written words are of limited value.

Imagine, for example, you're a novice sailor trying to cross the Atlantic with only a sailing manual as a guide—a certain recipe for disaster. If you've already mastered sailing through years of practice under the watchful eye of an old salt, then you can use the manual only as a resource for information on navigation, tides, and so on, and your odds of success skyrocket. The importance of a qualified teacher in such pragmatic endeavors as sailing is obvious, yet in the business of life, most people rely on haphazard reading and devote little effort to finding a qualified teacher.

That wasn't the case in ancient China. There, one's teacher was of paramount importance. Families sacrificed much to have their children tutored by acclaimed masters, and students worked for years as novices for the privilege of learning from such teachers. It was understood that any endeavor worth doing well required the tutelage of a wise teacher, and book learning was of secondary importance.

Lao Tzu echoed this sentiment by warning about the limitations of books:

> **He who neither values his teacher**
> **Nor loves the lesson**
> **Is one gone far astray,**
> **Though he be learned.**
>
> —*The Wisdom of Laotse*, 156–57

Consequently, Taoism has a long history of oral tradition as its primary means of instruction—a path requiring the guidance of a master.

Desires and Expectations

> **Therefore the Sage desires to have no desire,**
> **And values not objects difficult to obtain.**
>
> —*The Wisdom of Laotse*, 283

Achieving the perfect day involves first understanding that desires must be natural and not driven by society. This means discarding many of the values taught us during childhood by parents, school, and church, then replacing them with those most consistent with our true desires. For example, society labels success as owning a luxury car, though a reliable pickup truck may be adequate (and maybe more practical). Some religions identify a large family as a noble goal, while fewer children may be more appropriate and affordable. Society associates a large house (and its attendant large mortgage) with the American dream, while a small bungalow on a remote beach may be ideal.

The Conduct of Life

There are no right or wrong desires—only *natural* or *artificial* ones. Therefore, sorting though one's desires to construct the perfect day is a challenge for which Lao Tzu provides guidance.

Taoism's most poignant lesson in distinguishing true, natural values from artificial ones dictated by society is probably the Tao Te Ching's passage on the Three Treasures. As previously explained, the first treasure is love. Often misunderstood, the classical Taoist version of love is more accurately translated as "acceptance and caring action yields simple, natural emotions." Lao Tzu cuts to the heart of natural love or desire by defining it as that which is simple and elemental. It emanates from one's natural core, not from some external stimulus. The colloquial saying "Life's simple pleasures are the best" comes to mind. Acceptance and caring are how love manifests in action. For example, the true love of a spouse, friend, or pet is as essential as breathing. Loved ones are an extension of ourselves, as vital to happiness as our own limbs. We embrace them with undiminishing acceptance. By contrast, how many loveless marriages are the result of society's mandated love? In applying the first treasure, one reawakens the passions and emotions that were lost with maturation, for calculation has no place in the business of love. And without an understanding of love, one's desires are confused and the perfect day is lost.

The second treasure is "Never too much." This can be defined as "sufficiency," or adequacy. The American notion that "you can never be too rich" is an example of a societal value that creates desires antithetical to the second treasure. Lao Tzu warns us that our desires should be restricted to that which is sufficient. Unrestricted desires can never be met. The perfect day is impossible with such thinking, for we constantly chase unobtainable goals. This is a typical American mentality—one is never too rich, never too thin, never too popular. Lao Tzu couples the first two treasures—natural love and adequacy—to address desires:

> **Reveal thy simple self,**
> **Embrace thy original nature,**
> **Check thy selfishness,**
> **Curtail thy desires.**
>
> —*The Wisdom of Laotse*, 120

The third treasure is "Never be the first in the world." Here Lao Tzu tackles the urge to always be first. Society applauds competitiveness, and the typical American strives for recognition as the richest, most powerful, best looking, smartest, and fastest. Society honors those who excel and mocks "losers." Even more significantly, society offers no accolades for contentment, so Chuang Tzu reminds us,

> **The perfect man has no (thought of) reputation.**
>
> —*The Wisdom of Laotse*, 144

Desires related to being "number one" are a prescription for dissatisfaction and suffering. It's nearly impossible to become "the best in the world," and if you somehow capture this temporary status, you'll be targeted by jealous competitors dedicated to overtaking you. Chuang Tzu notes that the tallest tree is almost always the first to be cut down. Becoming the best in any endeavor requires a sacrifice of time and money—a devotion that foregoes any chance to experience the perfect day. He advises us,

> **Live sincerely and plainly like the others and suffer yourself sometimes to be called a fool.**
>
> —*The Wisdom of Laotse,* 144

Filtering your desires through the Three Treasures is an antidote to society's value-forming machinery. But an additional step is necessary to clear and prepare your mind for designing the perfect day: you must align your expectations with reality. Desires and expectations combine to form your mental outlook on life. Unnatural desires create artificial cravings, while unrealistic expectations translate those desires into anticipation of events that have no hope of realization. The perfect day is replaced with frustration and confusion as hopes and dreams are shattered.

> **Those who dream of the banquet, wake to lamentation and sorrow. Those who dream of lamentation and sorrow wake to join the hunt.**
>
> —*The Wisdom of Laotse,* 236

The link between desires and expectations is important. In the calculating mind, once any desire is born, an expectation is created. These expectations for future fulfillment—based on current desires—often fail because of fate's vagaries. For example, if a lonely young man purchases a sports car to gain more friends, he'll likely be disappointed with the characterless, shallow individuals he attracts. Our young man's understandable desire for friendship yielded a plan to fulfill his yearnings. Unfortunately, reality didn't cooperate with his fantasy, and only suffering resulted. As the old saying goes, "Be careful what you wish for—you may get it."

Lao Tzu combats unrealistic expectations with his concept of limitations. He teaches us that expectations need to be tempered by a solid understanding of our limitations. While people instinctively understand physical limits— few would attempt to lift a five-hundred-pound barbell or leap out of a skyscraper—they harbor no such concerns regarding life's principles. Indeed, "The sky's the limit!" governs the American psyche. Lao Tzu countermands that attitude, recommending that each person fully understand his limitations, temper his expectations, and adjust his lifestyle accordingly.

Once you appreciate your limits, you can design your perfect day within the constraints of your situation. Your goal is to devise a daily routine that allows for a more enjoyable existence—*today*. Understand that the perfect day of idle hours and unbroken recreation is probably unrealistic given your current limitations of time and money.

On a practical level, your financial resources are the greatest limitation in mapping out your daily life. This means that the perfect day is limited by your budget. Humans, as physical beings, have basic requirements such as food and shelter. But you alone decide to what degree you'll spend your hard-earned money on these needs. Take the example of housing: do the constraints of your budget allow for a mansion—or only a little shack? Perhaps renting a modest apartment is best, considering it relieves you of the expense and hassle of home ownership. Some may prefer the less expensive, more self-reliant country lifestyle. A few nautical folks live on boats, combining their love of the sea with the need for shelter. Indeed, there is no recipe, except to find a comfortable and affordable "cave." At all costs, avoid the Siren song of costly mortgages that burden you for decades with large monthly payments. And view all other expenses in a similar vein, weighing the pleasure they'll return against the work, stress, and resources they consume.

While many Americans are predisposed to overspending, others exhibit the opposite trait of excessive frugality. These people hoard money rather than using it to enjoy life. This bizarre psychology mandates a life of working hard and saving money, but not using it for daily enjoyment. For these unfortunates, pleasure is tied to the size of their bank accounts, leaving their souls bankrupt and their hearts dry.

Under no circumstances do you want to sacrifice all of today's enjoyment for an uncertain future, as does the typical American who forfeits everything between the ages of twenty-five and sixty-five for theoretical retirement bliss. The perfect day is actually the *perfect today*, reminiscent of the ancient warrior's motto: "Live every day as if it is to be your last."

Overall, clarifying desires and adjusting expectations can achieve the perfect day. As life unfolds, the Taoist filters major decisions through the perfect-day test. Each big decision will be evaluated as to whether it moves him closer to or further from his perfect day. By checking desires and determining whether they are implants of society or true to his natural core, he reduces frustrations and makes contentment more likely. And he doesn't throw away today for an uncertain tomorrow.

Dealing with Society

> Since good men are scarce and bad men are the majority, . . .
>
> —*The Wisdom of Laotse,* 123

In the conduct of his life, the man of Tao must deal with society. Not an easy challenge, for Lao Tzu and Chuang Tzu identified society as the primary culprit in destroying man's naturalness—dashing any hope for contentment. The two sages identified the values of *any* social structure as pollutants of natural instincts and agents of confusion. Thus, in creating a lifestyle that provides daily pleasure, you must inoculate yourself against society's manipulations.

Society's weapons of control include appeals to one's "humanity," pleas for "justice," and exploitation of one's pride and greed. This hasn't changed for many millennia, and Chuang Tzu warns us that this fixture of the human condition is unnatural when he writes, "It would seem that humanity and justice were not part of the nature of man!" (p. 60).

As the Taoist eliminates the fog of social confusion, he observes and comprehends reality. This clarity enables him to deal with the chaos of mortal existence and to react to threats. With clear vision he detects emerging problems before they become unmanageable. Instead of becoming frustrated with unexpected developments, the spiritual man addresses difficulties head-on and deals with them unflinchingly. By maintaining proper priorities, the Taoist determines the correct course of action. His expectation for life's chaos and absurdities prepares him for battle. He doesn't wallow in self-pity, crying over the world's unfairness.

Every community has social norms, and it is inadvisable to stand out as deviant from those standards. Modern America is tolerant of differing lifestyles, but the Taoist understands that social values can change dramatically. This was illustrated by Germany—a tolerant society in the late 1800s that became a bigoted realm of horror under Nazism in the 1930s. The man of Tao masks his beliefs to avoid becoming the target of a fickle society. Lin Yutang called Lao Tzu the first "philosopher of camouflage," because the Old Master advocated blending into the surrounding community so as to not draw its ire. He teaches us never to involve ourselves in affairs of state and to leave social issues to the confused masses. Avoid political revolutions, and head to the hills at the first smell of conflict. Pay your taxes, obey the speed limit, and hold the door open for old ladies.

The Futility of Argument

> A good man does not argue;
> He who argues is not a good man.
>
> —*The Wisdom of Laotse*, 312

While the principle of camouflage instructs us to disguise ourselves from potential adversaries, it also teaches that contention of any kind invites trouble. Probably the most practical manifestation of this is Lao Tzu's concept of the futility of arguments. He explains that arguing has no place in the conduct of life. While this concept is not popular with lawyers and politicians whose professions are steeped in a culture of verbal debate, the man of Tao knows that arguing is a fool's stratagem.

It is a common myth that truth and enlightenment can be reached through discourse. In this paradigm, rational people consider argument (dialogue) a valuable tool in the pursuit of knowledge—one in which everyone involved can explore the possibilities until they forge a greater mutual understanding. Dating back to the Socratic method of dialogue, such an approach is the cornerstone of inquiry used in our legal system, politics, and academics. As Chuang Tzu notes, civilization's progress has been accompanied by the dysfunctional use of argument:

> **Tranquil inaction has given place to love of disputation; and disputation alone is enough to bring chaos upon the world.**
>
> —*The Wisdom of Laotse,* 287

Why does argument fail? Why can't rational people engage in a logical dialogue, discussing their various views until a correct understanding is achieved? What is embodied within man's immutable nature that prevents constructive dialogue?

The answer gets at the heart of what motivates the herd of mankind. Ignorance and pride drive most human interaction. Chuang Tzu describes man's unwillingness to truly learn via discourse in his metaphor of "smugs, snugs, and humpbacks." Smugs are individuals who are so satisfied and pleased with their current understanding that they have no desire to accept outside challenges to their beliefs. Often they take segments of one theory, pieces of another, and combine them to form their own mental mosaics which they dub knowledge. These people create absurd eclecticisms, including "eight martial arts in one," "Taoist Confucianism," and "scientific Buddhism." For smugs, arguments are not a means to discover truth, but instead a means to reinforce their own intellectual positions.

Snugs, by contrast, are so comfortable within their safe environment that they can afford a confused version of reality. For snugs, a safe intellectual and physical environment allows them to discard external reasoning thanks to the shield of their short-term fantasy world. This is particularly evident in modern America, where affluence and safety have created snugs unwilling to listen to arguments that contradict their comfortable visions of reality. For example, the apparent security of daily American life enables snugs to disregard prudent warnings about personal safety, only to be surprised when they are attacked in dark parks. For snugs, no amount of rational discourse can overcome their intellectual indifference.

Finally, humpbacks are hypocrites who deceive themselves and exploit others, sometimes consciously, sometimes not. These hypocrites permeate modern media, politics, and religion. Humpbacks have no use for discourse other than to manipulate others for their own benefit; there is no quest for enlightenment, only self-promotion and monetary gain.

Regardless of its underlying motivation, argument fails when we examine its two possible outcomes. In the first case, you win the argument and your opponent resents being outmaneuvered—and is now an enemy. In the second case, you lose and your objective is foiled. Neither outcome is constructive, and no enlightenment has been achieved. As Chuang Tzu writes,

> **Granting that you and I argue. If you get the better of me, and not I of you, are you necessarily right and I wrong? Or if I get the better of you and not you of me, am I necessarily right and you wrong? Or are we both partly right and partly wrong? Or are we both wholly right and wholly wrong? Since you and I cannot know, we all live in darkness.**
>
> —*The Wisdom of Laotse*, 54

Argument is by nature neither good nor bad. Like a warrior's sword, the likelihood of victory depends more on the skill of the party wielding the sword than on the tool itself. A master swordsman can "win" his fights regardless of whether he is in the right. Likewise, a good debater can "win" his arguments without correct understanding. Chuang Tzu cautions us not to confuse arguing skill with true knowledge:

> **A dog is not considered good because of his barking, and a man is not considered clever because of his ability to talk.**
>
> —*The Wisdom of Laotse*, 173

Argument violates one of Lao Tzu's most fundamental principles—wu wei. This *doctrine of inaction* (discussed in chapter 4) dictates that we should not interfere with others since it may lead us from our natural path. In nature, there are no arguments among animals. They do what they do, until one animal's path interferes with another's. *National Geographic* has yet to film animals negotiating over food distribution. Thus, "Speech which argues falls short of its aim" (p. 54) is Chuang Tzu's warning that argument is counterproductive, because—regardless of its outcome—it results in one participant stepping off his natural path. Indeed, arguing is the verbal equivalent of physical confrontation, the ultimate form of interference. Lao Tzu advises us to let the self-satisfied herds wallow in their muck of confusion—they'll be happier and you won't raise their ire.

With argument as a chimera, how does one learn if not by discourse? Lao Tzu instructs us that learning can only occur when there is a proper student-teacher relationship. The student can learn from his teacher when he is open to the knowledge offered. You can't learn to drive a car by arguing with the driving instructor. The more critical the subject, the less you want to argue your way to understanding. Student pilots listen with great attention to their flight instructors, and young soldiers on their way to the front pay heed to combat veterans; no one has yet documented student-instructor debates on how to fly at thirty thousand feet or how to dig a foxhole while under fire. It's the same in learning life's principles.

Subjecting oneself to the discipline of a teacher requires a rare commitment. Most people have preconceived "knowledge" and opinions that weaken the resolution required to truly learn. Unfortunately, there is an ugly human tendency to cling to cherished personal beliefs and argue with any countervailing instruction. Perhaps due to pride, a potential student often requires a personal cataclysm to break those beliefs. The resulting humility opens the door to learning as the desire to argue is discarded along with conceit and ego.

> **(People) usually look at things from their respective points of view, and miss the truth by wanting to correct others.**
>
> —*The Wisdom of Laotse*, 74

Following classical Taoist principles, avoid arguments and achieve your objectives in other ways. In describing the conduct of life, the Tao Te Ching warns against embracing the common man's propensity to argue:

> **The true Sage keeps his knowledge within him, while the common men set forth theirs in argument, in order to convince each other. Therefore it is said that one who argues does so because he is confused.**
>
> —*The Wisdom of Laotse*, 53

Borrowing: The Ultimate Clarifier

You don't even own your self.

—*The Wisdom of Laotse*, 95

It's difficult to maintain a clear vision of the world while being bombarded by values that contradict spirituality. As simple creatures, we need uncomplicated tools to insulate ourselves from the brainwashing effects of television, church, school, parents, and politicians. Even New Age gurus have their own brand of confusion. Thankfully, we can reduce this murky confusion with a powerful clarifier: Lao Tzu's message that everything in the world—including life itself—is borrowed.

The idea that life is nothing more than a borrowed existence is powerful. The spiritual person recognizes that everything on this earth is on loan from the Great Ultimate. Even your most precious possession—your body—is a temporary vessel for the soul; when you die, you shed your shell of flesh ("dust to dust"). The realization that existence is borrowed and can end unexpectedly reinforces one's commitment to enjoy each day to the fullest and not to put off daily pleasures.

This concept also helps you put material possessions into proper perspective. By realizing that all you own will be lost when you die, you develop a healthier attitude toward ownership and eliminate the urge to hoard wealth. Anything purchased is a borrowed implement for daily pleasure. There is no merit in accumulating stuff. Possessions—like wealth—may come or go; it's of little consequence since they're only borrowed anyway. Contrary to society's materialistic urgings, you don't own anything—not your home, your land, your car, nor any other earthly goods. Given this truth, harboring anxieties over borrowed possessions is indicative of a lost soul:

> **If a man is unhappy because things loaned to him have been taken away from him, then it is clear that when he was happy, he had lost his true self.**
>
> —*The Wisdom of Laotse*, 95

Once the spiritual man embraces this concept, he frees himself from mortal ties and shrugs off many of the burdens placed on him by society. While certain possessions make life more comfortable, desires should be limited to those things that yield immediate contentment. All the effort exerted by our materialistic society to acquire more borrowed possessions is nothing more than a tragic comedy. How absurd to spend life's precious time to acquire things that, in truth, aren't really ours. Chuang Tzu recognized the logical bankruptcy of spending one's short life to pursue such borrowed possessions:

> **Those who lose their selves in material things . . . may be compared to people who stand on their heads.**
>
> —*The Wisdom of Laotse*, 95

Chuang Tzu extends the borrowing concept to the metaphysical, saying that your self "is a body lent to you by the universe" (p. 95). While we can't know what happens to the soul after we discard our borrowed physical form, we can deduce that it's likely the only "possession" retained at the conclusion of mortal existence is the soul. Therefore, if there is anything worth "investing" in, it's not stocks or a bigger house or a vacation home; instead, it's clarifying one's vision of reality so the soul becomes better prepared for its final journey. Thus, using the borrowing concept to live a better life makes the nonborrowed segment of our being healthier. In essence, physical and nonphysical realities are purified by this simple yet profound idea.

> ... the Sage rejoices in that which can never be lost, but endures always.
>
> —*The Wisdom of Laotse*, 98

Physical Conduct of Life

> One cannot live without taking care of the body, ...
>
> —*The Wisdom of Laotse*, 221

Man is a physical creature. For all of our illusions of superiority, we are wedded to our physical form just like our fellow beasts in the animal kingdom. Despite our pride in our intellectual prowess, our contentment is linked to a healthy body. A robust physique makes mental contentment possible. Place the most content mind in a body afflicted with disease and contentment is reduced to grim survival. Sadly, even when one suffers from less serious disorders—a migraine headache, intense flu, or an intestinal disorder—philosophy takes a backseat to dealing with pain. As Chuang Tzu observed,

> **When a man's body is at ease, and his spirit is recovered, he becomes One with heaven.**
>
> —*The Wisdom of Laotse,* 221

The man of Tao embraces an exercise program to maintain his body. In Taoist temple life, this traditionally included the practice of physical chi quong and kung fu. Ancient Taoists knew that optimizing chi flow throughout the body required a frame constructed of strong bones and cartilage. They emphasized flexibility and balance to counter the physical manifestations of aging. Muscles were strengthened using weights and heavy weapons.

According to traditional Chinese medicine, physical wellness is only achieved when the body possesses three healthy "burners," which power the rotation of chi. When the Three Burners function properly, chi moves through the body in a steady current, governed by a clear mind (hence, the mental aspect of health).

The first burner refers to breathing, whose proper performance involves much more than the mere inhalation of oxygen. Using deep-breathing chi quong, the Taoist coordinates specific body motions with the inhalation of fresh air (chi). Designed to accelerate chi throughout the body, physical chi quong can be gentle enough for elderly chair-bound patients or vigorous enough for warriors in training. Chuang Tzu documented this practice as a means "to control one's breathing, expelling the foul air and

The Conduct of Life

inhaling the fresh, to stretch like a bear and crane like a bird for the purpose of achieving a long life . . ." (p. 272).

The second burner encompasses the consumption of food and drink. Classical Taoists follow a nutritional program that reflects man's natural origins and bodily requirements. Even Lao Tzu was concerned about diet, and he cautioned against consuming too much grain-based food. Similar to Western nutritional guidance, the Taoist's well-balanced diet consists of fresh meats, vegetables, and fruits. Freshness is important because food intake involves the consumption of chi, and the fresher the food, the better the chi. Significantly, the American love of fast food is the chi equivalent of eating cardboard. Classical Taoists view vegetarianism as a bizarre concept, believing it is artificial to shun man's carnivorous side. This is especially crucial to those engaged in physical chi quong and martial arts; vigorous exercise dictates the need for protein to build and maintain healthy organs. The Taoist also augments his food intake with herbs, like ginseng, which are nutritional supplements and healing agents. Finally, contrary to many belief systems preaching so-called purity, spiritual Taoists *do* consume alcohol; as in anything else, however, they avoid excess.

The third burner involves the sexual aspects of our animal existence. Taoists aren't shy in advocating a healthy sexual lifestyle, as evidenced by their well-known Tantric exercises. Caring for the third burner mechanically rotates male and female chi (yin with yang), increases blood flow, and maintains a healthy emotional attitude.

Maintaining one's physical body must be a priority in the conduct of life. The God of Longevity is one of the most popular images in Taoist temples. Most major Taoist deities have powerful physiques. This shows that a healthy body is necessary to survive life's hardships and successfully fight one's way to spirituality. This important lesson is lost on an increasingly lazy America where the majority of the population is considered significantly overweight.

A healthy, functional body is sensitive to its surroundings, attuned to the physical comfort afforded by its daily environment. It exchanges chi with all that is around it. For this reason, it's important that the Taoist create a comfortable home. Whether it's a small rented studio or a mansion on the ocean, a person's home needs to be physically comfortable and appealing. It serves as one's "cave," a place to recharge one's energies after long days spent battling society. It should be a reflection of the inhabitants' personalities and configured, as much as possible, for the perfect day. Its design need not be extravagant or expensive; if you like to read, for example, you can create a small area with bookshelves and a comfortable reading chair.

One's physical environment deeply affects one's health. As the Taoist clarifies his likes and dislikes, he should be able to articulate the particulars of his desired residence. This is one of the most important ingredients in building a content life and must be factored into life's big decisions. For example, taking a job for higher pay in a large city may be a terrific career move, yet it would be a slow death for someone who loves life in the country. Similarly, retirees who leave their residence of thirty years for a retirement community in a different climate risk a dramatic—and possibly irreversible—shock to their chi.

The Conduct of Life

As the student of the Tao becomes more spiritual, his sensitivity grows. The manifestation of this change is an acute awareness of his health and physical surroundings. This is both a blessing and a curse: a blessing because it allows him to sense and embrace those things that improve his health, a curse because he grows less tolerant of those things that agitate his physical state. As a result, he will crave a physical state of well-being unknown to mankind's herd. Your inquiry into Taoism may begin as an intellectual pursuit, but once embraced, it affects your entire physical form in profound and unexpected ways.

Mental Conduct of Life

> The wise ones of old had subtle wisdom and depth of understanding, . . .
>
> —*The Wisdom of Laotse,* 106

While the Taoist understands that his physical body requires care, he also recognizes that his mental side needs similar attention. Indeed, Taoism as a philosophy is primarily concerned with man's mental outlook. Using Lao Tzu's collection of principles, one cultivates a mental attitude that ultimately leads to contentment. Harmony is struck between care for our animal/physical components and our mental existence. The Taoist avoids both extremes of the spectrum spanning from the ignorant athlete to the sickly intellectual. A proper mental attitude gives equal weight to maintaining both a robust body and a sound mind—"healthy body, healthy mind." Western doctors now recognize what Chinese healers knew thousands of years ago: there is a strong link between mind and body (as evidenced in psychosomatic illnesses). Indeed, the two are inextricably bound.

Taoism teaches us that society constructs "sins" to control its masses' behaviors at the expense of the individual and thus sustains its social structure. The Taoist therefore pays them little mind. According to classical Taoist theory, however, there is one indisputable "sin": confusion. The Taoist's ultimate mental goal is to see reality clearly and to use that vision to handle life's challenges better. In short, eliminating confusion is the most important step in attaining an enlightened state.

Achieving this mental "state of grace" requires a lifetime of cultivation. Fortunately, Lao Tzu's passage on "mental hygiene" shows where to begin:

> **When you are disturbed by the external senses and worried and confused, you should rest your mind and seek tranquility inside. When your mind is blocked and gets beyond your control, then you should shut out your external senses.**
>
> —*The Wisdom of Laotse*, 85

This technique discards society's dysfunctional values and replaces them with one's natural instincts; it quiets the mind and silences all of the calculating and planning required to meet society's artificial goals.

Lao Tzu and Chuang Tzu emphasize the importance of mental hygiene's calm and quietude. They observed people's propensity to constantly hustle and bustle, a trait as prevalent in today's America as in ancient China. Scrambling about frenetically, the mind has no time for reflection or contemplation. Accustomed to having its thinking dictated by others, the mind is deadened to its own natural desires. Sadly, people wouldn't know what to do with idle time if it were given to them.

In the conduct of life, one must embrace a quiet, calm state, leaving society's hustle and bustle to the confused masses. According to Chuang Tzu, "When the mind is overworked without stop, it becomes worried, and worry causes exhaustion" (p. 108).

Without the noise of confusing thoughts, the quiet mind grows more sensitive. It more quickly detects both internal and external forces that threaten one's contentment, be they social forces, trends in relationships, business developments, an impending assailant's attack, or the onset of a cold. This "sensitive radar" allows the spiritual man to detect emerging threats and counter them early.

Taoist sensitivity begets caution. Some faiths are forgiving of mistakes; Taoism is not. Missteps inevitably occur during the course of life, but they are to be avoided because they may carry consequences far beyond our mortal comprehension. Accordingly, the Taoist is a careful creature, always alert for trouble. Maintaining a low profile and using camouflage to mask his intentions, the Taoist treads softly "like crossing a wintry stream" (p. 106). Similarly, Lao Tzu warns Taoists not to take life lightly:

> He who makes light of many things
> Will encounter many difficulties.
>
> —*The Wisdom of Laotse,* 282

The cautious Taoist embraces the concept of wu wei, or noninterference. He takes only those actions necessary to maintain his content path and thus conserves energy for those occasions when something directly threatens his well-being. Accordingly, he doesn't interfere with others or stick his nose into the affairs of the world. Rather, he leaves the confused herd of mankind to wallow in its own muck.

Responding to emerging problems—taking action—requires flexibility. In his warning against excessive rigidity, Lao Tzu observed that inflexible trees were the most likely to be blown down by stormy winds. This concept is important because change is always present. Sometimes the change is gradual, sometimes sudden and traumatic, but nothing is static. The Taoist must adjust himself to situations, which requires flexibility of mind and body to survive in a world of chaos and absurdity.

Lao Tzu extends this concept of flexibility by cautioning against an excessive reliance on plans. His warning about their futility runs contrary to most Americans' belief in the sanctity of such long-range plans as the traditional forty-year retirement plan. One courts disaster by believing that plans will come to fruition as anticipated. One must understand that planning requires constant adjustment and, in some cases, outright abandonment. Whether making a life plan, business plan, or battle plan, adjustment is the key to success. And such adjustment can only occur when one's mind

The Conduct of Life

is tractable. Without this flexibility, one will meet life's inevitable surprises with paralysis. The result will be constant disappointment and frustration.

The man of Tao constantly attunes his desires and expectations to the reality of his situation. Always aware of his limitations, whether external or personal, the spiritual man explicitly keeps his expectations in check. And using the motto "life's simple pleasures are the best," he aligns his desires accordingly.

Limiting desires and expectations also dampens the need for wealth. Unlike other faiths, Taoism doesn't hypocritically disparage wealth; money is the means to buy a more comfortable lifestyle and is therefore considered a beneficial tool. The God of Good Fortune's prominent position in Taoist temples illustrates this. However, when one sacrifices a lifetime to acquire property at the expense of daily contentment, then wealth has taken on a life of its own and inevitably results in unhappiness. In the conduct of life, it's up to the Taoist to regulate how much time he spends earning money and how much time he spends actually enjoying it.

As the Taoist matures, his understanding of limitations becomes more profound. In essence, the unbridled exuberance of youth is replaced by the wisdom of age, tempering one's outlook on life. The invariable consequence for the man of Tao is a deep sense of humility. The spiritual man abhors the bravado of the obnoxious, self-assured herd. True humility is the Way and is reflected in how a Taoist conducts himself. Chuang Tzu summarized this mental attitude by describing the "Wise Ones of Old":

> The pure men of old appeared of towering stature and yet could not topple down. They behaved as though wanting in themselves, but without looking up to others. Naturally independent of mind, they were not severe. Living in unconstrained freedom, yet they did not try to show off. They appeared to smile as if pleased, and to move only in natural response to surroundings. Their serenity flowed from the store of goodness within.
>
> —*The Wisdom of Laotse*, 108

The humble Taoist understands life is hard and nothing is given free. He knows life is not a party, and it takes much work to survive and be content. This understanding leads him to a lifestyle that, while comfortable, isn't lazy. He recognizes the need for discipline—discipline to train and cultivate the body and mind. The spiritual person must constantly counter the natural human tendency toward weakness. Staring reality in the face, the Taoist works within his limits to develop himself in a steady, disciplined manner. The path to enlightenment is long, but gains can be made with discipline. In essence, enlightenment is a *process* whose benefits are accumulated over time. Chuang Tzu emphasized this reality by stating, "to preserve one's character is called self-discipline" (p. 75).

If there is an ideal model for the conduct of life, it is that of the warrior-scholar. Taoist temples depicted this by pairing the God of War with the God of Literature. The warrior-scholar duality is necessary to deal with both the hazards of physical reality (the warrior) and intellectual challenges (the scholar). Neither alone is desirable: the purely physical warrior is an unguided missile, the purely intellectual scholar an ineffectual wimp. Blending the two gives one a powerful physique aptly guided by a clear picture of the world.

> **. . . one who embraces the Tao has wholeness of character, from wholeness of character comes wholeness of the body, and from wholeness of the body comes wholeness of the soul.**
>
> —*The Wisdom of Laotse,* 268–69

This model of the warrior-scholar implies that one must bring passion to the conduct of life. Whether fighting with ferocity, painting with creativity, or dancing with feeling, the human animal needs to engage its emotions to perform its best. And when passion is controlled by clear-sighted intellect, one creates the ideal survival machine.

The Taoist's goal of achieving enlightenment can be thought of as a reawakening process, one that energizes the suppressed, natural core of man. While man's basic physique has changed little over the last five thousand years, his intellect has suffered from civilization's deleterious effects. Civilized thought has effectively reduced man to a largely passionless creature. Unfortunately for most Americans, the Judeo-Christian ethos has expunged life's passions. The natural instinct to "live for the day" has been replaced by the Protestant work ethic; the aggressive instinct to defend oneself has been replaced by turning one's cheek or dialing 911; and loveless marriages endure for decades so spouses can avoid the social stigma of divorce.

Modern America is perhaps the best of all of history's civilizations. With abundant prosperity and a legal system honoring individual liberties, you couldn't ask for a better place or time to build a content lifestyle. Ironically, most Americans voluntarily subscribe to soulless lives. They—who Lao Tzu designated the "herd of mankind"—don't even understand they are sacrificing their most precious asset, life itself. Indeed, the persuasive powers of society's social institutions have convinced the typical American to join the parade of life's walking dead.

As the Taoist builds a more content physical lifestyle, his animal nature becomes more vital. But the mental aspect of existence is where Lao Tzu's principles really demonstrate their power. As the Taoist embraces a philosophy dedicated to clarifying his vision of reality, he exposes society's misdirections. Like one escaping from the dark confinement of a cave, the emerging Taoist first flinches at the harsh light of reality, but is then compelled by its warmth as he claws his way to its embrace.

Spiritual Conduct of Life

The Perfect Man . . . is a spiritual being.
—*The Wisdom of Laotse,* 260

Taoism is both a philosophy and a religion (Tao of Man, Tao of God). Remarkably, the two are not in conflict. There is no contradiction between the Taoist philosophical mission to clarify one's vision of reality and its theology that deals with heaven's realm. Indeed, as Taoist philoso-

The Conduct of Life

phy clarifies earthly reality, its religion taps the unseen components of existence to do the same. Due to its pure, shamanistic origins, Taoism's philosophical principles are synchronized with its natural, spiritual side. Unlike Christian tenets—whose fantasies include the notion of universal love—Taoist theology is a reflection of unspoiled nature, the model from which Lao Tzu urges us to take our instruction.

In the spiritual conduct of life, the Taoist—with thanks to the harmonized "diamond of the Tao"—constructs a religious lifestyle that is completely consistent with his unambiguous philosophical tenets. This congruous situation makes it easier for the practicing Taoist to embrace a spiritual mindset while simultaneously building a content life. For once, the pious man can be as happy as the sinner.

The religion of the Tao urges man to find his spiritual core within the natural world. Its tenets are firmly grounded in reality, whether manifested in physical nature or in the unseen power of spirits. Unlike other religions, Taoism abides no confusion in dealing with the invisible forces of nature. Therefore, the spiritual man is able to deal with life by embracing Taoist theology. Religion and philosophy combine to help the Taoist build an arsenal of weapons to deal with life's absurdities.

Taoists are enlightened skeptics and therefore demand proof before embracing the unseen world. In short, religion's results must live up to its promises; it must function.

For the Taoist, enlightenment is that state achieved when one can behold the ultimate reality. Blind faith, therefore, is intolerable, because man's fallibility allows him to be fooled easily by his own ignorance as well as the misdirection of others. Thus, for ever-practical Taoists, even prayers must yield tangible results. There are no excuses allowed for failure, such as "God acting in mysterious ways." Historically the images of deities honored in Taoist temples had to yield concrete benefits to their congregations, lest they be destroyed. Reminiscent of its shamanistic origins, Taoism's prayers and ceremonies were required to produce tangible results because the survival of desperate clans were dependent on their success.

Apart from prayers, Taoists deal with the unseen side of existence in the everyday application of chi. Chi is an energy that is immeasurable by traditional scientific instruments, though it can be manipulated and experienced in concrete ways: in health with the practice of chi quong and in martial arts with kung fu, for example. Chi flows through all living things—animal or plant—and its cultivation is a practical consequence of Taoist sciences.

Chi, as the unseen component of existence, is enhanced by clarity. As the Taoist strips away confusion, his chi becomes clearer. Chi, whose qualities Lao Tzu likened to water, is enhanced when it flows through a healthy body directed by a calm mind. As the Taoist becomes more "enlightened," he improves his chi. It can be said that the man of Tao has "good chi." Thus, in the spiritual conduct of life, one cultivates healthy chi using both physical and metaphysical techniques.

> **Calm represents the nature of water at its best. In that it may serve as our model, for its power is preserved and is not dispersed through agitation.**
>
> —*The Wisdom of Laotse*, 77

The Conduct of Life

Man is a social animal. And the advancement of civilizations, including more organized social structures and more sophisticated technology, has fostered ever-greater interdependence. As such, the social aspects of existence have great importance for spiritual men. In this environment, the sensitive Taoist has an emotional soul, which reacts to everyone with whom he interacts. Thus, he is selective in choosing his companions. And because he marches to a different drummer than most of society, he carefully limits the number of people with whom he shares his thoughts and beliefs.

Metaphysically, every encounter with someone, no matter how casual, involves an exchange of chi. This can be beneficial, as when spending time with one's master or a loved one. Or it can be detrimental, as when dealing with society's "bad chi." The fatigue that one feels after a tough day in the office is partially due to being bombarded by the public's bad chi. Logically, chi exchange is more substantial with those around whom you spend the most time: family and friends.

A teacher is important for the Taoist seeking spirituality. Spirituality, as it involves dealing with the unseen world, presents many opportunities for confusion. For this reason, the teacher, priest, or master is the bedrock of one's spiritual lifestyle. Unfortunately, the world is full of "spiritual teachers" who promulgate beliefs that are, in actuality, the antithesis of enlightenment. Abusing their followers' blind faith, they create a facade of legitimacy through lofty titles and ceremonies or perhaps the buzzwords of exotic, New Age babble. The man who falls victim to these charlatans puts his contentment at risk.

On the positive side, one who is lucky enough to find a true spiritual teacher greatly increases the possibility of finding enlightenment by learning sound philosophical/spiritual principles. There is also a positive exchange of chi between master and student, which means that this relationship extends beyond simple instruction into the metaphysical realm.

When deciding with whom you should spend your time, you must weigh physical, mental, and emotional factors. You are struggling to ascertain the character of that person, be he master, friend, or spouse. The issue of character gets at the core of a man; it represents his soul, that immutable nucleus from which everything radiates.

But how do you evaluate character? Taoism cautions against relying on words. Words are cheap and the world is full of good talkers. Action alone demonstrates a man's true character. Ever-practical Lao Tzu and his disciple, Chuang Tzu, provided guidance for determining character by outlining the following nine tests:

> **Therefore (in the judgment of men) a gentleman sends a man to a distant mission in order to test his loyalty. He employs him near by in order to observe his manners. He gives him a lot to do in order to judge his ability. He suddenly puts a question to him in order to test his knowledge and makes a commitment with him under difficult circumstances to test his ability to live up to his word. He trusts him with**

The Conduct of Life

> money in order to test his heart, and announces to him the coming of a crisis to test his integrity. He makes him drunk in order to see the inside of his character, and puts him in female company to see his attitude toward women. Submitted to these nine tests, a fool always reveals himself.
>
> —*The Wisdom of Laotse,* 251

Like practitioners of any religion, Taoists use the power of prayer to find spiritual guidance. Because the Taoist recognizes his mortal limitations, he is eager to enlist the counsel of heavenly spirits to clarify his path. This means that in the spiritual conduct of life, one must use these channels of communication to help remove the sin of confusion.

Taoist temples use images of various spirits as communication channels to the Great Ultimate. Since the Taoist is a sensitive creature, he recognizes which of life's chaotic forces is blocking his natural path and then, using prayer, seeks counsel from the appropriate god. For example, he appeals to the God of War for guidance regarding an impending confrontation (business or otherwise), while he relies on the God of Longevity to rectify health problems.

Significantly, Taoist deities only help those individuals who help themselves. There is no free lunch in Taoism, which emphasizes individual responsibility. You invite trouble by praying to a spirit for help in rectifying a situation caused by your own laziness. If, however, the sensitive man of Tao presents himself on bended knee, sacrifices something of value, and humbly asks for clarification and support, he will find answers.

The Purpose of Life

> He who understands the music of heaven lives in accordance with nature in his life and takes part in the process of change of things in his death.
>
> —*The Wisdom of Laotse,* 196

Throughout the ages, man has asked, "What is the purpose of life?" So hungry is the world for answers that it has embraced philosophers and priests who performed divinations and created philosophies and religions with beliefs that flew in the face of mortal reality. By appealing to the confused herd's emotions, entire cultures were built on blind faith, with wars fought over unverifiable tenets.

Invariably, most religions define life's purpose as the attempt to bring certain heavenly virtues to earth. The most common of these virtues is "universal love," the cultivation of love for all mankind. Philosophers, by contrast, try to organize life's absurdities into some sort of rational structure. In either case, both philosopher and priest provide the drumbeat for their followers as they march toward a false vision.

As previously discussed, both religion and philosophy fail when they attempt to build belief systems that are inconsistent with man's natural desires. Traditional religions fail due to the immutable cruelty of the human animal, while most philosophies fail because life's chaos and absurdity cannot be rationalized, even by wise men. In either case, though, there is no merit for ill-conceived "purposes of life" that contradict reality.

So what then is the purpose of life? Certainly Lao Tzu, as author of a system that taps the power of the Great Ultimate, must have spoken to this central question. What does the Tao Te Ching say about man's cosmic purpose?

Since enlightenment involves clarifying one's questions in order to adjust one's desires, Lao Tzu addressed this subject to further his mission: the removal of the confusion regarding life's fundamental questions.

First, he states that, in the cosmic sense, the question is moot because we mortals are unable to test and verify any potential answer. He further warns that mere speculation gives birth to confusion and discontentment. Therefore, ever-wise Lao Tzu reminds us that, due to our mortal limitations, trying to ascertain the gods' intentions in putting our souls on this planet is an unpardonable sin. Why? Because, like ants trying to discuss aerodynamics, mortal man is ill equipped to grasp cosmic intents:

> **What we can know compared with what we cannot know is but like a squint (compared with the full view of a situation).**
>
> —*The Wisdom of Laotse*, 175

While the Old Master scoffed at the myriad "sage" speculations about this unanswerable "purpose of life," he wasn't silent about what Taoists should do with their short mortal existence. While simultaneously warning us to leave life's cosmic purpose to the gods, he explicitly articulated a logical paradigm for the way Taoists should live their lives. In essence, you have but two choices: you either live for yourself or you live for others. There is no in-between.

Unlike Taoism, the world's other religions and political establishments push an ideal world where living for others is the noblest virtue. Whether Christianity or Communism, these systems see sacrificing for the "greater good" as the essential characteristic of the "good man." In doing so, this "good man" earns society's praise while living and rewards from heaven in the afterlife. Even in America, a country built on the foundation of individual liberty, sacrificing oneself for "God and country" is revered.

Taoism is much more honest about man's true motivations and thus urges the spiritual person to recapture his *natural* desires and live for himself. Through mental cleansing, the Taoist strips away society's hypocrisy, revealing his natural desire to care for himself (and immediate loved ones) and leave the rest of the world alone. In essence, he embraces a healthy form of egocentrism. Because of the chaos, absurdity, and suffering of the world, it takes all of an individual's energy to live a content, self-serving life. Just as animals do not engage in crusades for God and country, so should the spiritual man avoid society's campaigns. Achieving self-contentment is a huge effort that is easily derailed by the false ideals shouted from religious or political pulpits.

This book has discussed the hypocrisy of those who claim to live for the benefit of others. But one point bears

The Conduct of Life

repeating here: if these "martyrs" don't understand how to live a content life themselves, then how can they possibly recommend a formula to others? Said another way, these oracles of "life's purpose" haven't *earned* the right to prescribe their remedies for mortal existence, for they only know how to endure their miserable existences through self-deception fueled by arrogant, self-righteous pride.

With this clarification, Lao Tzu's purpose of life is thus reduced to a simple goal: live each day the best you can. Use Taoism's principles to deal with the challenges of an absurd and chaotic world. Enjoy life and leave society to wallow in its own confusion. Develop a clear vision of reality. Embrace the oneness of mind and body. Surround yourself with those few people who share your values. Relish every precious minute on this planet. Get hit as little as possible by the chaos of life.

While Taoism may appear pessimistic—founded as it is on philosophical and religious tenets that reflect nature's immutable cruelty—it is really quite optimistic. It prescribes hope for the individual surrounded by a threatening society steeped in mass confusion. It offers choices and thus doesn't condemn the Taoist to a de facto life of misery. It doesn't allow its followers to blame others for a discontented life. Which is why, for several millennia, the adage "Every man is responsible for his actions" has been inscribed above the entrances of classical Taoist temples.

This attitude of responsibility and self-reliance is remarkably American. Indeed, Taoism may be the most "American" of the world's philosophies and religions. When this country's founding fathers stressed individual liberties and the pursuit of happiness, they were advocating a nation in which rough-and-ready colonists could follow their own paths without government interference. The creators of the American Constitution, as if following Lao Tzu's instructions for laissez-faire rulers, created a country that offers individuals a chance to carve out personal lifestyles in accordance with their natural core.

There are metaphysical implications in this attitude as well. Taoism's integrated system teaches us how to navigate optimally through mortal existence and thus attune ourselves to reality. As a consequence, the unseen components of the body—its karns—align with the pattern of the Great Ultimate. This is earthly preparation for our final journey. For that time when the mortal shell is shed and our soul returns home, earthly life has prepared us for existence without a body.

The human animal has freedom of choice, which is at once a curse and a blessing. It's a curse because mankind repeatedly squanders this freedom by concocting absurd social constructs and foisting them on the masses—destroying natural desires. It's also a blessing, because this freedom offers opportunity. For in the Taoist view of fate, you are presented with options throughout life, like a multiple-choice test. It is analogous to traveling along a wide, safe thoroughfare and happening on forks that require careful consideration. Choose correctly and you continue safely and easily along your way; choose poorly and you veer off onto increasingly narrower, more treacherous side roads. As you become more in tune with the Great Ultimate, you make better choices, and your path through life is less arduous and chaotic. Thus, while the gods control your fate, they allow you the opportunity—and with it the responsibility—to create some of your own luck.

> **Walking on the Main Path (Tao),**
> **I would avoid the by-paths.**
> **The Main Path is easy to walk on,**
> **Yet people love the small by-paths.**
>
> —*The Wisdom of Laotse*, 246

Life on earth is, in the truest sense, a prerequisite for entrance into "heaven." Admittance through heaven's gate is not achieved by performing good deeds, but instead by passing the test of mortal reality. Only by demonstrating the ability to live a content mortal life can you achieve the welcome embrace of the cosmos. Ironically, following the rhetoric of popular religious values "detunes" you from mortal reality and results in increasing misalignment with the Great Ultimate. The very folks who promised you heaven not only conned you into sacrificing mortal contentment, but also ruined your chance for a decent afterlife.

By contrast, the Taoist prescription for life offers a happier mortal existence while preparing your soul for an afterlife. This approach has no downside, for even if there is no life after our mortal existence, you have still lived the most content life possible on earth. Thus, Taoism's unified system couples the goals of mortal and empyreal existence. In essence, the man of Tao treats life like a training camp for the afterlife.

To have been cast in this human form is to us already a source of joy. How much greater joy beyond our conception to know that that which is now in human form may undergo countless transitions, with only the infinite to look forward to?

—*The Wisdom of Laotse*, 98

Afterword

The Truth of Tao has come full circle. We began the book by defining the goal of enlightenment and observed how the mythologies of the great quests had their explorers endure many hardships in the search for life's truths. The crucible of these quests tested the character of the searchers, challenging them both physically and mentally. The mettle of the heroes was strengthened by repeated challenges as they discovered that, in many ways, the journey itself was the source of enlightenment.

In the same way, classical Taoism explains that navigating through life's hardships is a quest for self-discovery and personal development. It is the chaos, absurdity, and suffering of life that makes mortal existence a continuous process of facing obstacles and adjusting to overcome them. This process of consciously adjusting to reality turns life into a continuous tuning exercise, increasingly bringing the Taoist closer to the Great Ultimate. Stated succinctly, life is nothing more than one continuous test.

The Truth of Tao

Fortunately, Lao Tzu not only explains *why* the fight for daily contentment is a metaphysical test, he tells us *how* to pass the test. For this reason, the Tao Te Ching is an instruction manual filled with principles and cautions for the Taoist to use in successfully overcoming mortal challenges. The Old Master, while abandoning the herd of mankind to its hopeless confusions, offers the emerging Taoist a great gift. It is his ancient voice that serves as a guide through the crucible of life and prepares one for the journey afterward.

The Truth of Tao

The Truth of Tao